# The TOI Story

Sangita P. Menon Malhan, forty-five, worked as a journalist with *The Times of India*, Delhi, *Mid Day* and *The Statesman* before turning to creative writing. She has published *Rastapherian's Tales*, a book of short stories for children and a collection of poems in Urdu, *Nusrat-e-Gham*. Formerly a private pilot, she is fond of languages and teaches French. She lives in New Delhi with her husband, Tejinder, and son, Avii.

# The TOI Story

## *How a Newspaper Changed the Rules of the Game*

Sangita P. Menon Malhan

HarperCollins *Publishers* India

First published in India by
HarperCollins *Publishers* in 2013
Building 10, Tower A, 4th Floor, DLF Cyber City, Phase II,
Gurugram Haryana – 122002, India
www.harpercollins.co.in

4 6 8 10 9 7 5 3



P-ISBN: 978-93-5029-663-9
E-ISBN: 978-93-5029-664-6

The views and opinions expressed in this book are the author's own and the facts are as reported by her, and the publishers are not in any way liable for the same.



Typeset in 10.5/14.3 Sabon by
R. Ajith Kumar

Printed and bound at
MicroPrints India, New Delhi

*For my parents and siblings*
*And for Teji, Avii and Kanwaldeep, who walked with me on this journey*

# Contents

# Prologue

THINK OF NEWS MEDIA in India and the image that comes to mind is of aggressive, racy, out-of-breath, near-paroxysmal anchors sharing screen space with scrolls, images, graphics and ads, coaxing news angles out of diligent correspondents – all this, done slickly, tirelessly, in real time, through all our waking hours.

The media[1] scene appears as a grand frenzy; almost shambolic. A flurry of images, ideas, updates – and the familiar in-studio panellists – mingle in a relentless churn, in the battle for the TRP. At the last count, more than 800 private satellite television channels[2] including 300 news channels[3] across several languages were vying for viewer attention.

The consumer is spoilt for choice when we also consider the print media that is on offer. While newspapers and magazines in the print form are in rapid decline in the West, they are more than holding their own in India. They may be less obstreperous than their television counterparts, but are not any less competitive.

As of 31 March 2012, the total number of registered publications in India was 86,754, with the combined circulation of newspapers standing at 373,839,764.[4] Their numbers, as well as circulation, have been growing handsomely over the years. The rate of growth of the combined publications over the previous year (2010-11) has been 5.51 per cent. And 4,545 new publications were registered in 2011-12.[5]

This media phenomenon in India is only a little over a decade old. Prior to that, the media was much smaller, more confined and far less competitive. Media players now are always at pains to make themselves distinct from their competitors (though to a lay viewer, they often end up looking alike). In contrast, newspapers in the 1980s and earlier, while having their individual and distinct personalities, had a lot in common in the way they looked at their business and the unstated rules around which they organized themselves.

It may be said that Bennett, Coleman and Company Limited (BCCL), which owns *The Times of India* and *The Economic Times*, among others, was the first to break the rules. That set the stage for a seminal change in the Indian newspaper industry in the 1980s and '90s. To be sure, several protagonists played a part in that transformation. But this one media group remained at the centre of it all.

The BCCL story is probably one of the biggest corporate growth stories of that decade. Strangely, it has never received the attention it deserved. All the interconnections of that change have never been brought out. It is ironic that a newspaper group that regularly chronicles the rise and fall of business empires – and all that happens in between – should remain relatively obscure from public attention.

Some of this has to do with the philosophy of the group as also the obsessively low profile of its vice chairman, Samir Jain. He is rarely, if ever, featured in his own publications. The photographers of the group are under instructions not to click his pictures for use in the papers. As for other publications and channels, his interactions are so few, with so many years between them, that opportunities to know his story through the popular media are practically non-existent.

The group's growth has not just been about its own numbers. It has profoundly impacted the media industry in India. If the media today is market-driven and profit-obsessed, the media before the 1980s was resolutely profit-averse. The market was rarely the media's priority and it almost seemed to draw satisfaction from the fact that commerce did not govern its decisions.

The transformation from an inward-looking and market-agnostic media, to the media as we consume it today, was led by BCCL. The media began breaking away from a sequacious past sometime in the mid-1980s. Until then, for decades, it saw itself in the role of a 'watchdog of democracy' contributing to 'building the nation'. It had been at the forefront of India's freedom movement. Although more than three decades had elapsed since then, and much had changed even within the media, its self-image was still tethered to its days of glory.

The break that BCCL triggered was built around the idea that the media was also a business like any other. Like any business, it had to identify who its customers were, how its products and services would bring value to them and how much the business would make in return. As in any other business, it would have to compete with other companies, create its own value proposition and safeguard its bottom line.

In many ways, this set the stage for what came thereafter in the media industry. With the advent of satellite television in the early 1990s and then the proliferation of news channels, the media has effectively gone to the other end of the spectrum in terms of following the dictates of the market. The BCCL's transformation, though resented and controversial at that time, now seems far more measured in comparison.

The BCCL story is also largely hidden from public view because one part of it had to do with the 'truculent' treatment of journalists in the group's publications. The company chose to get rid of those who did not understand, or agree with, its new line; they were unceremoniously removed. The controversies surrounding the exit of journalists from The Times Group were analysed at some length in the past. They hit the headlines because fellow media persons took up the issue with great vigour, even as they, more or less, ignored the other aspects of the transformation of the group.

The media in the 1980s was, of course, much smaller, far less competitive and a lot less to play for. Yet the moves were audacious for that time. Take, for example, changing the look, feel and content of *The Economic Times*, pricing it at a premium and then abruptly bringing down the price one-day-a-week to rake in the volumes – all this made for scintillating stuff.

The group's diligent but clever move to create a web of advertising rates for editions across the country also created new rules for the industry. Its move to cut the price of *The Times of India* and expand reach had a cascading effect on the industry. After some initial hesitation, many formerly sententious rivals followed suit. This meant that households in Delhi, for instance, could buy two newspapers for the same monthly bill. This, combined with certain other factors, led to an explosive growth in readership.

To carry all this through, it was important that the organization worked as one integrated whole, focused on the overall objectives. That was not easy. Newspapers consciously separate the news side of the organization from the advertising and marketing functions. This is to maintain objectivity and ensure that news is not influenced by those advertising in it.

While the same applied to BCCL, the separation had been taken too far. Each function operated as an island. The predominant position was with the lead writers. Many of its editors were erudite, well known among the intellectual middle class and respected in the corridors of power. Over time, however, this perhaps made them averse to change. They had strong, sometimes limiting, views on what was appropriate for a newspaper.

There was resistance, though less publicized, on the marketing and advertising side as well. People had to shed years of inertia and wake up to the new experiments being undertaken. There was upheaval there as well, with some in the old guard yielding to a new crop of professional marketing and brand managers recruited from other sectors.

All this action unfolded in the context of major changes in the media landscape, as also in the Indian economy. The latter half of the 1980s was an interesting time for the print media in India, which witnesed a magazine boom. There was also growth and expansion of newspapers, as some of the now prominent names entered the fray during that time.

The electronic media was essentially Doordarshan. Although government-controlled, it had opened itself up to commerce. It was smartening up, having gone colour in 1982. More importantly, it was steadily expanding its reach across the country and owing to its captive position, governments saw it as a potent weapon to shape and strengthen perceptions.

The Indian economy was taking its first wobbly steps towards liberalization. The new paradigm of openness and less government control had started to become visible. It would acquire momentum and clarity post-1991. But even in the mid-1980s, a new middle class was emerging in the metropolitan cities and large towns.

In hindsight, it appears that the transformation in the BCCL was timed to coincide with these mega developments. Some insiders claim these were a conscious response to the context as it unfolded. Others argue that they were foreseen. Yet others claim that to a large extent these changes were defined and shaped by the experts at BCCL.

What cannot be refuted is that the group experienced scorching growth in turnover, profits, reach and mindshare during the decade starting the mid-1980s. In 1985, it had a turnover of Rs 73.5 crore and a net profit of Rs 1.2 crore. *The Times of India* had three editions with a circulation of a little over 5.6 lakhs. By 2001, turnover had grown to Rs 1,214 crore. Net profit was at Rs 205.9 crore.

On 5 June 2005, *The Sunday Times* carried an advertisement which declared, 'Shakespeare sulks. Byron blinks. And Wordsworth wails...as *The Times of India* becomes the largest selling English newspaper in the world' with 2,438,115 copies. There was further growth.

As of March 2012, *The Times of India* is the largest circulated multi-edition daily in English in the country, with fourteen editions and a circulation of 4,575,895.[6] *The Economic Times* is the second largest-selling business daily in the world, after the *Wall Street Journal*. The group publishes thirteen editions of newspapers and several magazines from eleven publishing and twenty-six printing centres and dominates the country's English-language newspaper arena, which has more than 11,000 newspapers. All in all, the group has fifty editions across forty cities.

The group's financials too have come a long way. In the financial year that ended on 31 March 2011, the company earned profit before tax of Rs 1,489.2 crore on a total income of Rs 4,749.3 crore.

Along with its newspapers, the group forges ahead with its two news channels, Times Now and ET Now, an entertainment, film and lifestyle channel (Zoom), a movies channel (Movies Now) and a radio network (Radio Mirchi). It also has OOH (out of home) advertising and event management ventures; and its investments span various other sectors such as music, films and real estate, among others.

Much has happened in terms of the group entering new areas of business, catching up on the news television business, buying and selling new brands and putting a lot of focus on the web and Internet media.

But it is reasonable to argue that the seeds for this prolific growth were sown in the early 1980s.

## ONE

# The Grand Dame of Bori Bunder

## *The Times of India*: A historical background

THE FIRST EVER ENGLISH newspaper to be printed and published in India was called Hicky's *Bengal Gazette* or the Calcutta General Advertiser.[1] It made its maiden appearance in 1780 in Calcutta, the then capital of British India. It was a two-sheet, weekly newspaper. Its tag line announced, 'A weekly political and commercial paper; open to all parties, but influenced by none'.

It had been launched by an Irishman, James Augustus Hicky, who had spent two years in jail for defaulting on his debts, and then again been jailed for criticizing the activities of Lady Hastings, wife of the first Governor General of India, Warren Hastings. The paper carried news on current events in the city; it took potshots at the powers that were; it made space for advertisements on auctions and it offered a 'Poets' Corner' for aspiring bards. It was directed at the employees of the East India Company and European traders.

*The India Gazette*, *The Calcutta Gazette*, *The Madras Courier*, and *The Bombay Herald* were among the newspapers of that age. The first two were published in 1780 and 1784 and the last two, in 1785 and 1789.[2] Yet another weekly newspaper – the *Bengal Journal* and a monthly magazine, the *Oriental Magazine of Calcutta Amusement* were published from Calcutta in 1785 with the result that four weekly newspapers and a magazine were published from this city within six years of Hicky's maiden effort.

By 1833, the East India Company had lost its trade monopoly both in India and China, and Bombay was beginning to emerge as a major trading centre. Soon many newspapers began to be published from Bombay. The *Bombay Samachar*, a Gujarati daily, was established in Bombay in 1822. Then there was the Christ Church School (Bombay) Education Society magazine, a bilingual annual, which first appeared in Bombay in 1825. Among the centenarians of the Indian press, there was also the *Jan-e-Jamshed*, a Gujarati daily, established in Bombay in 1832.

*The Times of India*, in its earliest avatar – *The Bombay Times and Journal of Commerce* – was launched on 3 November 1838 by a syndicate of eleven British firms, two barristers and a doctor, to cater to the need for mercantile news.

Initially it was a biweekly, published on Wednesdays and Saturdays and Dr J.E. Brennan was its first editor. He was also secretary of the Chamber of Commerce. Its annual subscription charges were Rs 30, and it 'focused on collecting and providing intelligence on subjects of politics, science and literature' according to the newspaper's own documentation of its historical past. In 1839, after Brennan's death, George Buist became its editor.

In 1850, the newspaper was converted into a daily. The telegraph service had opened up in India in 1855 and the paper entered into a mutual agreement with the news agency, Reuters, to raise news coverage and lower subscription rates. In December 1859, it absorbed *The Bombay Standard*, and in June 1861, *The Telegraph & Courier*. Later that year, the paper was renamed *The Times of India*. Robert Knight, its editor, tried to give it a national character.

The year 1880 also witnessed the first magazine to be published by *The Times of India* called *The Times of India Weekly Edition*, and it was indeed that – a synopsis of the week's news and main articles. But with time, it came into its own and was renamed *The Illustrated Weekly of India* in 1929. In its earlier phase, it was also the first Indian newspaper in English to carry sketches and pictures, which were very well received by readers who hadn't seen this break from verbosity before.

With the arrival of Thomas Bennett, its first professional editor in 1892, the paper's holding company, Bennett, Coleman & Co. Ltd (BCCL), got its name. Bennett became the sole proprietor and later offered a partnership to Frank Moris Coleman. Bennett's successor, Lovat Fraser, expanded the reach of the paper to the furthermost boundaries of Asia. He travelled far and wide and covered myriad issues of international concern.

Stanley Reed who succeeded Fraser would go on to become *The Times of India*'s longest serving editor (1907–23). He improved its coverage even more, taking it to a level where no less than Lord Curzon, the then viceroy of India, called it 'the leading paper in Asia'. Reed is also credited with having extended the deadline for carrying news from 5 p.m. to midnight (earlier, news that came after 5 p.m. would be kept over for printing the next day).

During his tenure the cover price of the paper was reduced from four annas to one, which gave a phenomenal boost to circulation. (A drop in cover price to boost circulation would be attempted on two more occasions over the next century, the latter proving very successful.) The paper had to introduce the fast-running rotary machines to cope with the increase in circulation. This was a market-determined move triggered by the arrival of the *Bombay Chronicle* on the media scene in 1915. The *Chronicle* was an anti-establishment paper and provided a platform for nationalist leaders. It was B.G. Horniman, the *Chronicle* editor who bestowed the sobriquet, 'The Old Lady of Bori Bunder', on its rival,*The Times*.

The last two British editors of *The Times of India* were Francis Low and Ivor S. Jehu, both Scotsmen. The former witnessed the freedom movement and the passing of the paper to Indian owners. And the latter began as a junior assistant editor in 1935, left to work as a commissioned officer in the army's public relations directorate, and returned in 1945 to take over the editorship of *The Times*.[3]

During its journey thus far, *The Times of India* had already evolved into an institution on the Indian media scene. It was known as much for its content as for its linguistic style and focus. It moved office from the Parsi Bazar Street to Churchgate and then came to rest opposite the Victoria Terminus. And soon, its ownership would change hands.

In 1946, an Indian industrialist, Ramkrishna Dalmia, approached BCCL's then owners and offered to buy the company off them. India was on the threshold of independence from British rule. Dalmia felt that 'without establishing some big newspaper, I could not serve India effectively'.[4] The *Hindustan Times* in Delhi, and the *Amrita Bazar Patrika*, among others, in Calcutta were part of the nationalist press. *The Statesman* and *The Times of India*, on the other hand, were British-owned and Dalmia decided he will buy *The Times*.

To clinch the deal, Ramkrishna Dalmia worked with Sir Arthur Moore, ex–chief editor of *The Statesman*, and requested him to go to London to negotiate the purchase of *The Times of India* with its then owners. Dalmia subsequently met Sir Pearson, the managing Director of *The Times of India*. The interaction between the two is best described by Dalmia himself:

> Sir Pearson remarked to me, in Bombay, 'You want to snatch away my baby (*Times of India* and allied publications) whom I have nursed for forty years.' I replied, 'Sir Pearson, the baby needs two nurses instead of one.' Sir Pearson smiled. Then, he asked me, 'Do you want to buy for Rs 2 crores?' I put a blank cheque before him, and asked him to fill it. He remarked, 'Are you mad?' I replied, 'Look at the generosity of Indians.'[5]

The deal to purchase the paper was finalized within twenty-four hours at a little less than Rs 2 crore, 'at a meeting held at the Taj Mahal Hotel in Bombay on 24 March 1946',[6] much to the surprise of 'important industrialists'[7]. Dalmia also wanted to purchase *The Statesman* but did not succeed in his attempt. He was planning to buy more than one paper but that did not work out for him. He mentions that when the deal for the purchase of the *Leader* was almost complete, 'the Birlas appeared on the scene and purchased it.'[8]

Dalmia also got possession of *The Illustrated Weekly*. In April 1947, a Hindi paper – *Navbharat Times* – was launched in Delhi. A Bombay edition of the newspaper was begun in June 1950.

## Ramkrishna Dalmia (1893–1978)

Ramkrishna Dalmia was born in April 1893 in Chirawa, a small village of the Khetri state (now Jhunjhunu district) in Rajasthan but his family moved east, to Calcutta, when he was a young boy. His ancestors belonged to the village Dadma near Dalmia Dadri, later called Charkhi Dadri, in Haryana. They were originally called Dadmias but with time, somehow, they started being addressed as Dalmia.

Dalmia's father died in 1913. He had, by then, begun working for his maternal uncle, Seth Motilal Jhunjhunwala. 'Soon after father's death, during the First World War, I was financially hard hit; being a defaulter, I was despised and condemned as a criminal in the business world. To support a (large) family was quite a heavy burden for an uneducated, indebted and ostracized young lad of twenty-two,' he wrote in his book, *Some Notes and Reminiscences: A Guide to Bliss*,[9] published in 1948. Over the years, he became a 25 per cent working partner in a Danapur-based sugar mill in Bihar owned by a local judge. Ramkrishna Dalmia acquired sole ownership of the mill after the death of the judge. Gradually, he became confident enough to trade and speculate in commodities such as silver. One such speculation brought him his first windfall. And there was little to stop him after that. 'For some time, I was controlling the whole of the Calcutta share market in partnership with the merchant, Baldeo Dasji Dhudhwawala,' Dalmia wrote.[10] He also dealt in jute and cotton.

In 1932, his daughter from his first wife, Rama, was married into the Sahu Jain family of Najibabad in the Bijnore district of western Uttar Pradesh, to the younger of the two sons, Shanti Prasad. Dalmia took his son-in-law to Bihar, where he began setting up what would become one of India's fastest-growing groups in the latter half of the 1940s. The Dalmia-Jain group was formed with Shanti Prasad Jain and Dalmia's younger brother, Jaidayal, as partners.

Shanti Prasad Jain was an industrious administrator, with a distinct streak of imagination and innovation in him. His second son, Alok Jain,[11] remembers his father as a man of great imagination and full of zest. He was energetic, enterprising and sensitive to the creation of wealth. 'When the Dalmia-Jain group began expanding, it was babuji who went to Indonesia to strike a deal for the purchase of three sugar mills, which were installed at Bihta, Hathwa and Dalmianagar,' he said.[12]

Jaidayal Dalmia had a sharp eye for technology and engineering and contributed greatly in setting up the group's factories and plants. The group began its growth process around 1933 and by the end of 1940, it had acquired four more sugar mills, a paper factory, five cement plants (one of them in Karachi), chemical factories and engineering plants.

Ramkrishna Dalmia floated Rohtas Sugar, later known as Rohtas Industries, in 1933 at Rohtasnagar, later called Dalmianagar. He purchased majority shares of the Dehri Rohtas Light Railway and constructed a ropeway to bring the sugar cane to the factory at Dehri-on-Sone.

In 1936, he purchased shares of Bharat Insurance Company Ltd and appointed Shriyans Prasad Jain, elder brother of Shanti Prasad Jain to manage it. The same year, he entered the cement industry.

He sent Jaidayal to Germany and Denmark to purchase six cement plants. He also purchased a paper mill and two cotton and woollen mills, and established Bharat Bank.

He was also into civil aviation: 'I also purchased a three-seater aircraft'. He also bought up the Govan Brothers' interest, which comprised many industries including the Indian National Airways which was carrying passengers from Karachi to Burma.[13] Besides, he set up a Delhi-based airline company called D.J. Aviation, which folded up in May 1948.

Much of the early history of the group was told to me by senior Jain family members. The late Ramesh Chandra Jain, a former executive director of *The Times* Group, was one of them. Ramesh Chandra Jain's grandfather, Musaddhi Lal, was Shanti Prasad Jain's father Diwan Singh's elder brother. He was also Shanti Prasad Jain's guardian after Diwan Singh's early demise.

When I interviewed him, Ramesh Chandra Jain was managing trustee of the Bharatiya Jnanpith, which was established in 1944. After the initial round of queries about why I was writing the book, he opened up and spoke at length about the past. His was a treasure trove of information, mostly having to do with the years that had gone by. He spoke of the glory of those early years and of the wealth built over time.

The late 1930s was an important period for the Dalmia-Jain group.'The group, which was already doing well, benefited monetarily when World War II broke out in 1939. They had imported some German machines and were to pay in instalments. With the outbreak of the war with Germany, that money stayed with them and they earned interest. This also helped the company become cash-rich,' Ramesh Chandra Jain pointed out.[14]

He also spoke of the entrepreneurial acumen of the Dalmia-Jain group of those times. He talked about one of the first business battles the group ever won and how 'competing to stand out' runs in its blood. The Dalmia-Jains' increasing market share in cement production between the late 1930s and early 1940s brought them in direct competition with the number one cement manufacturer of the times, the ACC.

'The competition between the two companies rose to such a level that both began cutting the price of cement to sell more,' explained Ramesh Chandra Jain. 'A stage came when the Dalmias would have collapsed if they had continued to sell at the depressed price. But they held on to the lower price levels and then the unexpected happened: ACC agreed to an arrangement by which the two warring groups could share the market. And though the Dalmia-Jain group got control of only one-third of the spoils, they seemed to have emerged victorious in this episode,' he elaborated.

According to R.P. Jain, an eighty-five-year-old member of the extended Jain family, who was also a Rajya Sabha member from March 1964 and had been a board member of some of the group's erstwhile companies, particularly Bharat Overseas of which he had been managing director, 'Dalmia was a financial giant, although not very educated. He had interests in many sectors; he wanted to buy banks and insurance companies and even had eyes on the Indian Iron and Steel Company, which belonged to R.N. Mukherjee.'[15]

The Dalmia-Jain group also tried to diversify its publishing business. BCCL brought out the *Evening News of India* in 1948 (it folded up in 1950) and a children's weekly magazine called *Junior* for a few months in 1949-50. In 1949, the group started a Bengali newspaper called *Satyayug* from Calcutta. It also launched an edition of the *Navbharat Times* in the city in 1950 and an edition of *The Times of India* in March 1953. All three publications, however, ceased to publish from Calcutta after September 1953.

Soon, the ownership of Bennet, Coleman and Co. would pass on to Shanti Prasad Jain, in rather controversial circumstances. But even before that there was a formal break up of the Dalmia–Sahu Jain group. Alok Jain told me that the details of the split of the

Dalmia-Jain group were worked out at the family house of the Jains in Mussoorie on 12 May 1948. Hanuman Prasad Poddar, who established the Geeta Press, was the arbitrator. Going by Alok Jain's recollection, when the group split, the Jains got Rohtas Industries and SKG Sugars.

Sanjay Dalmia, Jaidayal Dalmia's grandson and chairman of the Dalmia group said that the group split because each of the three patrons had different personalities. 'Ramkrishna Dalmia was the creator. He took risks. My grandfather, Jaidayal Dalmia, was a cautious businessman. He was content with what we had. Shanti Prasad phoophaji (uncle) wanted to expand the business. Their styles were different. The business had become big and it was only prudent to split it. There was no fight. It was done very amicably. There has since been no straining of relationships,' he stressed.'[16]

The transfer of controlling shares in BCCL to Shanti Prasad Jain happened in 1955. About this time Dalmia had incurred a loss of Rs 2.5 crore in speculation gone awry. Dalmia had leveraged the funds of Bharat Insurance for his speculative activities and the finance ministry asked him to make good the losses. 'To arrange money, I was compelled to sell *The Times of India* and Jaipur Udyog. But there was no buyer in such circumstances. Then, my son in law Shanti Prasad's group of companies purchased the above concerns for Rs 2.5 crore,' Dalmia wrote.[17]

In his book, Dalmia hinted at a political conspiracy against him. He suggests that the finance ministry had instructed the 'Bharat Insurance Administrator to create obstructions in accepting the payment because they wanted to send me to jail.'[18] This is a charge that Sanjay Dalmia reiterated in his interview. 'What I do know is that my older grandfather (Ramkrishna Dalmia) got into trouble with the Nehru government and had to pay for that.'

Of course, charges of political vendetta may seem justified given the fact that Ramkrishna Dalmia had entertained political ambitions. He had strong beliefs on what he termed 'one God, one government', and he had launched a crusade against cow slaughter.

He was open and imprudent in his criticism of the powers that were and had no qualms about being politically incorrect. He was also openly critical of Jawaharlal Nehru and expressed his antipathy in the front pages of his daily for an extended period of time.

He blamed Nehru and his selfish ambitions for the Partition and held him responsible for the plight of the refugees. (Incidentally, Dalmia, who was a friend of Muhammad Ali Jinnah, was in favour of Pakistan: 'In 1940, I was the first Hindu to advise the country to accept Pakistan as being the only solution under the circumstances. For this, I was denounced as anti-Hindu and called all sorts of names for having played host to Mr Jinnah, who had stayed once at Dalmianagar for a couple of days. My sole motive in retaining friendly relations with Mr Jinnah was to secure favourable terms for Hindus in an amicable settlement between the two communities,' he wrote.[19])

Nehru returned the compliment in equal measure. 'Dalmia,' Nehru is reported to have stated, was 'an ugly man with an ugly face and an ugly mind and an ugly heart. Just because he owns a few newspapers, he claims to be an expert on foreign affairs.'[20]

It is an exaggeration, however, to say that Dalmia's troubles were the result of vendetta politics, although Nehru was well aware of the issue and kept himself abreast of the developments on the matter.[21] In 1955, there were reports of fraudulent transactions by the Dalmia group and the issue was raised in Parliament by Feroze Gandhi in December that year. An inquiry was instituted by the government to look into the charges.

The commission of inquiry was initially headed by Justice S.R. Tendolkar of the Bombay High Court and after his death by Justice Vivian Bose. He submitted the main report on the investigation to the government on 18 June 1962. The commission had inquired into the affairs of nine companies of the Dalmia-Jain group.

The Vivian Bose Commission Report[22] was presented to Parliament on 23 January 1963. It held the group guilty of 'fraud, manipulation of accounts, personal gain at the expense of the investor as well as the exchequer and avoidance of taxes'.[23] The commission allotted the largest share of blame for the malpractices to Ramkrishna Dalmia, describing him as the 'mastermind behind all the various malpractices'.[24]

The commission also indicted Shanti Prasad Jain. Describing Jain as the 'key man, second only to R Dalmia',[25] the commission mentioned at least four fraudulent transactions with which Jain 'was actively associated'.[26] Jaidayal Dalmia, Shanti Prasad Jain's brother Shriyans Prasad Jain and their nephew Shital Prasad Jain were also held responsible; the first two for fraudulent action and the last for 'most of the manipulations'.

In its findings, the commission recorded that the funds of public companies, banks and insurance companies were improperly used by the Dalmia-Jain group to buy shares of other companies with large accumulated resources to obtain control over them. 'This was done for improper ends. The public companies suffered and so did the investing public',[27] it observed.

'Loans and advances running into many crores of rupees were outstanding against the companies of the Group, the financial position of some of which was unsound',[28] it pointed out. 'Another way in which the investing public lost was the improper transfer of assets from one company to another,'[29] it recorded.

'In some cases, we found the same block of shares appearing as assets in the balance sheets of one company, and within a few months, by mere book entry, they appeared as assets in the balance sheet of other companies,'[30] it added. The commission gave details of the 'purely personal' gains amounting to more than Rs 2.60 crore made by Ramkrishna Dalmia as well as the gains by the other partners of the group by methods that it found fraudulent.[31]

In the court case that followed, where he was represented by the leading British attorney Sir Dingle Mackintosh Foot, Ramkrishna Dalmia was sentenced to two years in Tihar Jail. However, for most of the jail term he was unwell and was transferred to Irwin Hospital (now Loknayak Jayaprakash Narayan Hospital). He was released in May 1964 and his attempts to regain control of *The Times of India* were rebuffed by S.P. Jain. Though S.P. Jain's stand may have upset R.K. Dalmia, Sanjay Dalmia put a positive spin on it: 'It does not matter whether they were to be given back or not. What does matter is that they have remained within the family. We are, in a way, one big family.' In fact, 'the decision to keep Bennett Coleman within the extended family was actually a good one.'[32]

## The Sahu Jains: Shanti Prasad Jain (1911–77)

Shanti Prasad Jain acquired BCCL when he already had a large empire of his own. He had the largest of cement mills, jute mills and sugar mills — New Central Jute, Jaipur Udyog in Sawai Madhopur, SKG Sugars in Dalmia Nagar in Bihar and Rohtas Industries, also in Bihar. He had bamboo forests and interests in vanaspati, steel and plywood. The family had built and operatd a railway system which was running till the late 1970s and a power station, an airfield, colleges and schools. The newspaper company was but a small business interest, lower down in Sahu Jain's list of priorities.

Speaking about Shanti Prasad Jain, BCCL's former MD, Ram Tarneja said, 'He was the pillar of this empire. He was from an agri-business family; a pioneer in the pulp, paper, cement and sugar industries. When the British left India, he purchased some jute mills and plywood factories. The family also had independent interests in Bihar.

'There was also a Dalmia airline, started around the time Air India was launched, then called the Indian National Airline, sometime between 1946 and '49. The airline was based in Delhi. The family also had businesses on both sides of the Indo-Pak border. It had cement factories near the Karachi airport, and an insurance company in Lahore.'[33]

Shanti Prasad Jain made Calcutta his home, just as many Marwaris had done, choosing the city over Bombay, in the 1950s. His business had mostly kept him in Bihar and his home was in

Uttar Pradesh, before that. Calcutta housed many other Marwari business houses including those of the Surajmals, the Nagarmals, the Goenkas and the Birlas.

Here, he built a palatial home called Jain House on 9, Alipur Park Place, where it still stands. During its heyday, its opulence, grandeur and sheer size were the envy of friends and rivals in business and government. The Jain House was better than even the governor's mansion in Calcutta. It had Italian marble and Chippendale furniture in the bedrooms, suites for every member of the family and French bathroom fittings and sunken bathtubs.

With its many rooms resting on a generous spread of marble, a lavish dining area with a custom-made dining table that could seat twenty-four, and a sprawling spread of open area around it, Jain House hosted many gatherings and witnessed the daily arrival of dignitaries. In the 1950s and the 1960s, the prime minister and the president of India were said to have been house guests of Shanti Prasad Jain.

During a visit to Calcutta in July 2002, I had a chance to attend a prayer meeting there. Once the huge grey gates open, you can see the house in all its glory, painted grey and white. The grounds are spacious and covered with greenery. The path towards the house is lined with trees. There is a small temple to the left, within the premises, as you walk along the way that leads to the prayer hall inside the house. The reception-cum-lobby is lined with paintings and the foyer is decked with unusual mirrors. A small photograph of the late Nandita Judge (Samir Jain's younger sister, who lost her life in an air crash in Arunachal Pradesh in May 2001) rests on a mantle.

Further in, there is a sitting area with a sunken fountain with coloured lights built into it. A grey-and-white spiral staircase in Italian marble takes visitors upstairs. By the staircase, as one goes up, is a huge linear window, which lets the sunlight pour in. Visitors may also avail of a lift service. By the lift is a huge grandfather clock flanked by five-foot-tall vases of porcelain and metal.

The prayer hall is open on all sides, surrounded by lush green lawns. A huge overturned lotus in full bloom looks at you from the ceiling. Towards the right of this prayer hall is a drawing room with huge, framed, circular paintings. The room, which may have entertained many dignitaries and luminaries, is now unused and dark. Its sofas are covered with sheets. A part of the drawing room has a low stage built within it and a huge diamond-shaped mirror covering an entire wall. The room was used for performances held in-house, a member of the staff told me.

There is a huge dining room to the left of this prayer hall. It still has that mahogany table to seat twenty-four people and several extra chairs lined up against the wall, and huge carved-wood and ivory cupboards. Wooden candelabra-shaped lights outside mark the hallway leading eventually to the green area in the house, where one finds a small lotus pond.

As one steps out of the house after the prayers, one sees yet another temple. There are some green outhouses with quaint white windows. Lush palms and hanging flower pots dot and decorate the rest of the space. The Jain children, Alok, Manoj and Alka, were born here. The eldest, Ashok, was born at the Jains' Najibabad house in Uttar Pradesh, when that was still their home in 1934.

Alok Jain remembers his father as an intrepid man, full of ideas. 'His graph began rising after he joined his father-in-law at Danapur, at the refinery. He got the idea of setting up sugar factories and went to Indonesia to purchase four sugar mills. He began Kalinga Tubes in partnership with Biju Patnaik. And he set up the country's first fertilizer plant in Benaras, among other things,' Alok Jain said. 'He was featured in an early 1950 issue of *Time* magazine as being one of the four men who built modern India along with J.R.D. Tata, B.M. Birla and Sabin Mukerjee,' he proudly stated.[34]

The pride in his voice was unmistakable, although he lay slumped on a sofa in Ramesh Chandra Jain's Bharatiya Jnanpith office. Alok Jain was trying to relive his glorious past. The Jain empire was 'counted among India's top ten business houses along with the Singhanias, Goenkas, Mafatlals, Anant Kilachand, Keshubhai Lalbhai, and the Thapars by the mid-1950s,' he said.

'As far as BCCL was concerned, Babuji did not think of it as an industry or as a way of wielding political clout or power like Dalmiaji. He never attempted to project himself through his publications despite the fact that he had sympathizers in government,' he insisted. But he confessed that Shanti Prasad Jain did have it in him to beat Ramnath Goenka (1902–91) of *The Indian Express*.

Goenka was a friend of Ramkrishna Dalmia's brother, Jaidayal, and Shanti Prasad Jain knew him well. 'Yet Babuji wanted *The Times of India* to be better and ahead of *The Indian Express* and he was keen that BCCL become more profitable than the Express group. That was his one motivation. His rivalry with Ramnathji was striking. They met for the first time in 1944 and were close friends, and yet, they were rivals,' he noted.

R.P. Jain, too, echoed these sentiments. 'Shanti Prasad Jain was good at both economic matters and social interactions. He had a lot of well-placed friends and acquaintances but there was always some tension between him and Goenka. They often met at the former's home in Calcutta and were cordial. But we were aware that there was an element of one-upmanship involved,' he said.

'Shanti Prasad Jain gave all power to his executives. He was intelligent; not too interested in details but adept at finance. He would collect information based on conversations he had had with people and take quick decisions. And, he was liberal. Above all, he liked winning,' R.P. Jain continued.

At *The Times of India,* Frank Moraes had succeeded Ivor Jehu to become the first Indian editor of the paper and was at the helm from 1950 to 1957. Moraes had joined *The Times* in 1936 and became an assistant editor by 1938. He was then its war correspondent between 1942 and '45. In 1949, he was also named editor of *The National Standard* by Ramnath Goenka. But in 1950, he took over as editor of *The Times*.

He was followed by N.J. Nanporia, who edited the paper for the next ten years, and also got into an infamous tussle with the management when he wrote a confidential letter to the then prime minister, Jawaharlal Nehru, narrating the misdemeanours of those who owned and ran the company. Both these editors had a great understanding of international affairs and their editorials were eagerly awaited and lapped up by their readers.

Bennett, Coleman and Co. Limited also launched several Hindi magazines and journals, which were to become popular with a large segment of the readers in the following years. These included *Vama* and *Sarika* among many others. Alok Jain credited his mother Rama Jain for this contribution. 'Amma's thought pattern about the media was different from Babuji's. She wanted to use the medium to promote Hindi and the other national Indian languages. She encouraged the translation of Indian writings from all regional languages into Hindi,' he said.

Rama Jain is believed to have acquired some of her aesthetic taste and her fondness for literature and the arts from her early days at the Jamnalal Bajaj household. She spent a substantial part of her childhood and teens with Rahul Bajaj's father's family in their house in Nagpur and Bombay, and she had acquired her sanskaar (culture) from their family, according to Ramesh Chandra Jain.

In 1944, Shanti Prasad Jain, inspired by his wife Rama, set up the Bharatiya Jnanpith to promote research into, and the study of, ancient Indian texts and to encourage their publication. The institution was also meant to appreciate original, contemporary literature and culture. Its inaugural project resurrected a rare manuscript, written on palm leaves in Prakrit, called 'Mahabandh'. This book carried the eleventh-century Jain scholar and sage Bhagwant Bhootabali's thoughts on Karma. Epics such as the Ramayana and the Mahabharata were published in a set called the

'Moortidevi Granthamala',[35] and the annual Jnanpith Award was instituted in 1965.

In 1952, Rama and Shanti Prasad Jain launched *Filmfare* from Bombay; a Hindi fortnightly, *DharamYug* in 1957, a Hindi monthly, *Parag* from Delhi in 1958 and *Femina* in 1959. While Rama Jain concentrated on launching more publications to cultivate and appeal to readers' tastes, Shanti Prasad Jain strategically tried to push up the circulation of his papers in nascent markets. Delhi was one of them. And Shanti Prasad Jain was painfully conscious of *The Times of India*'s unenviable position in the Delhi market. The paper was the readers' last priority in Delhi with the *Hindustan Times*, *The Indian Express* and *The Statesman* leading, in that order.

'Shanti Prasad Jain was a remarkable man; rich but modest. He had great regard for journalists and for professional competence,' said Inder Malhotra, a former resident editor of *The Times of India*, Delhi. 'He was greatly interested in what was going on; he was a man of great curiosity. He would invite people like Kuldip Nayar and me for breakfast and discuss politics. On the newspaper front, he let the editor handle operations; he did not say a word to Sham Lal,' he added.[36]

Baljit Kapoor, who joined the company in 1957 and stayed with it for thirty-two years, eventually becoming head of circulation, had an interesting story to tell about Shanti Prasad Jain's strategies at boosting circulation to beat his counterparts. 'The focus on boosting circulation has always been there, and one sure way to achieve growth in these numbers is to cut price,' he began. 'So, Jain tried the price-cut strategy in 1958 much before his grandson Samir would try it in 1991. This was when both the *Hindustan Times* and *The Times of India* were priced at sixteen paise.'[37]

Shanti Prasad Jain reduced the price of *The Times of India* to thirteen paise and *Hindustan Times* followed suit. And both these newspapers held on to this revised price for about six to eight months. Surprisingly, however, the circulation did not increase. And both papers reverted to their old prices. The pricing strategy was tried out in Delhi because *The Times of India* had already established itself in Bombay and it was the Delhi market that the Jains were trying to capture.

With an eye on attracting a new segment of the readers' market and catering to businessmen's interests, Shanti Prasad Jain launched a financial paper – *The Economic Times* – that would later be used for Samir Jain's first bold pricing experiment. *ET* was first published from Bombay in 1961. P.S. Hariharan was its first editor. D.K. Rangnekar took over in 1964 and headed it till 1979.

Ramnath Goenka also launched a financial paper – *The Financial Express* – in Bombay the same year. In fact, Goenka managed to launch *The Financial Express* just ahead of *The Economic Times*. R.C. Jain had an aside to share on the launch of these two financial dailies. He said that talk about launching a financial daily came up during a meeting of the Jain family where Ramnath Goenka was present. 'Shanti Prasadji mentioned that he was thinking about launching a financial daily in English from Bombay. Ramnathji was listening keenly but did not say anything. He however inquired about the launch date. The next thing we knew was that he had launched *The Financial Express* about a fortnight before *ET*. He was like that; a fierce and unapologetic competitor,' he said with a shrug and a mischievous chuckle.

Like his father-in-law, Shanti Prasad Jain too had his brushes with the law. Trouble courted him in 1958 after a trip to Europe and the United States. He and his wife were accused of possessing foreign exchange beyond the then permissible limits and of violating provisions of the Foreign Exchange Regulations Act (FERA).

The case went all the way to the Supreme Court. 'It was alleged that Babuji had taken kickbacks for some machinery purchased abroad. We were in talks with some German companies,' said Alok Jain. 'After that, it was a struggle,' he added.

Inder Malhotra had this to add. 'When Shanti Prasad Jain landed at the airport, nearly fifty people came there to receive him. And the authorities were about to arrest him. So, a staff member requested the customs authorities to let him go out of the premises with dignity, and assured them that Mr Jain would be brought back after having driven a certain distance, to avoid embarrassment. That was allowed.'

But this was relatively minor compared to the implications from a previous set of enquiries by the Vivian Bose Commission. Apart from the wrong doings attributed to the Dalmia-Jain group as a whole, the commission had made specific charges against Shanti Prasad Jain.The government had gone on to file a petition against the group which pleaded, among others, that a special officer be appointed to manage the affairs of Bennett, Coleman and Company and that the then management be restrained and removed from employment.

In response to this petition, Justice J.L. Nain of the Bombay High Court, while noting the allegations made in the petition, passed an interim order on 28 August 1969 that would prove decisive for Bennett Coleman over the next seven years. 'Under these circumstances, the best thing would be to pass such orders on the assumption that the allegations made by the petitioners that the affairs of the company were being conducted in a manner prejudicial to public interest and to the interests of the Company are correct,' the judge ruled.[38]

In accordance with the high court ruling, the existing board of Bennett Coleman was disbanded and a new board was constituted. It would stay in place for the next seven years, a period that came to be called the 'zero years' in the company.

In the new board, Dr L.M. Singhvi, Narendra Kumar and Mouli Chand Sharma were the nominees of the company. R.K. Hazari, S.M. Kumaramangalam and H.M. Trivedi came in as nominees of the government. And Kantilal T. Desai (who would also serve as chairman), S.M. Dahanukar, Kai Khushru, S. Engineer and G.V. Desai were appointed as nominees of the Bombay High Court. Shanti Prasad Jain was no longer on the board.

Dr Ram Tarneja, a professional and in that sense the only

outsider 'to the closely held, family-run company', came in as general manager. There were two deputy general managers – Ramesh Chandra Jain and P.R. Krishnamoorty.[39]

Krishnamoorty had started out as Shanti Prasad Jain's stenographer and later became the executive secretary of the company. Shanti Prasad's elder son, Ashok Jain joined the company in September 1969, and became member of the board of directors representing the shareholders. Shanti Prasad Jain had, more or less, retired by then and devoted himself to social welfare and philanthropy.

## Ashok Jain (1934–99)

Ashok Jain was born in 1934. He was sent to the DAV (Dayanand Anglo-Vedic) School, Lahore, in 1942 from where he did his matriculation. Later, he graduated with an honours degree in science from Presidency College, Calcutta. Jain family members and his contemporaries say he was soft-spoken and liberal.

'He had business acumen. He was good with numbers. He wanted to expand the publishing business but was thrifty. And he ran this concern in the traditional manner of Marwari businessmen,' said a relative. 'Ashok Jain did not like to invest so much,' said Inder Malhotra. 'When Sham Lal was a director on the board, and post-government-control, in 1976, when the paper had become bureaucratic, we suggested getting our proofreaders trained in a four-to-six-weeks training course. But Ashok Jain said "No". His father was keen to improve the intellectual level for the newspaper. But for Ashok Jain, the status quo was good enough,' he pointed out.

Ashok Jain also retained a lot of managers from the Sahu Jain group; kept an eye on costs and avoided taking risks. 'He was a bad paymaster although he could handle troubles very well,' said R.P. Jain. 'He was skilful but not too keen to induct people from outside. There was no major policy change or prosperity but no loss either. He was extremely cautious too,' he noted.

'Ashok had begun work around 1963. Prior to that, Alok had been more important, although he was younger. He had been looking after the jute mills in Calcutta and in just one year, he had given the company a profit of Rs 1 crore. His father preferred him. And until 1969, he was more important than his elder brother,' R.P. Jain said.

New editions and publications were launched. The company stayed profitable. But Ashok Jain was not hell-bent on rewriting industry rules to increase profits phenomenally. For him, press was not a hard-core business, where the survival of the fittest meant the annihilation of the counterpart. But he was mindful about his business interests and ensured that his newspapers were not in conflict with them. He interacted with his editors and managers and let them manage the day-to-day affairs. And he remained that way even after his son, Samir, had brought about changes in the organization, although he was interested in national developments and enjoyed engaging with his editors on issues.

Ashok Jain pursued and promoted the spread of literature and scholarship. He took a healthy interest in politics and government. He socialized and moved in business circles, and he was associated with the setting up of the Associated Chamber of Commerce and Industry.[40] In the course of researching this book, I met Dr Sanjaya Baru, who has held senior positions at both *The Times of India* and *The Economic Times* and been media advisor to Prime Minister Manmohan Singh. Over a cup of coffee at a Khan Market cafe, he gave me an inkling into the way Ashok Jain operated. 'In 1996, I was accused of being tough on the BJP government and soft on Narasimha Rao during the time of the thirteen-day BJP government. Ashok Jain wanted to support the BJP and Vajpayee. He called me upstairs one day. I went up and sat with him for two hours just listening to Vajpayee's speech. He did not say anything directly. But he would ask, "Don't you agree with this point?" "Don't you believe that is a strong argument?" "What do you think of the speech?" The hints were all there but nothing was said directly.

I responded by saying, "Vajpayee is a great speaker but he is in the wrong party."'[41]

'He made his point so subtly,' Baru noted.

'Ashok Jain was a soft-spoken man who was keen on fostering a harmonious working relationship between journalists and the management, and he nurtured journalists and journalism; never interfering with the editor's job and giving them a free hand,' said Pritish Nandy, who was inducted into the world of newspapers and magazines by Jain.[42]

To ensure this harmonious working relationship, to give readers a forum for redressal and to improve and monitor the functioning of the company, Ashok Jain also inducted into BCCL an ombudsman – Justice P.N. Bhagwati, a former Chief Justice of India.

During the time the court-appointed board oversaw the functioning of the company, there was hardly any technological advancement or forward planning and the organization lagged behind by two to four years. After the 'zero years', control of the company was returned to the Jains in August 1976.

Alok Jain claimed that he and R.P. Jain played a constructive role in accomplishing this. 'The company would have otherwise been given up as lost to the government,' he said. And he recounted how he had tried to get friends in government onto his side, and finally managed to get help from Vidya Charan Shukla, Fakhruddin Ali Ahmed, and finally Indira Gandhi, who had by then been prime minister for nearly a decade.

'The children (Ashok Jain's sons, Samir and Vineet, who are now the owners of BCCL) either do not know how we managed this near-improbable task or do not care,' he lamented. He credited Ramesh Chandra Jain and Dr Ram Tarneja with having played stellar roles during that phase. 'Ram Tarneja was an outsider but he did not misuse power. And although technically there was little control of the family, these men ensured that it effectively stayed within their grasp,' he noted.

R.P. Jain, on the other hand, said that Alok Jain had created trouble. 'Indira Gandhi had decided to give the company back to us much earlier and that had been conveyed to the Bombay High Court. Fakhruddin Ali Ahmed was the minister for company affairs. Shanti Prasad had gone to meet him. Alok was also there. He started saying all sorts of things to Ahmed, asking him why he had not acted quickly. Alok kept saying, "Who are you to stop it after the Cabinet has decided upon something?" Things got out of hand. Meanwhile, the judge got time to appoint a new board for a specific period,' he added.

Ram Sukhraj Tarneja, a professor of management, had taught at a university in America before joining BCCL. Subsequently, he was one of its non-executive directors. His career graph at Bennett, Coleman and Co. began rising when he became director, personnel, in 1963. By 1976, he was a general manager. From 1981 till he retired in 1991, he was the managing director of BCCL.

During our meeting at the Ashok Hotel in New Delhi sometime in June 2001, he was not amused by the larger-than-life image that the media had drawn of Samir Jain. He browsed through a synopsis of this book I had drawn up in early 2001, and gave me a hard look. Part serious and part in jest, he asked me, 'Do you believe that Samir Jain is the architect of *The Times of India*'s success?'[43]

I asked him for his point of view. 'Perhaps you should know that the first steps to strengthen this inherently strong organization began in the early to mid-1960s,' Tarneja began. 'Between 1963 and 1964, the company's HR department hired its first batch of trainees and we started revamping HRD. We also brought in technology and professional management into the company and have kept upgrading these ever since,' he said.

Without having articulated it, Ram Tarneja had conveyed what he believed. To him, *The Times of India* was already a strong institution. It had been strengthened further during the 1960s and

1970s. Those who managed the affairs at BCCL during these years had put in place a large network for the company to further expand. And, if the fortunes went up phenomenally after the mid-1980s, it was because the *TOI* stood on solid ground and because it had a solid foundation.

Dr Tarneja also laid emphasis on the early work that had gone into the making of this company. 'The foundations of *The Times*' growth were laid during Shanti Prasad Jain's times. I strongly believe that. Whatever was done after that was just building upon that early strength and consolidating it further,' he stressed. 'He was the pillar of this empire.'

'*The Times* was in the extended family. And then, Shanti Prasad Jain bought BCCL from his father-in-law, Ramkrishna Dalmia, for an official amount of Rs 54 lakh, and appointed J.C. Jain as GM. And even before the entire machinery could be put into high gear, the cases happened and there was a rough patch,' he said.

'The period between 1970 and 1976 was a challenging one as control over BCCL remained with the government after some cases were filed against some members of the family. It was the management of the company that was taken over, not its ownership. Yet, BCCL, in the real sense, came back to the family only in 1976 and Ashok Jain became its chairman. After this, *The Times*' empire was again built. Ashok Jain had great expansion plans for *The Times* and it was he who wanted to see the paper's presence all across the country,' Dr Tarneja added.

He also noted, 'The year 1988 was a turning point for *The Times*. All the apex activities were institutionalized. There were the year-long celebrations of the sesquicentennial. Besides that, between 1986-87 and 1990, there is a technology story. This was when we introduced state-of-the-art suburban printing for the first time and brought about a huge technological upgrade in the company.

'Eventually,' he said, 'The Times Group has failed in almost everything except its newspapers. Is *The Times* really a brand? Will a Times T-shirt sell as well as a Times newspaper?' Incidentally, he might be wrong on both accounts. The group has pushed ahead in its multimedia ventures with equal vigour and the its brand-building exercise is a case in point.

Around this time, *The Times of India* had one of its finest editors at the helm – the unparalleled Sham Lal: writer, thinker, philosopher; erudite and reclusive. This 1912-born doyen of Indian journalism worked with the *Hindustan Times* and the (now defunct) *Indian News Chronicle* before joining *The Times of India* in early 1950. In 1967, he took over as editor of *The Times of India*.

'Although they continued to keep a close watch on the activities at BCCL, the government let Sham Lal run the paper,' Inder Malhotra reminisced. However, during the Emergency (1975–77) the government wanted M. Shamim to be the editor. Prime Minister Indira Gandhi also brought in Rajni Patel as the chairman of the board of directors at BCCL.

Sham Lal edited the paper from 1967 to 1978 and his column, 'Life and Letters', written under the pen name 'Adib' had a huge following as did his other column, 'The National Scene', which was written under his own name.

When I met Sham Lal,[44] he spoke about his experiences at *The Times of India*. 'The chairman,' he told me, 'would sit in the building and chat with the editors. The owners would ask me what time suited me for a discussion and then meet me, and talk general politics. On no occasion was a policy directive given. I remember when (film actor) Raj Kapoor's daughter got married and they wanted to put in a picture, I said no, and that was it. We did not carry the photograph.

'There was only one manager during my days, and no executive managers. The relationship between owners and editors was cordial. The owners let the editor handle the paper entirely and rarely interfered. Of course, they maintained an interest in what was happening on the political scene and at an international level and enjoyed discussing these matters with us, but that was it,' he added.

Sham Lal retired in 1978 and was followed by Girilal Jain as editor. Inder Malhotra, who had joined the *TOI* in February 1971 and had been posted in Bombay, came to Delhi as the *TOI*'s resident editor. Newer publications continued to be launched from the Bennett Coleman stable. *The Times of India*'s Ahmedabad edition was started in 1968. And a Marathi newspaper, *Maharashtra Times*, was launched from Bombay in 1972. Delhi and Calcutta saw the entry of *The Economic Times* in their respective arenas in 1974 and 1976.

The day after the Jains regained control over BCCL, they held a meeting to take stock of the situation and lay down an agenda for change with Ashok Jain in charge. Inder Malhotra, who frequently dealt with Ashok Jain, said, 'He was a well-mannered owner. He respected journalists and journalism and rarely ever interfered in the paper editorially. There may have been stray instances of an unexpected interest in how a news report appeared in the paper or did not. But that was done with utmost decency and caution,' he said.

'He may have rung me up, just twice, but he never tried to influence me,' recalled Malhotra. 'The first time I got a call from him inquiring about editorial content was when Indira Gandhi came back to power. Swraj Paul was, at that time, making a bid to take over Escorts. The Ambanis were coming up. There was a raid on the Nandas at Escorts. In 1983, we started the Lucknow edition, and Giri was in Bangalore to start an edition there.

'The news editor showed me a message that on the raid on the Nandas we should not feature it prominently and only carry an agency copy. Giri was taking a position against the raids. That is when Ashok Jain asked me, "Why is there no item on the raids?" He wanted to know why the omission had happened,' Malhotra recounted.

On another occasion, although Ashok Jain was involved, it was Samir Jain's reaction that Malhotra remembers. 'When Rajiv

Gandhi came to power in 1984 and V.P. Singh was the finance minister, the Kirloskars were raided and the patriarch of the family, S.L. Kirloskar, was arrested. But the story went unreported. The next day, when asked, Giri said that he had got the story covered as per the Kirloskar's reaction to the raids.

'Samir's reaction was strong. "Why has *The Times of India* been reduced to become the Kirloskar's Gazette," he shouted. He ran Giri down. I decided to leave,' Malhotra said.

By the time Ashok Jain became BCCL chairman, the rest of the Sahu Jain businesses had almost been frittered away. Most industries were either sick or dying, and almost all of them beyond repair.

Ashok Jain's elder son Samir, who went to New Central Jute Mills to revive it, failed to turn it around. Besides, he was keener to be in an urban setting rather than in the back of beyond, in a commodities market. That is when *The Times of India* and BCCL assumed greater significance for Samir Jain. It became all the more important to the scion who was beginning to understand the domain, and envisage a different role for it.

BCCL continued its plans for expansion by launching *Khel Bharati* to cater to the sports reader. It brought out the *Indrajal Comics* for young children, and *Science Today* and *Career & Competition Times* for teenagers. Profits at BCCL were Rs 49 lakh by end-July 1977 against Rs 216.45 crore by end-July 2000.

Bennett, Coleman and Co. launched *Sandhya Times*, a local Hindi evening tabloid in Delhi in 1978 as a part of its expansion plan. By 1979, *The Times of India* was being published from three centres – Bombay, Delhi and Ahmedabad.

Circulation-wise, BCCL's papers were not doing badly. But they were not outstanding either. *The Times of India*, the company's flagship newspaper was selling almost 2.5 lakh copies daily in Bombay, nearly 1.7 lakh a day in Delhi and almost 47,000 copies a day in Ahmedabad between January and June 1979. But the *TOI* was much behind the market leader, the *Hindustan Times* and even *The Indian Express*, which played a stellar role during the Emergency (1975–77) and after.

*The Express* not just saw a boom in its circulation but won many loyalists. It was the favourite of the masses and had a particularly good stint between mid-January 1977, when the then Lok Sabha was dissolved and fresh elections were announced, and mid-March 1977, when the elections took place and the Emergency (26 June 1975 – 21 March 1977) was withdrawn. '*The Express*' circulation in Delhi almost tripled during this period,' media analyst Sushil Pandit[45] noted. Guided by the combative Arun Shourie as its editor, it continued to ride on that wave much after Emergency. And *The Times of India*, known for its centrist, moderate stand was still at the number three position in Delhi.

Just like his father, Ashok Jain also found himself on the wrong side of the law. He was arrested by the Enforcement Directorate in July 1998 from his Bombay residence for alleged violation of FERA. Even as the family – and his newspapers – rallied behind him during a prolonged legal battle, he underwent a bypass surgery in Cleveland, US. He died in February 1999.

In the 1980s, the newspaper would undergo a phenomenal change with a new entrant stepping into the saddle. This would be a time for much turmoil in the group but also for a renaissance of sorts. The old order would change. Conventions would be thrown to the winds and the rules of the game rewritten. The newspaper industry would truly become an industry; a bona fide business in the real sense of the term, with no apologies for the way it would function and a very clear reorientation of its mission.

TWO

# VC with a Third Eye on the Fourth Estate

*'When you are inspired by some great purpose, some extraordinary project, all your thoughts break their bonds. Your mind transcends limitations; your consciousness expands in every direction, and you find yourself in a wonderful, new world. Dormant forces, facilities and talents come alive and you discover yourself to be a greater person than you ever dreamed yourself to be.'*

(The quote is attributed to Patanjali. But its ownership is uncertain.)

IT WAS A HIGH-PROFILE meeting, sometime in 1984, in the conference room of the Times House, Bombay, convened by Ashok Jain, chairman of the group. Attending the meeting were the top brass of the company including its MD, Ram Tarneja, Executive Directors P.R. Krishnamoorthy and Ramesh Chandra Jain, *The Times of India* editor, Sham Lal, who was also a director, and head of circulation

Baljit Kapoor. Also present were Girilal Jain and the legendary cartoonist R.K. Laxman. The objective of the meeting was clear, although not spelt out. Ashok Jain would formally introduce his thirty-year-old son, Samir, to the top brass.

A slim, average-looking young man walked in and took centre stage. All of them relaxed. Samir did not seem overbearing or boorish. He spoke in a soft voice. His story had been unremarkable so far. Not that he was a stranger. Many in the audience had known him for years; one of them was to go on to say that he had seen Samir from the time he was in shorts as a four-year-old. But none would have anticipated what was in store.

Invited to speak a few words that day, the young scion did not soft-pedal a proem. He came straight to the point and said, 'Newspapers are vehicles for carrying advertisements and news is what we print to fill in the gaps between the ads.'

For an audience that included, arguably, some of the top editors of the country, this statement was disparaging, if not downright insulting. Even if you were not a journalist, the line was heretical and profane at a time when newspapers saw themselves as missionary. Editorial news and opinion – not advertising – is what accorded power and prestige to proprietors. This opening remark was to be quoted over and over again for at least the next decade as the mark of a man who was believed to be vehemently 'anti-journalist'.

Anti-journalist or not, it did sum up Samir Jain's approach to how he would manage his media empire over the next two decades. It also signified his clarity of thought and vision, even if it was starkly different from how newspapers were run and perceived at that time.

Nearly three decades later, Samir Jain, the owner of the world's largest-selling English newspaper, remains resolutely reclusive. He is determined, almost stubborn, about shunning the limelight and keeping away from the public gaze. While you might occasionally see a photograph of his younger brother, Vineet Jain, in his newspapers, Samir Jain is elusive. On the other hand, photographers of certain other organizations are under instructions to capture as many shots of him as and when possible.

Given this context, my efforts to meet him at the start of this project, and again some years later, were bound to fail. But his people, serving and separated, have been more than forthcoming in talking about him. They have each shared the dimension that they were aware of. Here, I piece together the multiple shades to attempt a sketch of one of the most famously enigmatic personalities of the Indian media.

I realized that it is not easy to have a balanced view of Samir Jain. He evoked extreme reactions. Some associates were completely in awe, almost mesmerized, by what they considered his sharp intellect and his ability to connect the dots to create the big picture. They marvelled at his penchant for challenging the conventional, courting controversy and criticism and, eventually, taking a detached view of it all.

Many alluded to the mystique around him and the agony of deciphering his codes and signals. Equally, there were others who had suffered (or relished) his long and oblique monologues, laced with references to the scriptures, and how it all made sense at some later time. Reference was also made to his spirituality, his 'conversations with God' and his interactions with his gurus.

Clearly, there is no *one* Samir Jain who can be put in a box. There are tales where he has demonstrated deep empathy, sometimes taking people by complete surprise. At the same time, there are anecdotes of ruthless action in 'total disregard of values' prompted by business interest or just plain ego.

It appears that Samir Jain was brought up on his grandfather Shanti Prasad Jain's principles of playing to win. Early enough in his career, he learnt not to trust any individual too much, too long. He comes across as one focused on self-learning, self-realization and improvement. Beneath the reclusive exterior is a simmering, raging ambition to make it against all odds. No one likes to lose.

One is struck by his unconventional approach and execution, in particular, his proclivity to take decisions based on gut feeling, instinct and intuition and then having them tested out. He also maintains a keen desire to weed out as many flaws as is possible from every idea, proposal or initiative that comes to him for perusal, to make it truly viable. He seems willing to experiment and to take calculated risks. He detests failure. Samir Jain is calmly aggressive, detachedly involved; and above all, aware that fame and success are ephemeral and that the temporary is the only permanent.

Samir Jain was in his late twenties when he first joined BCCL. He was an introvert, shy, modest-looking and tentative. He had been through school in St Xavier's, Calcutta. By the time he was at St Stephen's College, Delhi, studying English literature, political science and economics, he had developed an appetite for reading.

At BCCL, there is not much information about the early years of Samir Jain. I met Akhilesh Jain, one of Samir Jain's cousins, at his home in Gulmohar Park in south Delhi, as a part of the interaction with the extended family, to know a little more about the man. Akhilesh Jain was not very comfortable at first and it took a while before he felt he could say anything. But I had interacted with his father (Ramesh Chandra Jain) at length, and that reassured him. 'I could share a lot of stories with you,' he began.[1]

I would like to know what motivates Samir Jain; what propels him to become who he is; and a little bit about his days as a college student, I told him. Akhilesh lived at Safdarjung Enclave in his youth. Samir Jain was a few kilometres away at 6, Sardar Patel Marg. 'I first met Samir properly when the family shifted from Calcutta to Delhi. Before that, as children, we may have occasionally met at social gatherings but I cannot recollect talking with him. My grandfather, who was the head of the family, would invite the entire extended family to weddings and other functions.

'When the family decided that Calcutta was dying as far as industry went, it moved to Delhi. That is when I met Samir a lot.

We were average students, and more friends than cousins. I used to go to his house and we would go to college together in a chauffeur-driven car. Around 2 p.m., we would return home, and sometimes study. Before our exams, we sat in the library at his house and burnt the midnight oil. At other times, we would go to a five-star hotel for coffee. He was always careful about what he ate and drank. His throat is rather sensitive,' Akhilesh said.

'Kuku[2] was the quiet type. He did not interact with those around him and he had practically no friends. In fact, I remember how scared he was of being ragged when we began college. A friend of ours, Shashank Raizada, whose family owned the Delite Cinema in Delhi, accompanied him for almost fifteen days,' he added.

Shashank Raizada remembers how Samir Jain would pick him up from Sundar Nagar in south Delhi in his white Datsun while going to college to beat the threat of ragging. 'I was already in college; his senior by a year. Although we managed to protect him from the ragging, there were people who called him "Datsun" because of the car,' he said.[3]

'He was a very quiet person who could be outspoken if he wanted to; never loud, yet assertive. He is also extremely analytical; he could argue with panache; he studied everything in great detail; he was open to suggestions and he read voraciously,' he elaborated.

'I do remember that he was very fond of reading, and his expression of English was strong. "Use the proper words and you can express yourself well, briefly," he would say. He wanted effective usage of words, and spoke very little himself. That made it difficult for us to understand him sometimes. He also laid particular stress on making great presentations. "These help one understand the subject better," he believed. The presentations might have even served the purpose of testing the skill of his managers,' Akhilesh added.

People who worked with Samir Jain in his early days at BCCL recalled that he did not display any overt signs of the aggression or the single-mindedness with which he would later transform the company. 'In the beginning, he seemed affable, nodding his head deferentially when we spoke to him at meetings and social gatherings. And we treated him just as one would treat the owner's son,' recalled Baljit Kapoor.[4] 'But when it came to carrying out his decisions, many of them unpopular, he was surprisingly resolute and calm in the face of all opposition,' he pointed out.

When his father Ashok Jain initially inducted him into the newspaper business in 1980, Samir Jain was placed under the tutelage of Ramesh Chandra Jain. He was probably piqued by that and left and did not return until a few years later when he was designated executive director.

In the first few months after his induction at the Times House, Samir Jain maintained a low profile, mostly keeping to himself. He had even confided that he found the newspaper business boring. He understood very little of it and he felt there was no risk involved.

Several senior members of the company saw him as a novice in need of training and guidance. Ashok Jain reinforced this impression by asking them to help put the young man at ease. The management information reports started to be sent to him but he went largely unnoticed. The seniors were mostly indifferent to him at first; almost dismissive, even recalcitrant.

'Many executives from the past, who had served in the Dalmia-Jain group, were still attached to the family's businesses. The old guard made Samir Jain feel that he did not know how to run companies and that really bothered him. He was resolute in his conviction to prove them wrong,' said Vijay Jindal,[5] who joined the Sahu Jain group in the early 1980s, working at one of the paper factories, and went on to become a member of the board of BCCL by the mid-1990s.

For a number of reasons, Samir Jain was determined to make it work. He had tried his hand at the family's other businesses, many of which were in decline. In that sense, he may have encountered failure early in his career. From the family's point of view too, the stakes in the newspaper business had become high: its future, as a business group, hinged on the success of its newspapers.

'When Samir started to take interest in the family's media business, most of the other businesses of the Sahu Jain group were in a state of decline,' Ramesh Chandra Jain said. 'Samir had served in Rohtas Industries in Bihar, where the family owned one of India's largest sugar factories.

'He even tried his hand at the family's New Central Jute Mills in Uttar Pradesh as executive director (administration). But by that time, the jute business, which had flourished during the 1933–50 period, was in bad shape. Labour problems plagued the industry. Samir tried to revive it, but in vain. He returned to the family's home in Calcutta,' he added.

'Although his family was from a commodities background, he had mentally rejected that area. It could have had something to do with his St Stephen's background. He did not want to be working in a remote area in Bihar. He wanted a city-based business,' Ramesh Chandra Jain observed.

Those at BCCL who took him lightly during that early phase obviously overlooked the young inheritor's resolve. But there were others who got a whiff of his complex nature. There was something about him that showed that he meant business and that he wanted to be taken seriously. Unlike his mild-mannered father, he wanted to command authority, take firm decisions and boldly push ahead with his plans.

Inder Malhotra was one of those who saw it coming. 'In the beginning, his full potential was not seen. But by mid-1984, Samir had shown that he and he alone would run the newspaper for the next 30–40 years,' he said.

For a long time, his family and relatives had been dominating. When he joined the newspaper business, Samir Jain found journalists virtually dictating terms, as was the practice in most newspapers. This experience seems to have stayed with him for many years.

There are several anecdotes to suggest how the editor at that time had the supreme position and the proprietor was meant to play second fiddle. For example, there was no way Samir Jain –

or anyone for that matter – could casually walk into the editor Girilal Jain's room. It was well known at the Times House that a peon, positioned outside the editor's cabin, guarding it, would say something to the effect of 'Sahib editorial likh rahe hain' (The boss is writing his editorial). A red light would be on to indicate that the editor was occupied, and that he couldn't be disturbed. Samir Jain may have found this hard to take.

The current managing editor of a financial daily, who was a correspondent with *The Economic Times* in the 1980s, recounted an incident of how Samir Jain's early attempts at sharing his point of view with the editors met with opposition, almost indifference.[6]

'I was a young correspondent at *ET*. Manu Shroff was the editor. He was located at the Bombay office but would visit Delhi once in a while. Shroff was an economist and had served as a bureaucrat. He had a stiff upper lip, and wasn't an easy one to crack.

'During one of Shroff's meetings with his correspondents, Samir Jain walked in and began talking about some changes he wanted in the newspaper. Shroff did not pay any attention to him. He looked away; almost in contempt. And, because our editor wasn't engaging the owner's son, we journalists did not initiate a conversation with him either. Samir Jain spoke for a while but when he realized that he wasn't making any headway, he left the room. This is how most senior editors treated him during those early years.'

Samir Jain would go on to confront the editors at a later date. But before that, one of the first things he did was to put himself through a rigorous internship. He knew very little about the industry he had joined. He demonstrated an acute desire to understand the market in which newspapers operated. He built a small team, including journalists, and used it as a sounding board.

Gautam Adhikari, a former executive editor of The *Times of India*, was close to Samir Jain during that phase. Recounting those days, Adhikari said: 'He was very curious. He would take me on long walks through Delhi's ridge area. The environment was conducive. We could talk without much traffic or other distractions.[7]

'We would dwell at length about the newspaper industry. He was learning and he was inquisitive. And he was most certainly well read. He asked several questions. He wanted to know everything about the media and he absorbed information very well. He would assimilate and churn all that we discussed, and in subsequent meetings, ask more questions... He has an incredible mind,' Adhikari noted.

Samir Jain backed up those conversations on the media with voracious reading on the subject. He read extensively on the relationship between advertising and the newspaper industry, and on marketing, of course. He was willing to collect material on every newspaper in the world.

Around this time, he had an opportunity to visit the United States in connection with treatment for his son, Vardhaman, who had a problem with his vision. By many accounts, Samir Jain formulated several of his ideas on the basis of what he saw abroad, notably at *The New York Times*, in the mid-1980s.

Mostly unnoticed by the high lords of his creed and by his peers, Samir Jain had started to develop his own set of convictions about the newspaper business and about how BCCL ought to be managed. He also had his own comprehensive way of looking at life, his own Weltanschauung.

Jain soaked it up from more than one source. Pradeep Guha was someone for whom he is believed to have had a lot of affection. Guha had a long stint at BCCL which culminated in his becoming executive director and president. He had a major role in the turnaround of the company's newspaper and magazine brands.

He is credited with ringing in the glamour quotient in the newspapers, including the famed 'Page 3' concept. Guha is well known in the film fraternity, as he was closely associated with the makeover of *Filmfare* and *Femina*. He is also known to have worked with Samir Jain as the two sought to redefine media marketing and build their newspaper brands.

Early in his tenure as executive director, Samir Jain made several visits to Calcutta to supervise the company's eastern operations.

That is where he came into contact with Guha, who had been sent from Bombay to handle the operations in that region. Jain's induction into advertising could have begun there.

'Samir Jain had just taken over as executive director and I had moved to Calcutta as manager of the eastern operations. This was sometime in March–April 1983,' Guha recalled.[8] 'We interacted a lot and began understanding the business together. My family would stay over at his home in 9, Alipur Road. There would be several discussions and many long talks on what we could do with *The Times of India*.

'We were spending a lot of time together, and we connected at multiple levels. Sometimes, there would be a visit to a nightclub. Samir was the one who introduced me to the Pink Elephant in Calcutta. We worked together on The Times Eye Foundation in the city. He was so passionately involved in everything he did and knew that he could bring about change,' Guha reminisced.

When I asked Guha about how Samir Jain went about transforming his business, he said: 'It was not as if he picked up things and copied them; his is a very curious and focused mind. So, he would look at one situation and relate it to a completely different context; and that would still work.

'During those days, I remember he was also a fun-loving man, modern and progressive, and looking keenly at the future of his business. He recognized his newspapers as products which had been undervalued and he felt that we needed to extract more revenue out of them. He felt that gold was being treated like tin,' Guha pointed out.

'The fact that the company had no money too weighed on his mind. We had limited resources, virtually no profits and more people than chairs in some of the centres. 'I would tie my chair to the table with a bicycle chain before leaving office lest someone take it by the time I returned, would you believe,' he asked. 'Things were not really gung-ho'.

About Samir Jain's learning style, Guha said: 'He was very

open to ideas and discussions. In fact, he thrived on them; intently listening to every suggestion and assimilating everything. I think his greatest strength lies in being able to comprehend everything that happens during a discussion, pick up all the relevant pieces from here and there and convert that into a big picture, which then becomes clear to everyone around him.'

Once Samir Jain began to get into the thick of things, it appears that many around him discovered that it was not easy to decipher him or to put him in one category or another. Even for those who worked closely with him, it was not easy to break through his enigma. There was a certain aura, a mystique about him. He was his own man. You could never get a hold on his personality. At most times he came across as reticent and private. At other times, they discovered, he liked to sit in on meetings and hold forth for several hours on his 'thoughts' about the business to audiences much older and experienced than him.

'Working with him was never comfortable. That was true then. That is true now', observed a journalist who worked at *The Times* in the 1980s, and like many others who spoke about Jain, did not want to be named. 'As a person, he is highly complex. Very few can claim to understand him, be close to him or be his confidants. He will never share his vision or plans fully with anyone. Different people may know different parts, but never the whole picture. Sometimes, you think he deliberately causes the confusion.'

One of the most striking features of his work and personality was being staunchly apolitical. That was most unusual for a newspaper proprietor at that time. Most of them saw their papers as instruments to secure power and political influence. But Samir Jain had no taste for those things. This was decisive during his reinvention of the company.

T.N. Ninan is well known for his role in the transformation

of *The Economic Times* in the late 1980s, before he left the group abruptly for the rival *Business Standard*. It was difficult for me to meet him. I called his office and mailed him a questionnaire with a detailed introductory note, following which he met me at his Link House office on New Delhi's Bahadur Shah Zafar Marg.

'Unlike many of the other media proprietors, Samir Jain has always been staunchly apolitical,' Ninan said. 'He had no collateral objectives, while other publishers had political aspirations. Instead, his was a sharp financial focus. He broke rules, he kept trying and he was not afraid of making mistakes. He kept experimenting. His is a story of ceaseless experiments,' he remarked.

His apolitical position was a major factor in shaping the new direction for The Times Group. On the one hand, Samir Jain was very clear that his newspapers had to give up their 'missionary' role. They would have to operate as businesses, with a modern and progressive approach.

At the same time, publishers would have to give up playing the power game, leveraging their newspapers to secure favours from the government. Samir Jain was able to firmly shift the focus of his publications from the state to the citizen. 'He did not want any of that (political clout). He did not like that at all,' observed N.P. Singh,[9] a former advertising director of the group.

The Jains, like most leading business families of that time, had political contacts across parties and were in a position to negotiate and have 'parleys' with the government. But Samir Jain's stance was different. He did not genuflect before the politically powerful. He did not even 'keep friends' in politics. And he did not think that politicians were superior.

In some ways, that approach proved costly in the late 1990s when cases of FERA violations were pursued with vigour against Ashok Jain. While the business fraternity did its bit in support of Ashok Jain, the family found few friends among political circles and the bureaucracy. When Samir Jain did finally seek the occasional appointment to meet a top bureaucrat who had once been close to the family, he and his brother were kept waiting in the visitors' room at the ministry.

A former editor, who did not want to be named, recalled that when Girilal Jain, one of *The Times of India*'s last legendary editors, was asked to leave, some members in the ruling Congress party had approached the then prime minister to secure a fresh extension for him. They were also averse to bringing in Dileep Padgaonkar as executive editor owing to his so-called Left leanings.

The then finance secretary invited Ashok Jain for a chat. Samir Jain accompanied his father to the meeting. The finance secretary said something to the effect that if Girilal Jain's tenure could be extended the government would go easy on some cases against the Jains. While Ashok Jain was ambivalent, Samir Jain is believed to have told the finance secretary: 'You mind your business, and I'll mind mine.' Girilal Jain did not get the fresh tenure, and Dileep Padgaonkar stayed.

Samir Jain's distance from state and authority was evident early on and he relished challenging the holy cows. Ramesh Chandra Jain had told me: 'I have had trouble putting up with Samir. I could have parted ways from the company long ago. But I did not do so for Ashok (Samir Jain's father).[10]

'Sometime in the early 1980s, when the queen (of England) visited New Delhi, I had been invited to the prime minister's house for dinner. Samir had just returned from a trip to the US. He asked me to go to Calcutta for something, and I said I could not do that because of this pressing engagement. He was angry. "The queen? Why is the queen so important," he wanted to know. Soon after, there was a *Filmfare* party at 4, Tilak Marg (a Jain family property in central Delhi). Samir had already briefed Ashok about our conversation. Ashok asked me to give in. I had to miss dinner at the prime minister's house and go to Calcutta,' R.C. Jain recalled.

By many accounts, Samir Jain had a definite spiritual streak. Long before he took up a position at BCCL, he frequented ashrams and devoted himself to meditation. According to one version, there was a phase when he is believed to have told his family that he wanted to be a sanyasi. But his father threatened to disown him if he chose to be an ascetic.

He came around. But it appears that the spiritual dimension continued to influence his approach to business, making him a difficult person to predict or decipher. Some of his employees speak about it in glowing terms. 'His spirituality has to be experienced to be understood. It is self-reflection, self-awareness and a deep sort of meditation,' said Bal Mukund Sinha, an editor from *Navbharat Times*.

Samir Jain's home in central Delhi is called Sujagi (self-awakened). The editor went on: 'When the VC is here in Delhi, he is hyperactive (the editor made gestures of boxing in the air), fighting everything out. Then he retreats to his home in Haridwar, where he could be resting, reading, watching television or just thinking. He interacts with those around him there. He will speak to the watchman, to anyone and pick up nuances and analogies for his business,' he said.

An associate of Samir Jain from his younger days also mentioned this at length. 'He is known to have a rather detached approach to life. He believes one should keep control of one's life in one's own hands, and not be moved by events. "See everything that happens in your life as a film," he would say,' this associate said.

While Samir Jain has had a remarkable success rate with his business moves, he has been unemotional about letting go of initiatives which may have gone wrong. Some explain this, again in spiritual terms, as an example of his 'detached approach' to the business. 'He is in the thick of it all and yet appears unaffected,' they say.

'There is bondage when the mind is attracted to the visible. And liberation, when that is not so,' says the *Ashtavakra Gita*, which

I ended up reading to understand the lead actor of my story. Even with difficult situations such as death, Samir Jain is believed to have a completely unique approach. The above-mentioned scripture also says, 'Liberation is when the mind does not desire, does not grieve, does not sacrifice, does not accept, is not pleased or get angry.'

Samir Jain lost his son in tragic circumstances. At a prayer meeting at Sujagi, he held his sister Nandita's hand and started to dance, as if in a trance. Some senior *TOI* editors who were there were taken aback. But to him, it meant that his son had now become part of the universal energy that is eternal.

Samir Jain, indeed BCCL, has always had an eye for talent, in journalism as well as marketing. He had his own criteria for choosing the people at the top. One of the people he brought in to edit *The Times of India* and usher in the new paradigm, in 1988, was Dileep Padgaonkar, the Sorbonne-educated, erudite savant, who is probably as well versed with the Vedas as he is with Victor Hugo.

'Samir Jain likes people who can look within,' Padgaonkar said when I met him at his Defence Colony home in South Delhi in February 2003. 'He is an *antarmukhi* (inward-looking) in every sense. Samir Jain will accept you even if you seem somewhat weird or bizarre, if he is able to size you up. He likes contrarians. He does not like people who plough the same furrow. He looks for quicksliver minds,' he pointed out.

'Samir Jain has the ability to look at any problem from all its dimensions. When he calls you in for a discussion, he has not only studied the subject at hand thoroughly, he has also thought of all the possible objections to it,' Padgaonkar noted.

Bal Mukund Sinha, the edit page editor of *Navbharat Times* recently told me, 'He is fundamentally a scholar. Had he not been in the media business, he would have been a great professor. He always has the big picture in his mind.'

Stories abound of how he intervenes in his newspapers, often with bizarre insights that work out in the end. A few years ago, for instance, he suggested that the front page of his newspapers be packed with many more news reports and articles. They ought to be crisper and shorter in length. This was much to the discomfort of his editors who (besides seeing this as a direct attack on their long, verbose pieces) feared that the page would become too cluttered.

Samir Jain's argument was: 'Indians like clutter.' He went on to explain his logic. 'Give Indians a thaali (a plate) with twelve katoris (small cups for holding vegetables and curries) to sample. They'll like that. They may not eat everything but they want the choice. The more, the better,' he had said.

'Bring in at least ten or eleven stories on the front page. If you are constrained by ads, put in seven or eight pieces,' was his suggestion. Besides the thaali argument, he was also sensitive to the fact that his readers were becoming busier and could spare on an average only 18–22 minutes for the daily newspaper.

Bachi Karkaria, a columnist known particularly for her wit and distinct wordplay, was not with *The Times of India* when I met her in Bombay in December 2001. She had moved to *Mid Day*. 'You know, by the mid-1980s, Samir Jain had come in and faced wallows of controversy,' she began.

'I found him to be all that he was made out to be – and more: the bogeyman, out to sell all journalism down the rivers of commerce, had arrived. But people did not see that he has a phenomenal mind. His mind is like a huge sponge. There is alchemy in it, all the time. He has the capability for lateral thinking and his every action is premeditated. He can never be impulsive; he is completely in control, always,' she stressed.

I remember being advised to read Edward de Bono's *Lateral Thinking* to understand Samir Jain. What Karkaria said next explained why. 'I saw how his mind functions. It is completely unique,' she said, and proceeded to give me an illustration.

'During some conversations for a potential tie-up for Planet M (the group's music retail venture), Samir Jain was talking about fashion. But the interesting element was that he had elevated it to a very cerebral, multidimensional level. He spoke of how fashion had a cultivated, mafiosi look. You had to be present there to experience how he does that,' Bachi recalled. 'He was a bit of a radical. He spoke of customer delight. In those days, that was subversive; completely unheard of.'

There are some who can see the depth and complexity of his personality, and also its dark shades. In my quest to understand this story better, I contacted Dr Chandan Mitra, currently the owner-editor of *The Pioneer* and a BJP MP. He was once a star journalist of *The Times of India*. He had observed Samir Jain at close quarters and had original insights on the man.

Recalling his days at the Times House, Mitra told me in November 2001: 'His is one of the finest minds, post-Independence. He wanted a corporate culture for Bennett, Coleman and Co. Ltd. His ideas were sometimes bizarre but his logic was irrefutable. His mind works everything out to the last detail.

'Yet, working with Samir Jain was a destabilizing and disturbing experience, although there was much to learn. People developed a phobia about him. Samir Jain liked those who were argumentative; he was a consummate angler. He would stalk the fish all the time and lose interest in them once they were hooked. He just sought the intellectual thrill in doing this,' Mitra said.

There are numerous anecdotes of Samir Jain's unpredictable, almost maverick bearing. Ramesh Chandran, a former Washington correspondent of *The Times of India* recalled[11] a luncheon meeting that Samir Jain had with an editor of *The New York Times* many years ago.

'Samir is a frugal eater. So, while we ate, he just sat there quietly peering at this *NYT* editor, who was talking non-stop,' he began. 'While he spoke about his company and about his paper, Samir kept a blank, disinterested, faraway look. At the end of an hour or so, the *NYT* man was quite disappointed that Jain had been so distant.

'As the man was about to leave, Samir Jain began talking. In less than twenty minutes, he had worked out some mind-boggling numbers and made some brilliant suggestions to the *NYT* representative. You should have seen the look on the latter's face; he was completely bowled over,' Chandran said. 'He later told me that this man (Jain) should have been on *The New York Times* board, with a brain like that,' he added.

Satish Mehta, a former marketing director who played an instrumental role in the transformation of the organization, recalled[12] the sense of urgency and restlessness on the part of Samir Jain. 'He had a lot of ideas. His imagination and enterprise may have been suppressed in the past. So, it looked like he wanted to try out each one of them; it seemed like he wanted to break free.'

Some interesting insights into Samir Jain's personality emerge from the days when he was taking on the venerable editors of The Times Group. In many ways, it was also a decisive phase in that it laid the ground for the changes that happened later.

He may have developed some dislike for journalists and the predominant position they enjoyed. He was uncomfortable with the fact that while the newspaper's proprietor kept a low profile, it was the editor, his employee, who was in the limelight. Politicians and bureaucrats pandered to the journalist while the proprietor was a mere bystander.

There are yet others who concede that there may be a 'hidden agenda' against journalists, besides the imperatives for change. An editor, who worked closely with Samir Jain after the reorganization, but did not want to be named, admitted that Samir Jain did hold journalists in 'deep disdain' at that time.

He recalled that sometime in 1986, The Times Group hosted a party in honour of Krishna Kumar, then a Union minister in Rajiv Gandhi's government. When it was time for dinner and the guests were being ushered in, Krishna Kumar pulled a chair for Girilal Jain to sit. 'I was standing close to Samir Jain,' narrates the journalist; 'he (Jain) said, "This party is thrown by the company and me. Is it not strange that the minister should pull the chair for the editor and not the owner of the paper?"'

So determined was Samir Jain to prove that he was superior to the journalists and to keep them in their place that he issued a directive that everyone be addressed by their designations. So, senior editors, who until then had been calling him by his first name, had to switch to calling him JMD (joint managing director) and later, VC for vice chairman.

When the government had taken control of BCCL for seven years, Samir Jain, then in his early twenties, believed that certain journalists of the paper had started it all by first making allegations of irregularities against the company to the government. It had been a difficult phase, and Samir Jain blamed the paper's own journalists for creating the mess.

'Samir carried the memory of those years. He thought the editors had to be shown their place,' recalled Baljit Kapoor. 'He thought they considered themselves too important. "After all," he said, "the editor is just one of the employees of the company. He is just a processor of news."'

Samir Jain wanted more control over the newspaper. Editors were taking their autonomy too far. Jain found that he could not appoint people of his choice; that it was tough to get something of his liking included in the paper, among other such 'restrictions'. These stumbling blocks bothered him.

In his early days, one of the top editors tried to belittle Samir Jain by treating him like a probationer. '*Ladka theek hai. Lekin usey abhi padnaa hai, seekhnaa hai.* The boy is okay but let him educate himself first,' he said. Samir Jain hated that. As a counter, he began circulating articles from *The New York Times* and other newspapers. He wanted it to be known that he was already educated, and contrary to the editor's comments, well read.

He began taking the editors head-on. At one interaction, he is believed to have said: 'Please, all you editors listen. If you have an appointment with the prime minister, and if I call you, you must cancel the appointment and come to me.' That quote has stuck. Although editors now make reference to it in a light-hearted way, it is unlikely that anyone violates that diktat even today. When the sensei says something, it is followed.

He had trouble over the fact that while the goodwill generated by a newspaper accrued to the editor, the negative fallouts went over to the owners. 'He would often say, "The balance of inconvenience is always with me." He wanted his team to be completely on his side and fully with him, no matter what he did. And, when that did not happen, there was friction between the sides. Such situations bothered him, and they did not end well,' recalled Pradeep Guha.

Independent observers outside the organization have also corroborated Jain's dislike for journalists. In his acclaimed book, *Paper Tigers*, Nicholas Coleridge writes: 'Samir Jain views his editors and journalists as elements whose power needs to be constantly diffused ("those blue-blooded Brahmins of the editorial floor"). He takes pleasure in giving the best offices to his managers instead.' [13]

A rebellious streak, a certain amount of irreverence for convention and tradition – that constant and regular inverting of the pyramid persist even today. Does he go about it in an authoritarian, my-word-no-matter-what manner?

Here again, there is no single or simple view. There are those who believe that in his single-mindedness, he brooks no resistance though his manner and approach may be understated. One of the edit page editors at the Times House said, 'Samir Jain has established his own regime. His staff has to understand and accept him. The VC will not interfere in the day-to-day functioning of the newspapers. He is more the Puppet Master. He will throw an idea at you and have you figure it out. But you *are* expected to figure it out.

'He likes high-quality discussions. He will never call a reporter for a discussion. It will mostly be editors or people on the edit page. He will size you up and treat you accordingly. But he is soft-spoken and gentle and will never give you a direct command. It will all be hints and subtle suggestions, and you will have to pick up cues. That makes him both interesting and difficult, depending on how much you are willing to invest in him.'

I asked this editor whether Samir Jain is temperamental, as is often alleged. 'I have never seen him lose his temper. The VC likes equals. One would often see Swami (Swaminathan Aiyar, former editor-in-chief of *The Economic Times*, who continues to write a column for the paper and is a consulting editor) and the VC standing in the corridor and talking like old friends. When in a good mood, the VC will start his conversations with his Bengali editors with "*Kaemon aachho?*" (how are you?).

'The problem is that most journalists don't like to be given sermons, and certainly not by their publishers. They will not listen. And that becomes a point of conflict,' he said.

Shubhrangshu Roy, editor of the *Financial Chronicle*, who earlier served at the *ET*, drew up a sketch in a matter-of-fact way. 'Samir Jain is not the despot he is sometimes made out to be. He is not an anarchist. In fact, he is down-to-earth. I have never seen him lose his temper with anyone. He is actually a compassionate man. People have this terrible habit of demonizing him. One either hero-worships him, or tries to make a monster of him.

'Samir Jain is an editor-publisher; he isn't anti-journalist. He is, in fact, a better editor than most editors I've known; he knows his journalism. Samir Jain is the Holy Ghost of *The Times of India* – intelligent, intellectual,' Roy added. He believed that editors have had trouble with him because of their own vested interests somewhere down the line. 'Every editor who has worked with him has done so with a huge self-interest and an even huger ego,' he argued.

'In the contest between the publisher and the editor, the publisher wants to be the editor of the newspaper as much as the editor wishes to step into the publisher's role. There is the classic confrontation between the two. But he tried to delink or demystify this. He transcended it. As an observer of journalism, I truly believe that Samir Jain is indeed a quintessential editor,' Roy said.

It is quite clear from talking to his editors that Samir Jain takes a keen interest in what gets carried in the editorial columns of his newspapers, even to this day. The intervention could be subtle – a gentle cue or a hint, sometimes leaving the editor to struggle with deciphering the full import and intent behind it. Or, given his fascination with good language, Samir Jain could actually get down to performing the task of a sub-editor.

T.K. Arun, who was the edit page editor at *ET* when I met him, told me: 'The VC is an excellent sub (sub-editor). Occasionally, he reads through articles published in the paper and goes about marking out superfluous words and expressions. He is very particular about the correct use of the definite article. In the old days, one thought that the lalas did not know anything about journalism, leave alone language. But he is exceptionally well read'.

Abheek Barman, consulting editor at *ET*, seconded his colleague's comment. He said: 'The VC is a great one for semantics. He particularly likes interesting words and is very fond of neologisms. Once I used the word "zeitgeist" (German for the spirit of the times) in his presence, and he remarked: "No one uses words like this any more." On the one hand, he wants the language in his newspapers to be simple and easily understood. But at a personal level, he likes using words that would make a person think'.

Bal Mukund Sinha of the *Navbharat Times* said: 'He pushes your boundaries. He will drop a hint, a clue, and you are encouraged to interpret it. If you get it wrong, he will gently tell you what he had envisaged. He will also often pretend that he knows little about the subject being discussed, and as you wax eloquently, he will listen patiently. Then, he will spring a "guru mantra" at you which will sum up the entire matter. His mind is so powerful...also...because he is so spiritual.'

In many cases, the intervention initially leaves his editors aghast, until they come round. Samir Jain once came up with the line that it is alright to use words from the English language in the group's Hindi newspaper. He believed that newspapers are not meant to nurture language. '"That is why in our English newspapers, we do not carry Shakespeare; we carry (author) Shobhaa De's line which says, 'That neighbourhood boy is very *namkeen*.' People understand this language and speak like this. And we must be able to relate to them," he would say,' said the editor from *NBT*.

On another occasion, Samir Jain suggested that his Hindi daily do a story that English should be pursued by *NBT* readers for better career prospects. He wanted the newspaper to conduct a survey, asking readers whether their children studied in English-medium schools, and if so, why? "Expose the puritans," he would say. "Be real; be practical."' His suggestion wasn't taken very well but the survey was undertaken. 'We found out that he was right. Most *NBT* readers, who were questioned, did aspire for their children to be fluent in English. This is how he intervenes,' Sinha explained.

A member of the editorial team at *ET* said: 'The VC is civilized and evolved. He will share his views with you. If you understand what he is saying, all the better for you...for you will have all the freedom you need to write your edits. And if he likes what you've written, you might even get a small note, with just an 'S' for a sign-off, and a couple of points written almost illegibly.'

Autocratic he may not be. But Samir Jain can be overbearing, like handing out diaries to all the editors, asking them to bring those to their meetings with him, take notes, and refer to them at subsequent interactions, and, being a little uncomfortable when the process isn't followed by the oddball. Notebooks are promptly arranged for those who come to meetings without them. One is also supposed to write in them as he talks and shares his perspective.

Here again, some parts of his speech could seem nebulous. 'Trying to make sense of what he says could sometimes be an uphill task. That is true,' said an editor at the Times House, without wanting to be identified, of course. 'He often cites some Vedic philosophy or complex analogies. His *gyan* (knowledge) monologue sessions are called "chemotherapy sessions" because it becomes very difficult to put up with them.'

'When he doles out some religious funda, and sees that our eyes are glazed over, he would say, "I know you are non-religious people, if not atheists. Even so, you must read the *Ashtavakra Gita*, which was written as an atheists' manifesto." He loves it and knows it by heart. That is clearly his favourite book. But he will never insist on any point. He will generally suggest something like "Perhaps you could take a look at it, and see if you can write something,"' the editor said.

'But the sessions with him have to be endured. Those are unstructured monologues. They could start with just two or three people. But if the conversation got interesting, he would keep calling more and more people. He would mention some names and say, "*Unko bhi bulaa lijiyey*" (Call them as well).'

'And no matter what you are doing or are about to do, you are expected to just go upstairs, to the fourth floor,* equally perplexed, scribble pad in hand, of course, and listen to him basically talk to himself. But the sensitive part of all this is that he will never call you late in the afternoon or evening because he knows that that time is crucial for the edition to leave.'

The editor went on: 'One way to escape the gyan overdose is to feign a cough or perhaps sneeze in his presence. If you do that, he will immediately tell you, "You are not well. Perhaps you should leave." By the way, he fusses over his health a lot, sometimes bordering on the hypochondriac. He has a sensitive throat. He is acutely averse to pungent smells and scents – perfumes, pickles and scented hair oils.'

I was also told that Samir Jain has a time fetish. He will not be late. He usually comes in to office around 10.30 in the morning when the News Management Committee (NMC) meeting is supposed

---

* The Fourth Floor is the Mount Olympus at the Times House, Delhi – a hallowed precinct that houses the offices of Chairman Indu Jain, Vice Chairman Samir Jain, Managing Director Vineet Jain and the top management of The Times Group. Visits to this part of the building are, more often than not, eventful. Special guests are entertained in the lunch room here. Entry is 'by invitation only'.

to start, and, if by any chance, it isn't on, he is disposed to being rattled. On occasions, he will mutter that they are 'slackers'. 'He doesn't take very well to this lack of order and discipline,' said one of the members of the NMC at the Times House.

The other thing about his morning ritual is that he will walk into the editorial side of the office, put his head into a cabin and talk a bit with one of his editors. Or he may choose to 'prevail upon' the NMC. 'He will sit and watch each and every one. Even if he is not directly looking at you, you better be aware that his eyes are on your every move,' chuckled the man.

There is a lighter side to Samir Jain, as emerged during a conversation with Gautam Adhikari. I met him in New Delhi in February 2002, the first of three meetings. 'One thing that most people do not know about Samir Jain is that he has a funny bone in him; he has a huge sense of humour; he can be an absolute imp. Sometimes during meetings with the staff, depending on what struck him as funny, particularly all the nodding and yesmanship, he would wink at me, and later, we would talk about it, and he would burst out laughing,' he remembered.

'There is so much to the man. He used to enjoy the comic, Asterix. Inspector Clouseau from the Pink Panther series was a character he was fond of. He liked Agatha Christie's books and stories with suspense and wit. He has read every book written by P.G. Wodehouse and is very fond of Wodehousian words and sentences. Being from the same school, we spoke a similar, stylized language sometimes. So, we understood each other very well. He had also read enough Shakespeare to quote him back at me. Our conversations would be explosive,' Adhikari reminisced.

'He loved the stage, drama and musical comedies just as much as he loved the serious stuff. He would ask me to explain the central theme, the essence of a play to Meera (his wife), and then come up with his own interpretation,' he recalled. 'But very few people get to see that side of him. They think that he is either a radical innovator or a media mogul who floats in a sort of religious ether.

But Samir Jain is far more interesting, far more intriguing,' Adhikari maintained.

Jug Suraiya is a raconteur with a sense of self-deprecating humour, who in his writings will take potshots at all things 'sacred' including The Times Group itself, always going for the 'jugular'. Senior editors talk about the equation between Samir Jain and Suraiya, who could be the best of friends one moment and arguing animatedly the next. That makes Jug Suraiya one of the chosen few who can provide an incisive look into Samir Jain. I met this aloof, pensive, almost reclusive writer at the Times House when he was in charge of the edit page. He vaguely recognized me from my days at the paper, heard me out and proceeded to answer my questions dispassionately.

'Samir Jain is a visionary,' Suraiya said.[14] 'He wanted to cater to an entirely new readership. He did not want to listen to precepts,' he added. 'When Gorbachov (former president of the Soviet Union) was going to visit America, I wrote a singeing editorial which was supposed to be the third edit (the slot meant for light, off-beat editorials). But Samir liked it so much that he made it the first edit, and said this is how editorials need to be written,' he recalled.

'He is a maverick genius. He likes to take risks. Money means nothing to him. Like a samurai, this is, for him, a game. It may even be a spiritual exercise,' Suraiya surmised. 'Samir Jain belongs to no one particular school of thought; he comes from the world of imagination.'

Another person with a long association with Samir Jain, this time from the marketing team, had this to say: 'Samir Jain is the Howard Hughes of India; a mystery man with an incredible mind. He has no material or worldly ambitions and that seems strange considering his focus on the business. He has no passion for sport, art or money in the raw sense of the word. He is, therefore, highly focused only on his goal.'

Samir Jain is also mentioned as being empathetic and compassionate. But here again, there are sharp paradoxes to the man. He could swing between supreme unconcern, and an empathy that is so extreme as to be almost unnerving.

Guha still cannot get over Samir Jain's 'acts of empathy and kindness'. When he spoke to me in August 2011, Guha remembered two instances with emotion. The first was when Guha's father passed away. Samir Jain landed up at his home in Mumbai with home-cooked meals in boxes, saying, 'None of you must have eaten. Please have this.' Samir Jain and Guha may no longer be as close as they once were. But the latter insisted he can never forget that gesture.

'And on another occasion,' Guha recalled, 'he came back from a trip. He had bought shoes for me, and proceeded to fit my feet into them. He had an idea of the size and of the fit. How did he even do that? It was very surprising.

'As a person, if he likes you and knows that you are with him fully in everything he does and that your interests – the greater good of the company – are aligned with his interests, then his is an association to cherish,' Guha maintained.

'He will look after your needs, your comfort – almost dote over you. He will let you be and allow you to take risks. And he will go all the way to support ideas that are aligned with the overall goal,' Guha added.

Several editors I met spoke of how the VC would personally serve food on to their plates at parties, or call for tea and proceed to make it for them. There have also been instances of a gentle reprimand at work, being followed by an invitation to dine at his home.

This perceived duality or split may have foxed some people who worked with him. He seems to have some fierce critics too.

Poet, writer, painter and a producer of Hindi films, Pritish Nandy was direct. 'Samir Jain's basic theory was to "de-journalistize" things, and make the group one that would efficiently sell both chewing gums and newspapers. He saw *The Times of India* as an FMCG (fast moving consumer good) product,' he said.

'He hated journalists. He thought they were intellectually superior to him. He destroyed the role of journalism in India. He realized that the trivialization of information was very seductive, very sexy. He anticipated the diminishing reading habit and the delegitimization of print. He anticipated the need to create an alternative platform which could absorb the new generation's tastes.

'Commercially, however, he was the best thing that could have happened to the *TOI*. But he destroyed an institution and made it a great big factory,' Nandy said.

I'll let Baljit Kapoor have the last word. 'In the pre–Samir Jain era, the newspaper was a social institution. Post–Samir Jain, it is a business. He had no illusions about it. His methods have been shamelessly copied. And that has been the most defining clause of the times.'

## THREE

# Building Blocks of the New Regime

SAMIR JAIN'S STRATEGY FOR change, which unfolded over the next decade, covered all aspects of the media business. He was convinced that his publications were far more valuable than they were given credit for. And that he would realize that value and make Bennett, Coleman and The Times Group profitable. For that to happen, all areas of the business had to respond.

First, he wanted to change his paper's approach to news reporting and content. Rather than be oriented towards the state, as was the unwritten norm for newspapers at that time, his papers would accord primacy to society and the citizen.

This was a major shift. Their primary target audience had so far been ministers, bureaucrats, politicians and the academia. These were the influential classes at that time, and they were staunch loyalists of *The Times of India*. But now the *TOI* was to change its focus from these sections to professionals and the middle-class households. It would focus more on the consuming classes rather than on the influential ones. With this new positioning, his newspapers did a 180-degree switch.

This transformed, first, the way his newspapers prioritized

news. Until then, they had primarily been passive mouthpieces for government proclamations and political rhetoric. This was understandable, given the central role accorded to the state. Opinion and comment revolved around matters of policy and state. But now, Samir Jain wanted his newspapers to cover and report daily developments from the point of view of the middle class.

His journalists had to develop sensitivity to what was relevant for this emerging middle class. They were required to trawl through the clutter of policy declarations and, rather than report them verbatim, understand their relevance for the new target readership. Local issues, for example, would gain importance in the paper as they were considered important to this class.

Developments would now have to be interpreted and presented in ways that this category of readers could relate to. This orientation also required changes in the writing style, language and flavour of reportage. Jargon and officialese had to make way for more lively and interactive reportage.

The most critical area Samir Jain focused on was advertising, or the selling of space in his newspapers. If he had to make the company profitable, this was going to be decisive. He believed space in his newspapers was not getting the price it deserved. His papers were delivering far more value to the advertiser and could command a better price. He needed to look for innovative ways to capture that surplus. At the same time, he had to ensure that his publications continued to enhance value for the advertiser.

In fact, the orientation towards the consuming classes and changes in content had to move in tandem with efforts to enhance value for the advertiser. It was a complete package. The nature and texture of content had to be such that it attracted the right kind of readers, the kinds preferred by the advertiser. Samir Jain was clear about this connection. If there were people in his organization who were unwilling to make this happen, like some of his journalists, they had to make way.

His other priority at that time was to find ways to bring in more readers. In addition to his focus on content and advertising, he would have to price newspapers attractively to invite new segments of readers. He did this in many innovative ways, and expanded the market manifold. Distribution too had to be strengthened for this purpose. It was important to reach the newspaper to newer markets, and to reach there in time, to widen and deepen readership.

Linked to these priorities was Samir Jain's other major preoccupation – closing down unprofitable publications. Some among them were hugely popular, though not profitable. They did not fit into his overall game plan and had to shut shop. If he had to transform content, redefine the rules of space selling in the industry and expand the market, he needed management bandwidth and focus.

He could not afford to be distracted by numerous publications. He realized it was not possible for him and his management team to act upon all the publications with intensity. The changes he envisaged required single-minded focus and drive.

Many of the publications had an emotional or nostalgic association for his family members. And these publications had a loyal readership. Their closure was resented. Many saw this as commercial interest taking precedence over media freedom and plurality. But Samir Jain was undeterred and quite clinical about closing down publications that did not fit the plot.

Over the next decade, he was able to achieve most of these objectives. His initiatives had a profound impact across the industry, and in many ways, defined the media business as it is managed and consumed today.

Besides its impact on the media industry, the transformation paid rich dividends for Bennett, Coleman and Co. Ltd. Starting from the mid-1980s, it was to experience scorching growth in both its top line and bottom line over the next fifteen years.

Some of this growth had to do with the overall buoyancy in the Indian economy and the boom in the corporate sector during this period.[1] But the company also did much on its own to create new opportunities for growth. Besides, economic buoyancy was no guarantee that it would automatically improve its prospects. The specific steps that it took enabled it to capitalize on the positive moves in the economy.

## The Context

In the mid-1980s, when Samir Jain entered the scene, there were multiple factors that made change imperative for BCCL. Some of these had to do with the profound transformation taking place in the Indian economy and society at that time. These changes, spurred by major policy shifts and global developments, created new opportunities and threats, and businesses would have no choice but to respond to them.

The Indian media industry, for its own reasons, was also in the throes of change. BCCL, a fortiori, could not survive without reinventing itself.

The third set of factors that triggered change in the company was specific to the family and to Samir Jain. Most of the other businesses of the family were in decline. Samir Jain had served on some of those businesses. His stints had been uneventful. He had no choice but to make the media business work. It had to be revived to serve as the family's cash cow.

Samir Jain was in a hurry to change. It seemed as if he had no choice but to make a success of the media business. 'Samir had to perform at BCCL. There was no other option. On the one hand, he had failed to revive the ailing jute mill in U.P. On the other, most of the Sahu Jain businesses had either lost their relevance or gone to seed,' said T.N. Ninan.[2]

At that time, the Indian economy was taking its first tentative steps towards liberalization. The big bang reforms of 1991 were still some years away. But the state had started to loosen its stranglehold over business and industry. There were early signs of consumerism, entrepreneurial activity and inflow of foreign investment through collaborations.

New consumer goods were beginning to be launched and consumerism among the upper-middle class was taking root. Besides the existing multinational companies in consumer goods, the government had encouraged Japanese collaboration in the automobile industry. These were laying the foundation for modern manufacturing in the country, creating jobs and consumers.

In the mid-1980s, Rajiv Gandhi took some bold though tentative steps to open up the Indian economy. He spoke in terms of modernizing industry and integrating it with the rest of the world. The Indian economy, stuck at the 'Hindu rate of growth'[3] of 3 per cent for nearly three decades, was starting to cast off its mould and achieve a more respectable 5 per cent trajectory.

For a while, the political landscape also acquired a fresh hue. The rhetoric was more inclusive and made appealing to the younger generation as well. The eligible age for voting was reduced from twenty-one to eighteen. Youth and the issues affecting them came into focus. The response to these changes from corporates, investors and the consuming class was, for that brief period, euphoric.

Although this optimism was confined largely to the top few cities, it created an opportunity for the media. Advertisers were looking for suitable platforms from where they could secure exposure for their products and services, at least in the urban centres. They now wanted their product communication to have a multi-city reach, if not a pan-India impact. Samir Jain was to exploit this need to the hilt.

New breeds of professionals emerged. Until now, the older generation was preoccupied with its concerns, and this was reflected in the media. With the younger generation joining the flow, new themes and issues came to the forefront.

Attitudes towards consumption had began to change. For years, socialist India had been opposed to, almost contemptuous of, consumption. Now consumption had started to acquire legitimacy. Media content had to orient itself to these new demands. India was yet to be unshackled from socialist controls and the licence-permit raj. That would happen in the 1990s. But the mid-1980s provided a glimpse of what was possible.

The media industry was on a new, more creative trajectory of its own. This was marked by a magazine boom and emergence of a new range of newspapers. And BCCL, drained and demoralized after seven years of government control that had ended in 1976, was on the recovery path.

In the early 1980s, newspapers continued to be styled in the traditional mode as platforms to transmit government pronouncements and comment on government actions. But a band of magazines had emerged. They too had political reporting at their centre. But they were well produced with special emphasis on sophisticated layout, design and graphics. They also had a healthy sprinkling of light-hearted features and lifestyle articles. They caught readers' attention in the late 1970s and early 1980s.

'The mid-1970s to the mid-1980s was the magazine era. *Sunday* had been launched by Ananda Bazar Patrika group in 1974 and was well into its own by the mid-1980s. Edited by M.J. Akbar, it banked on a strategy of "low price–sound distribution" and had touched a circulation of 190,000 in two years. By 1981-82, it had crossed 3 lakh copies a week,' observed media analyst Sushil Pandit.[4]

'The 1980s also saw the growth of television. And the period between 1985 and 1995 saw a rapid growth in circulation for the print media. During this period, *The Hindu* launched its Delhi edition not necessarily to acquire more readers or make money but simply to mark its presence in the capital. During the magazine boom, *The Deccan Herald* in Bangalore started *The Herald Review* under its former editor K.N. Harikumar. It had an all-India launch. *Malayala Manorama* launched *The Week* in 1983 to look national and to address the chatterati. It also wanted to bring the group some clout and presence in political circles. *Business India* launched

*India Week*. The Eenadu group launched *Newstime* but with limited success.... Change really began when the oligopoly of newspapers ended,' he said.

ABP had successfully launched a financial daily, *Business Standard* in the mid-1970s. Partly using that experience, and encouraged by the success of *Sunday*, it launched a business magazine, *Businessworld*, in 1981. Two years later, it launched *Sports World*.

Another magazine, launched around the same time as *Sunday*, was making waves in the mid-1980s. This was *India Today*. Prior to 1975, it was a glossy, an eye-candy product printed to be kept at Indian missions abroad. But that changed in 1977, when Emergency and a brief two-year period of government censorship of the media came to an end. The demand for information was so high in the domestic market that 75 per cent of *India Today*'s readership started to come from within the country against 25 per cent earlier.

After the Emergency, the *India Today* came into its own and positioned itself as a 'complete news magazine'. It was to bring India to Delhi, as it were. It became free and critical. In less than five years, it was heading for the top slot in the magazine market, seriously threatening *The Illustrated Weekly*, and giving stiff competition to *Sunday*.

'The tension between *India Today* and *The Times of India* was interesting. *India Today* became a hit. It made newspapers uncomfortable. But it went ahead aggressively. Its cartoonist Ajit Ninan (who later joined *The Times of India*) caricatured an old hag who was, presumably, the old lady of Bori Bunder,' said Pandit.

Among newspapers, the dominant Eenadu group in Andhra Pradesh launched *Newstime* to take on *Deccan Chronicle*, but with limited success. The Express group was on an expansion spree, starting editions in Chandigarh, Pune, Ahmedabad, Baroda, Vijayawada, Vishakapatnam and Hyderabad, among other places. Vinod Mehta (currently editor-in-chief of the Outlook group) brought out the country's first Sunday paper – the *Sunday Observer*

– in August 1981. He went on to edit the *Indian Post* (1987) with much elan until things went out of control there and he was forced to move on. Mehta joined BCCL in mid-1989 and briefly edited *The Independent*.[5]

There was a crop of regional English dailies as well, including *The Sentinel* and *Assam Tribune* in the north-east. In the east, while *The Statesman* had started to trail, *The Telegraph* grew. It brought in new technology and changed the way newspapers looked in those days. It was modern, irreverent and classy.

Founded in 1982 and edited by M.J. Akbar, *The Telegraph* experimented with layout, design and content among others. It was also the first English newspaper to segment its sections and give each page a separate identity and theme. Its tag line, 'Unputdownable' was prophetic.

Speaking of *The Telegraph*'s technology story, Pandit said, 'There was a time when newspapers were produced on hot metal presses. There were biscuit-sized columns which went to the composing table. Pages were created in metal. And, an ink roller was taken over them. Proofreading was an important department, and most proofreaders were aspiring sub-editors. The proofs were taken and corrections done with loose metal letters. Then flongs were taken and impressions made. That was an intermediary process. Two newspapers were put on a cylinder for direct printing. They hit the bed at midnight and got into printing at 3 a.m.

'But *The Telegraph* was the first daily newspaper to move to the linotype, between 1984 and '89. A rotary set machine was used. It was also the first newspaper to go offset and into photo composing, as also the first to have its main issue go colour,' he pointed out.

The popularity of the newspaper was also a sign of the metamorphosis that would soon overcome the print media of that age. The Lucknow-based *Pioneer* was taken over by industrialist L.M. Thapar in the mid-1980s. 'The *Pioneer* was bought,' says Pandit, 'because every industrialist wanted to be a Ramnath Goenka, and make politicians crumble before him.'

Many consumer brands that wanted to reach out to the emerging middle class found a handy tool in magazines. Their writing and presentation were often more upmarket and racy compared to the staid style of the leading newspapers. Most important, the magazines came in colour, making them that much more attractive for the advertiser.

Magazines nudged newspapers to look different. These two had a kind of face-off. Each got very aggressive with advertising. Newspapers pushed magazines to be more 'scoopy' and the latter forced newspapers to have more 'attitude'.

The dent from television had not been felt yet. While satellite television was almost a decade away, state-controlled Doordarshan had started to make inroads. It had turned colour in 1982. It was allowed by the government to acquire a certain commercial orientation. Its sponsored soaps, variety shows and programmes on popular mythology enjoyed a huge viewership among the emerging middle class. In addition, it was deepening its reach admittedly because the Congress government, which had had unsavoury experiences with privately owned newspapers, saw the state-controlled tube's potential as a propaganda tool.

The leading newspapers had started to focus on stepping up content to stave off the twin competition from television and magazines. There was, of course, little effort to manage the newspaper as a brand, or even to treat publishing like a business to be evaluated on the basis of usual parameters like profitability or return on investment.

The competition was far from cut-throat. Several key decisions were taken collectively. Newspaper publishers still believed that they could wield considerable power through the press, serve personal and social interests and have a say in a state-dominated economy. Newspapers were clearly in a comfort zone and it would take some effort to pull them out of inertia to cope with a fast-changing world.

BCCL was a large media house in the country. But it did not present a pretty picture for someone who wanted to make it a thriving, profitable enterprise. It had a portfolio of seventeen news-related publications and nineteen non-news-related publications. These ranged from *The Times of India*, *The Economic Times*, *The Illustrated Weekly, Navbharat Times* and *Khel Bharti* in the former category to *Indrajal Comics*, *Career and Competition Times*, *Science Today*, *Filmfare* and *Dharmyug* in the latter.

After the government demitted office, as it were, Ashok Jain had assumed complete responsibility at the Times House. Senior managers had tried to break the state of inertia that had overcome *The Times of India*. A period of growth had set in. Employees were told that they were now working for a corporation. The marketing department had been strengthened. Budgets were made. The management became professional.

Although there was no quantum jump in growth, there was nevertheless a steady pace of growth. BCCL's annual revenue had risen to Rs 61.6 crore by July 1982, a growth of about 30 per cent over the previous year. Net profit doubled to Rs 1 crore.

Its flagship newspaper, *The Times of India*, had three editions and a circulation of nearly 562,000 in 1985. While BCCL's turnover was the highest for any Indian media company, it also had a presence across the country in major metros and smaller cities. But its cash cow was the *TOI*'s Bombay edition with its overwhelming domination of India's financial capital.

In Delhi, it was still a distant second to *Hindustan Times*. At 2.15 lakh copies in 1986, *TOI* was 55,000 copies behind *Hindustan Times*. Bangalore was dominated by regional English-language newspapers and *The Times of India* barely did 19,000 copies. Jaipur was in the range of 12,000 copies and in Patna, it sold just about 35,000 copies. Chennai was a stronghold of *The Hindu*. The east was dominated by *The Statesman* and, of late, *The Telegraph*.

Despite the efforts of the past few years, Bennett, Coleman and Co. was still an old and slothful organization, which had to be energized and shaken up if it had any chance of being converted into a successful business. *The Times of India* was akin to a venerable aristocratic matriarch – respected, acknowledged and classical. By the 1980s, it had had a legacy of nearly 150 years of reporting on events, informing the reader on national developments and handing down opinion through her retinue of distinguished writers and editors. The language, especially of the columinists, was high-brow. Feature articles on lifestyle or social trends, which are now an integral part of newspapers, were shunned.

Within the organization, there was very little interaction between the editorial, advertising, circulation and production staff. Each department maintained an inward-looking attitude and rarely interacted with each other. Each wing was operating as an independent entity and the consciousness of being one grand ensemble moving forward seemed to be lacking.

The production of the paper and the 'minor' details of sales were left to the lesser mortals within the organization – the marketing and circulation managers. It was the job of these people to ensure that they sold what the journalists wrote. It fell upon them to sustain operations by getting advertisers to pay for space. Those who wrote were hardly concerned with this aspect of the business. For them, it was all about their 'stories', their bylines and their exclusives.

The big break that Samir Jain made was to treat the media as a business like any other. 'He saw the makings of a fruitful business in journalism when few others were willing to see it or imagine that it was possible,' said Gautam Adhikari. 'It was a novel approach,' he remarked.[6]

Samir Jain started to pay attention to parameters of profitability and return on capital. He wanted not just his marketing teams to focus on that, but also align journalists to the needs of the bottom line. For an organization basking in the glory of its leadership and legacy, blissfully unaware of business imperatives, it was hard to come to terms with this new paradigm.

Of course, other media houses were not any better off and the impact of Samir Jain's decisions inevitably affected them too. 'In a clear, candid, resolute manner, he forced the newspaper industry to regard itself as an industry,' noted Dileep Padgaonkar.[7]

When Samir Jain came into BCCL, concepts such as marketing, financial management, technology, expansion, pricing and brand management were almost alien to the newspaper industry. He had to induce fresh thinking on these lines among his managers and journalists.

But alongside building the case for change, he himself needed to be clear of where the opportunities lay. It was important that he knew the strategy and what new direction to take. Before making a case for change and articulating his thoughts to his people, it was essential that he was convinced of the path forward, the points of departure from the past and the implications for the future.

The company had been making a modest profit of Rs 1.5 crore to 2 crore a year. But Samir Jain believed that the potential was enormous. 'He was convinced that BCCL could become a cash cow at a time when the other companies of the old empire were languishing and had little potential for recovery,' observed Adhikari.

Newspapers at that time focused mainly on circulation. They believed that the more copies they sold, the more money they would make. The cover price as a source of revenue was insignificant. In fact, it was often lower than the cost of producing the newspaper. But higher circulation numbers were used as a pitch for advertisers. Higher circulation enabled the advertiser to reach more people, and hence he ought to pay more per column centimetre to insert an advertisement in the paper. It was almost as simple as that.

It followed from this that newspapers paid a lot of attention to ways of boosting circulation. Content was of course a major factor in this. It was assumed that the better the quality of journalists and the more credible the news and comment in the paper, the more popular would the newspaper be. On the flip side, allegations of proprietor interference or a reputation of pandering to vested interests in government could work against the prospects of the paper. Journalists and commentators of repute thus had a direct contribution to the business, though they were not supposed to be overly concerned about it.

The focus on circulation also meant that newspaper organizations built adequate capacity to print more and more copies, and do it on time. So they invested in machines and infrastructure. They needed more people as they scaled up. Newsprint was under tight control of the government and was doled out as per designated quotas for each publication or media house.

Distribution was also critical. Newspapers needed to cover larger territories if they had to grow circulation. They first inched beyond the metro cities to satellite towns. Later, their option was to move to other urban centres and tier-two cities. All the while, logistics and distribution kept getting complicated. Growing the newspaper business was thus an exhausting game. It required proprietors to sink in ever more resources to fund expansion.

Samir Jain could have persisted with this model. But he could see that this was a losing game in the long run. Since the cover price was much lower than the cost to produce the newspaper, the more copies you printed, the more money you lost. If the objective was to improve profitability and return on capital, this strategy would not take you there.

Besides, boosting circulation required the newspaper to attract new readers. Many of these new readers would have to be young, upwardly mobile, middle-class families. Samir Jain was perhaps not sure whether his journalists could yet fully reorient content to appeal to these sections. He would make a successful effort to recruit new readers. But that was some years away. For now, he chose to focus not on circulation but on creating value for the advertiser.

His premise was simple: advertisers should pay according to the value they derive from any newspaper. Circulation was one determinant of value but not the only one. Not even the most important one. The value that an advertiser could derive, he argued, depended on the kind of readership that a newspaper commanded.

The more relevant the readership provided by the newspaper, the more value it offered to the advertiser.

By his logic, while the number of readers as measured by circulation figures was relevant, more relevant was providing the *right* kind of audience to the advertiser. Companies wanted to communicate with their target audience, those who would consider purchasing their product or service. Overall circulation was irrelevant for companies. They would choose their advertising medium accordingly.

In this framework, a consumer goods company would prefer a newspaper that reaches the upwardly mobile, urban, middle-class families. Even if another newspaper sold more but was read by people outside the consuming class, it would be of little interest to the consumer goods company.

This was a straightforward argument, waiting to be made. It made sense for Samir Jain to emphasize value over sheer numbers. This was targeted mainly at *Hindustan Times* which was the leader in Delhi. Its circulation was almost double that of *The Times of India* in Delhi. People had been reading *HT* for years and it was difficult to make them switch to another paper overnight. But a case could be made that the reader profile of *The Times of India* was upmarket and more relevant for corporate advertisers compared to that of *Hindustan Times*.

In Bombay, there was no such debate. *The Times of India*'s circulation was more than the circulation of all the English newspapers there put together. It was not just the leader; there was practically no competitor in the English-language space in that city.

Having made this point about value versus circulation, the challenge before Samir Jain was multifold. First, he had to ensure that his newspapers indeed delivered the right audience to the advertiser. This meant realigning the news content to appeal to these audiences. The content of his newspapers had to touch issues that were important to this category of readers. This meant a lesser dose of politics in the newspaper, to start with. The newspapers had to speak a language that these audiences could connect to. They had to be sensitive to the choices, concerns and priorities of this relevant middle-class audience. This was never going to be easy.

Besides, they could not be content having met this promise once. Much of this was dynamic. This class of readers was fast evolving in their lifestyle and perceptions. Their preferences and concerns were changing rapidly. To keep pace with them, newspapers had to be flexible. They had to have speed. They needed to have a finger on the pulse of this audience and an acute appreciation of their likes and dislikes. That was the first part.

The other challenge for Samir Jain was to convince advertisers that his newspapers were indeed delivering relevant audiences compared to other newspapers. He had to show that his readers were younger, more affluent and with a higher propensity to spend and consume.

Bashab Sarkar, who was at O&M when I met him in October 2001, said: 'Samir Jain zealously promoted *TOI* as a premium product. To start with, he did not prove it. He just claimed it. There was a certain amount of arrogance and assertion in his claim. He asked media planners to pay more for space. In a subjective argument, you do not explain how you can claim to be a premium product, can you? But the message sent out was that *The Times* was now charging the value its product deserved; that there had been a reorientation of pricing.'[8]

To make his point, Samir Jain cited that according to the Thompson Urban Market Index, Delhi's market potential was sixty-six compared to Bombay's 100. In fact, Delhi was third after Calcutta. This meant that broadly, if an English-language newspaper in Bombay had a circulation comparable to an English-language newspaper in Delhi, the former should be entitled to a higher advertising rate.

The Index falls under the aegis of market research and postulates the market potential of a town or a city using many demographic and socio-economic variables. This quantitative assessment is crucial for market planning as it elaborates in detail the number of consumers in these areas, the means they have, their demonstrated buying behaviour and their awareness levels. Knowing what the Index has gathered is therefore of great value and Samir Jain knew that.

Not only had he to convince the advertisers that his audience was more relevant, he had to get them to actually pay more for advertising in his publications. Here too the industry was in a comfort zone. Like journalists, the advertising part of the media business was operating within a legacy.

Media agencies, who advertised on behalf of their corporate clients, had standard rate lists from publications. These were primarily based on circulation. The media agencies, advertising companies and the media houses were all comfortable with this arrangement. The advertising rates were decided by all publications in broad consultation with each other, keeping the media agencies in the picture. This too was one cozy world where everyone lived by rules and change came slowly, if at all.

Samir Jain's logic of designing advertising rates according to relevant audiences created discomfort. Circulation figures were hard numbers. There was a certain comfort in using them as a reference, even if they had ceased to be a true index of value. The media agencies and advertisers were now being compelled to cast away that parameter and switch to intangible measures like 'value' offered by one publication over another. It also meant often paying more for space in a newspaper with a lower circulation. This was bound to shake up the system.

The economics apart, Samir Jain's moves were ushering in fundamental shifts in the media business. It was no longer enough for newspapers to just expand their network and circulation. They would have to target specific markets and customers as well. They would have to devise innovative ways to reach these segments of the readership effectively. Newspapers would have to convey certain values and personality traits consistently to make themselves appealing to those sections of readers.

This meant that newspapers would have to transform themselves from a commodity-like behaviour to products with distinct characteristics that differentiated them from competitor products. They would have personalities and a feel about them that was specific to the audiences they were targeting. They would become 'brands'. 'Samir Jain saw the importance of branding in media much before anyone else,' noted T.N. Ninan. 'He built brands.'

In this 'market-driven' framework, all parts of the organization would have to align and work together towards building and reinforcing the personality of the brand. The organization would have to shed the watertight compartments that had characterized it so far. It would also have to build in dynamism in its functioning, so that it could anticipate any changes in its target group and adapt quickly. Those within his organization who could not fit into this new ecosystem had to either leave or take a back seat. This applied to editors and equally to managers and those in the administration.

He genuinely believed that the newspaper was marketing-driven, not editorial-driven. '"Marketing sells the paper," Samir Jain would say,' recalled Baljit Kapoor.[9] 'In fact, he believed that superior marketing could sell even a lousy product although he made sure that his products were upmarket and trendy. "We are not product sellers," we told him. "We are not selling toothpaste or soap." We were very uncomfortable with his terminology of the newspaper as a product. But he would use his authority to get things done,' Kapoor said candidly.

'Samir's emphasis on marketing techniques to improve the company's performance led to numerous tensions, both within the editorial and the marketing sides of the group. These tensions were responsible for clashes with editors and the subsequent restructuring of the editorial side's management structure,' Adhikari recalled.

While his framework of focusing on value over sheer circulation numbers made sense on paper, it had to be tested in the marketplace. Would advertisers be willing to pay more for a better profile of readers? Samir Jain tested out the argument by going in for a massive hike in his advertising rates during 1986-1987. Traditionally these hikes had been to the tune of 5–10 per cent a year. But he took it up by between 25 and 50 per cent. The rates in *TOI*, Bombay, went up a whopping 68 per cent in one year.

In doing so, he disregarded the other industry practice of privately consulting media agencies before effecting a hike. 'As far as Samir was concerned, there was absolutely no question of a discussion with the advertising agencies before the revision in the advertising rates,' recalled N.P. Singh,[10] who had been BCCL's all-India head of circulation before taking over as advertising director. 'We just announced the hike.'

There was absolute bedlam in the advertising and media world. It was not just the outsiders who resented the hike. Samir Jain also had to overcome doubts within his organization. Many in his marketing and management team felt it would not work. They too had been brought up in the old ways.

But his logic was the same: the value delivered by the *TOI* to advertisers was much higher than what they were paying. His newspaper deserved more. Incremental increases of 5 or 10 per cent would not do any more.

This bold move to revise advertisement rates ranks as one of the major shifts in trajectory for the group. 'This created a furore in publishers' circles but Samir was unmoved and pushed ahead shrewdly. He realized that the rates were too low and the market could absorb a 100 or even 200 per cent increase,' Singh recalled.

As it turned out, after the initial protests, the advertising and media industry accepted the hike. It was almost as if the market was ready and willing. Someone had to muster the courage to make it happen. Perhaps the changing demographics of Delhi and Bombay, with a growing middle class and a booming consumer market, helped his cause. The absence of a viable alternative may have also persuaded the advertisers to accept the hike.

Over the next few years, Samir Jain would go on to announce a number of rate hikes. But it was not a one-way street. He made far-reaching changes in his newspapers to justify the higher rates. 'Aggregating relevant audiences for advertisers' became the credo of the organization. This was reflected in changes in content. With the focus on design, layouts and packaging, the tone and texture of the papers underwent a major transformation. He invested first in creating glossy colour pull-outs that were ideal platforms for advertisers. Later, he went all-colour, well ahead of his competitors.

The columns were regularly chopped, changed and redesigned. Innovation abounded: all directed towards providing a better exposure and stickiness to the communication by advertisers. As it emerged later, these hikes in advertising rates were not stand-alone or arbitrary. They were based on a keen sense of the market and were aligned to major innovations in the pricing of space which would shake up the industry.

We shall take that up in another chapter soon. But before that, there was some work to be done within the organization's editorial echelons.

FOUR

# Stop Press! Reflong!

*'Now is the dramatic moment of fate, Watson, when you hear a step upon the stair which is walking into your life, and you know not whether for good or ill.'*

From Arthur Conan Doyle's
*The Hound of the Baskervilles*[1].

IN EARLY 1986, AN eight-page note was circulated among the top management of Bennett, Coleman and Co Limited. The note discussed certain changes that were required in the editorial structure and content of the company's flagship English daily, *The Times of India* and its Hindi newspaper, *Navbharat Times*. The note had been prepared by Samir Jain.

A copy of the note was printed in *Sunday* magazine (6–12 April 1986) under the heading 'The Samir Jain Plan' as part of the magazine's cover story 'The Signs of The Times'. Most of the points suggested in the note were straightforward. For one, the organization needed to recruit fresh talent to be able to support its growth. And existing employees needed to be put through regular training. Career paths had to be defined.

There were also a few suggestions regarding content. There would have to be more feature articles as against news reports, especially on weekends. In fact, it was suggested, the weekend papers should evolve as independent editions run by a separate editor. Samir Jain also asked for a more 'modern look' to the newspapers. The importance of graphics, layout and design was emphasized.

Many of these ideas were new and far-reaching for newspapers of that time. They were implemented over the next couple of years. These steps were part of a larger transformation that was being brought about at Bennett, Coleman. By and by, they impacted other leading newspapers in the country as well.

There was, however, one suggestion outlined in the note, which kicked up a major controversy. It put the note in jeopardy for a while. It threw the company in turmoil.

The suggestion was: the news and the views sections of the newspaper should be separated. There should be one editor for news, and another for views. Their domains should be clearly demarcated. It was further laid down that the editor for news, to be designated as executive editor, would have nothing to do with the edit page, which was the views page. All the news teams, covering politics, business, city affairs, sports and so on, would report to the executive editor. The editor for the edit page, on the other hand, would have a separate team of deputy editors and assistant editors reporting to him.

For a person unfamiliar with the newspaper industry, this would seem like a normal corporate reorganization. While it would change a few equations here and there, people would by and large settle down to it in time. But in this case, that was not to be. The journalists took umbrage at this. They resented the fact that the owner was interfering in matters of content and editorial which were in the domain of the editor. Besides, they argued, the owner's proposals were designed to undermine the position of the editor, with the ultimate aim of the owner assuming control over the editorial.

As the *Sunday* article reported, senior journalists, numbering about forty, signed a petition resenting this change. They said the note had created a 'veritable upheaval' in the organization. They handed this petition to the editor-in-chief of *The Times of India*, and asked him to take up the matter with the chairman. Their brethren in other publications joined in and roundly criticized the move.

For a brief period, it seemed the note would have to be dumped in its entirety. That was perhaps a lesser concern, given that BCCL itself was now in turmoil. Over the next few months, most of the petitioning journalists quit. Some of them were asked to leave. Within two years, the company came to be led by a completely new set of people. This also paved the way for major changes within the organization and with that, in the Indian newspaper industry.

This controversy had deep roots. It was not about just that one contentious point. It had taken a while for the situation to build up to this. Both sides – Samir Jain and the journalists – had come to realize that they had separate agendas, and conflicting ones. Suspicion on both sides had been growing.

The note, while a genuine blueprint for the company, was also Samir Jain's way of asserting himself. The journalists, on the other hand, were confident, perhaps almost smug, that they could resist the management's moves for change. They believed that they had enough influence and clout outside the organization – in political circles, bureaucracy and the intelligentsia – to be able to thwart Samir Jain's pugnacious moves. They decided to strike back. As it turned out, they seem to have underestimated Samir Jain's resolve. Even more, they may have failed to see the imperative need for change in the industry.

At that time, the newspaper industry revolved around editors. While there were several editorial heads in a newspaper manning individual domains, the overall charge was with one individual. The editor was responsible for the entire newspaper, including both the editorial and the news pages. He was seen as the veritable commander-in-chief. Samir Jain's proposal, seeking separate editors for news and views, was attacking this central role accorded to the editor.

In practice, the editor may not always have been the commander-in-chief he was being made out to be. The views side of the newspaper was effectively distinct from the news side, long before Samir Jain proposed it. This was due to the temperament of individual editors of those times. They, by and large, took interest in the edit page while the news side was left to an operational head like the news editor.

In that sense, the corridor separating the news side from the views side was already in existence, even if not defined in writing. Editors were far removed from the hurly-burly of daily news collection and reportage. They treated the editorial page as their domain where they wrote lofty editorials and opinion pieces. It was their channel to communicate with the political leadership, the cream of the bureaucracy and academia. The rest of the world, including the proprietor, would merely look on.

Within the newspaper, it was rare for someone from the news side to venture into the cabins meant for the editors on the views side. The news teams had to confine themselves to their task of gathering and presenting daily developments, as they happened, to the reader. There is an apocryphal story of an editor, an intellectual of great depth and reach, failing to recognize his news editor! Of course, such division of roles was more on account of the elevated, almost Brahminical stature accorded to the intellectuals in control of the edit page rather than a conscious separation of news and views in the paper.

Many editors were larger than life. They were men of erudition. They were revered in the corridors of power. Their views were seen either as reflecting the mood of the public or, at any rate, were the sage pronouncements of the wise.

This pre-eminent role of the editor also had to do with the fact that in many leading publications, ownership and editorial were separate. Owners respected this distinction and often chose to keep a low profile. Barring occasional situations where their personal stakes were involved, proprietors kept off the day-to-day affairs of their publication. They let the editorial unit function more or less independently.

The halo around the newspapers, and by extension editors, was also a legacy of the freedom movement. Leading freedom fighters, notably Mahatma Gandhi, Bal Gangadhar Tilak, Bipin Chandra Pal and Jawaharlal Nehru had used newspapers as a medium to communicate with the people and the government.[2] They discussed not just the freedom movement but also used newspaper columns to share their social and economic agenda for the country.

Long after Independence, newspapers continued to be seen more as institutions than just as businesses. They had a social role. Instead of supporting the freedom struggle, they were now required to safeguard democracy by informing, educating and airing opinions freely. Terms like 'watchdogs of democracy' and 'fourth estate' were taken seriously – and adhered to with utmost sincerity. Rudyard Kipling has summed up the sentiment the best:

> The Pope may launch his Interdict,
> The Union its decree,
> But the bubble is blown and the bubble is pricked
> By Us and such as We.
> Remember the battle and stand aside
> While Thrones and Powers confess
> That King over all the children of pride
> Is the Press—the Press—the Press![3]

The editor, therefore, was the one at the helm of this glorious institution that was steadfastly objective, honourable and at an arm's length from the Establishment. The freedom of this institution was seen as sacrosanct for a healthy and lively democracy. It had to be safeguarded from all possible encroachment. The obstacles to airing opinion freely and frankly could equally be from the government, the proprietor or crass commercial interests.

The editor was given all the space he needed to air his views – and words of counsel to the political leadership – on the issues of the day. He could make public his dislike or otherwise for the ruling dispensation and yet was trusted to be objective. It was taken for granted that he had no selfish or personal interest and that he genuinely believed in the views he propounded.

In most cases, the editors lived up to this faith. Their opinions were independent of any extraneous allurements or influence. The intellectual class was sensitive, almost touchy, about any violation of media freedom. Every time an editor, especially of a leading newspaper, aired his discomfort about 'interference' by the proprietor, it unfailingly caused concern in the intellectual class. The Press Council would frequently step in. The government, though not interfering directly and openly, was at hand. Occasionally, the courts were brought in to intervene.

Governments, another potential threat to media freedom, also had to be cautious, then as now, not to be caught in allegations of 'muzzling the press'. The government was (and is) a major advertiser. It also had control over the distribution of newsprint among the media. It may have tried to lure journalists and threaten proprietors more than once. But all these attempts were subtle.

As for commerce, another potential threat to editorial freedom, editors were zealously insulated from the real world. The content and approach of newspapers was delinked, often consciously, from what advertisers (or even readers) would prefer. Editors considered any talk about the business performance of the newspaper an assault on their sensitivities.

At the same time, the reputation and success of a newspaper seemed to be tied to its journalists and the editor. Just as clinics are known by their best doctors, and technical companies by their best IT engineers, newspapers were mostly known by their editors.

Samir Jain was completely at odds with this framework. But other proprietors had played their part well in this arrangement. Most of the leading English-language newspapers were owned by rich Marwaris, who had dominated trade and banking in the early twentieth century. They had either started the newspaper on their own or, as in the case of *The Times of India*, acquired them from their British owners. Their journalists, as intellectuals, enjoyed a higher social status. Even where the proprietors were established businessmen, they were comfortable respecting the editors and according them the limelight.

Barring one or two instances, the proprietors were reluctant to lay down even an editorial policy. They hardly undertook any initiatives to professionalize their organizations. Their intervention in their newspapers was as Girilal Jain had mentioned in the *Sunday* article: 'spasmodic, arbitrary and related to personal or family or friends' interests...they were not general or purposeful or ideological (interventions)'.

If newspapers behaved as lofty institutions above concerns of commercial success and profits, it was the proprietors who made that possible. The proprietors were in diverse businesses, and the newspaper was rarely the cash cow for their business empires. It was never the core enterprise generating wealth and profits for their group. Other businesses performed that role.

For many proprietors, the newspaper was more a means of exerting gentle pressure over the government, eliciting favours or just enhancing social status. They were happy if the newspaper made money. But even if it did not, it was more than compensated for by the clout and prestige that a newspaper offered. India was a state-dominated and over-regulated economy in the 1980s. A newspaper, which could make and mar reputations of politicians, was an invaluable asset for any businessman.

To be fair, some proprietors kept a healthy distance from their newspapers because they were committed to editorial freedom. Separating ownership from editorial control was the way to gain credibility for the publication and that is how they wanted it to be. Each media house was distinct in its editor–owner relationship and its profit objective. But by and large, the newspaper was perched comfortably on the periphery of business empires, and could afford to give virtually a free run to the editor.

The editors relished their pre-eminent role. According to Sunil Jain, his father Girilal Jain was offered the post of ambassador to the US by Indira Gandhi when she made a comeback as prime minister in 1980. He had declined the offer, saying there were only two important posts that he would like to take. 'You hold the first, and I, the second,' he had said.[4]

Indeed, the editor of *The Times of India* was one of the most privileged positions in the country. Frank Moraes and Sham Lal were towering personalities in their own ways. At the time Samir Jain came up with his proposal, the editor was Girilal Jain, an ardent supporter of Hindutva and Hindu hegemony. He was also someone who was cast in the mould of the mighty editors of yore.

While the editors at BCCL were invariably men of stature and erudition, the mild-mannered proprietor at that time, Ashok Jain, made a special effort in according them respect and freedom. He ensured that his role and relationship were always in line and above board.

Inder Malhotra, who saw the protest against Samir Jain unfold, emphasized that Ashok Jain was a 'well-mannered owner' who did not interfere in the editorial affairs of the newspaper.[5] At the height of the controversy caused by the Samir Jain proposals, the *Sunday* story mentioned above also had an interview with Girilal Jain. His responses offer many insights into the nature of owner–editor relationship at that time. Girilal Jain said he did not regard *The Times of India* as a family-owned or company-owned newspaper. 'I regard it as a national institution... If it were to be run as a company-owned concern, I won't fit in. For me, it is national service with a certain amount of payment. As it happened, *the personality of the chairman (Ashok Jain) has matched this requirement* (emphasis added). He has never interfered.'

By way of an example, he cited that the chairman 'has been a supporter of Rajiv Gandhi (the then prime minister), and I, his critic. We have discussed the matter half a dozen times but at no stage has it come to even attempting to influence my policy.' Girilal Jain said while the publisher was free to make his choice of editor, once the choice has been made he should not intervene. 'I would consider it very irksome if the owner breathes down my neck and keeps telling me what to do and what not to do,'[6] he had said.

Even after the reorganization plan was released, Girilal Jain seemed confident that Samir Jain would not interfere in editorial policy: 'Samir has said so many times, and he means it, that the editorial policy is not his concern.' He, of course, acknowledged that this kind of relationship (between him and the chairman) 'did not exist in most places'.

Within this overall context, Samir Jain's proposal to separate the news and the views sections was radical. The protesting journalists' central concern was that through these proposals for change, the owner was interfering in editorial matters of the newspaper. By suggesting changes in content and editorial structure, he was crossing the sacred line separating owners and editors. It was the editor's prerogative to decide how the content side of the paper was to be run. Interference by the owner was inappropriate.

There were many points in that note that the journalists disapproved of. The tone, tenor and approach were unacceptable to them. But all that came much later. The central issue, they argued, was impinging on the rights and role of the editor. This process had started with this eight-page note. If it was allowed to go on, the position of the editor would be made totally subservient to the agenda of the owner.

They could already spot the hidden agenda in the note. Not only was Samir Jain challenging the pre-eminent role of the editor, they argued, he was doing so with a motive. According to them, he was clearing the way for the owner to replace the editor and usurp the central role in the newspaper.

Suddenly, the separation of news and views was not merely a subject of organizational change. It became an issue of editorial freedom and proprietorial interference. At that time and era, this was potentially explosive. This was one corporate restructuring that got everyone interested.

Samir Jain's counter was that what he had proposed was nothing unusual. It was already happening. This is how newspapers were being run in the West, notably in the US. *The New York Times*, for years, had separate editors for news and views. Samir Jain had recently completed a tour of newspapers in the US and he was impressed by what he had seen. He also admired Rupert Murdoch.[7]

As for him interfering in the domain of the editor, he was clear and blunt. He was the owner of this business and it was for him to decide its course. This approach was a marked departure from the way owners had treated their media companies, and by extension their editors, until now. This is where Samir Jain started to change the rules of the game. It was a change his journalists found hard to stomach.

'One morning in January 1986, Samir Jain called me to join him for tea. He said, "Become my advisor. And let Girilal Jain run the paper." Later, on another occasion, he said, "Unko samjhaiye" (Get him [Girilal Jain] to understand). I resigned in April 1986. But was there till September that year,' said Inder Malhotra. He continued to write for the *TOI* for nine years.

'Between April and September 1986, some sub-editors had to be recruited. Samir brought in his own people, saying he wanted to democratize the recruitment process. I did not like to be bypassed. And Girilal Jain wrote to Ashok Jain,' Malhotra recalled.

Samir Jain's note had not stopped at separate editors for news and views. It had also proposed that editorial heads of individual functions such as sports, business and city affairs be also designated as 'editors' of their respective areas. So in addition to the editorial-page editor and the executive editor, the paper would have a sports editor, photo editor, metro editor and so on.

In this new framework, the edit page would continue to carry opinion. But it would do more than that. It would publish multiple opinions on an issue. At the same time with multiple editors heading various sections, the paper was being designed to take up multiple issues, not just those which the edit page team considered important. News reports in each of the sections would be interpretative and analytical, not just an objective chronicling of events. It appears that alongside reorganizing the editorial team for better results, Samir Jain was also taking away the myth and mystique surrounding the word 'editor'.

This was completely unacceptable to his top journalists. They could see that the new framework would erode the halo around the title 'editor'. While Samir Jain's reasoning was that multiple views and multiple editors would bring in plurality to the paper, the journalists perceived that this would diffuse power and influence across the organization rather than centre it on an individual.

'Samir Jain changed the editor's position. He was like Copernicus in reverse. It was heresy,' noted Bachi Karkaria. 'He was in the business as a business. Therefore, all the power structures needed to be changed and business became the predominant concern.'[8]

In 1986, a move was also initiated to change service conditions of journalists. They were hired now on a contractual basis. It was done a few years down the line. But when it was first proposed, there was uproar in and ouside BCCL. Well-known writer and journalist, the late K. L. Nandan,[9] who had been the editor of BCCL's magazines such as *Parag*, *Sarika* and *Dinman*, and who was also the features editor of the *Navbharat Times* told me: 'I was in Bombay in 1986. Ramesh Chandraji came to see me. He mentioned that a decision to bring us under contract was being considered.

'"You too may have to sign a contract," he told me. I was really angry. *Mein thekay par sampaadkee nahin kartaa hoon* (I am not a *contract* editor), I retorted. I approached Ashokji to discuss the matter. Meanwhile, I had been offered the editor's job at *Dainik Hindustan* with three times the salary. Rameshji asked me to meet Dr Tarneja. Eventually, I was asked to meet Samir Jain.

'Samir said, "We have nothing against you. But the difference is that you are a very strong editor." Subsequently, they created a new post for me at the *Navbharat Times*. I was in charge of the magazine section of the newspaper; in charge of the feature pages. I became the features editor. Ashokji was a fair person. But he had come under some pressure. His son had begun to assert himself. Some editors of some of the magazines, he said, will have to be shunted out...but gracefully,' Nandan recalled.

Besides, with fresh recruitments expected at that juncture, journalists were convinced that many of the key positions, like those of the executive editor, would be filled by recruits from outside the organization. This added to their discomfort. They felt that Samir Jain would bring in pliable people to man these key positions and thereby achieve his objective of assuming complete control of the editorial side of the newspaper.

They did not think much of Samir Jain's argument that this model had been successful in the US. The division of responsibility there, they argued, had not meant dilution of the editor's power. The separate editors there reported to a single authority. That single authority happened to be the publisher.

But the publisher there was either a full-fledged journalist or at any rate, one who took a keen interest in the running of his newspaper. Publishers like Rosenthal[10] were also journalists. They operated like professional journalists, not as proprietors. They devoted time to their newspapers. For them to take the central role in their publications was therefore appropriate.

That was not the case with BCCL in India. Here, it would only amount to the owner, a non-journalist, taking over greater control, making the newspaper subservient to the proprietor and, by implication, diluting the institutional role of the newspaper as an impartial and responsible pillar of democracy.

Clearly, Samir Jain and his journalists were approaching the issue from opposite ends and failed to see each other's point of view. The journalists' position was that allowing the proprietor to take control would mean letting him abuse the institution. If the powers that be and the intelligentsia held on to every word written in the editorial columns of the paper, it is only fair that the editor crafting those editorials be kept free of any external influence, including that of the proprietor.

This was a fair argument as far as it went. A proprietor at that time could have been tempted to misuse the clout and credibility of *The Times of India* for short-term gains. The checks and balances ought to be maintained.

Veteran journalist H.K. Dua,[11] who got into a tussle with the *TOI* management over his dismissal in 1998, and who has held editorial positions at four national newspapers – *The Times of India*, the *Hindustan Times*, *The Indian Express* and *The Tribune* – was the media advisor to the then prime minister, Atal Behari Vajpayee, when I met him. He spoke at length, although his moot point was that the proprietor's attempts to establish control over the editor have been harmful for newspapers. 'If profit is the motive, obviously managers become more important. They run the newspapers on commercial lines. And people's interests get diminished.... Once papers become products like toothpastes they do not reflect social concerns. They begin catering to an elite class and treat readers like consumers. Idealism becomes the casualty. Newspapers become less of a force to reckon with. Their social obligation gets diluted. The commercial interests of proprietors have distanced newspapers from the people. And this gap makes newspapers less of a force. Journalism has an edge because it is a public duty. But if you subordinate the editor's authority, editorial freedom will suffer,' he asserted.

But Samir Jain turned the argument on its head. He was interested not so much in using the *TOI* to build clout and influence for himself, but to generate profits. He was clear that he wanted a growing and profitable newspaper. For him, it was a business like any other, and it had to generate wealth. If, in the process, it meant giving up the 'institution' that communicated with the influential sections, so be it. He would rather have his paper talk to readers and citizens about their local concerns and aspirations than pontificate on esoteric subjects to a small section of the influential classes. He was happy to strip his paper off any halo or conceit, if it came in the way of connecting with his customers and creating wealth.

If the journalists feared that he would misuse the institution to garner influence and clout, Samir Jain was clearly not interested. Far from influencing the powers that be, he wanted to take his newspapers' focus away from them. Unlike other proprietors of the day, he did not see any purpose in treating the newspaper as a tool of influence. Rather, he saw much more gain in turning it into a medium connecting with the emerging middle class. As it turned out, that proved to be a far more profitable call. But many of the journalists either did not see it this way, or did not understand this shift in approach or refused to leave their comfort zone.

For readers of my generation, the late Girilal Jain is the last of the great editors of *The Times of India*. He was opinionated, an ideologue, known for his signature editorials. I decided to look at the controversy through the eyes of his son, Sunil Jain, a leading columnist in March 2002 and now the managing editor at *The Financial Express*.

'My father had worked for *The Times of India* for several years before he became the editor of the paper. He had seen several political ups and downs. Ashok Jain would request him to get a few things done. But it was never more than that. The editor was given a free run to manage the paper. But, for Samir Jain the paper is a corporate entity and news and views are two different things. My dad believed that the editor should be in absolute control of the paper. He believed that even the executive editor was second to the editor. The conflict was ideological. Who was really in charge of the paper? Samir Jain decided what the policies of the paper ought to be. His view was that the owners and the board would decide the future course of action. But my father said: "I am the editor and I will decide." He also said that it was incidental that the Jains owned *The Times of India*. It was not their family fiefdom. It was a national institution. These were the fundamental differences about the office of the editor and they kept arguing for their interests.'[12]

Soon after Samir Jain's proposals were released, it became the subject of heated discussions within *The Times* and also beyond, to cover large parts of the national media. Resentment among his journalists mounted. It was important for them to group together and channelize their reaction. This was done by the resident editors of the paper's Delhi and Bombay editions. They raised the banner of revolt and the journalists rallied together. The petitioners were from various sections of the newspaper and had their differences in terms of attitudes, backgrounds and world views. But they ignored their differences and came together against the reorganization because they felt that at that point in time, 'larger issues' were involved. They perhaps realized that the attack on the editor's position would soon cascade down to the rest of the editorial team.

A petition against the proposal was drafted and a voluntary 'signature campaign' was undertaken. There was no pressure to sign on the dotted line but efforts were made to convince journalists. The petition was placed in Inder Malhotra's room and people were free to walk in and sign it.

The protesting journalists did not stop at mobilizing people within the company. They invited their peers in other newspapers to help in the cause. There were also reports of a rival newspaper offering to recruit all the top *Times* journalists at the same terms and conditions, should they choose to quit or be asked to leave.

The issue simmered for a couple of weeks. Samir Jain decided to meet a group of senior journalists and explain the reasons for the change. The meeting was held at *The Times of India*'s office in

New Delhi in February 1986. Some thirty-five senior journalists attended the meet. Girilal Jain was absent.

Samir Jain laid down the context for the reorganization. However, he seemed to treat all the changes he had proposed as one package, rather than single out any specific point. He spoke at length about how competition was emerging to challenge the leadership position of BCCL. Newspapers like *The Telegraph*, launched by the Ananda Bazar group from Calcutta, were strong in both news and features. Their production and layout was of high quality, rarely seen in India before. He said he knew many Marwaris in Calcutta who had switched to *The Telegraph*.

His primary concern, of course, was that *The Times of India* had failed to overtake the *Hindustan Times* in Delhi. The latter still led by a significant margin in the capital. Again, while *The Times of India* was the leader in Bombay, he said there was 'scope for improvement' there as well.

The *TOI* editions in Jaipur and Bangalore were not doing well. *The Hindu*, unchallenged in the south for decades, was now considering a Delhi edition. *India Today* wanted to bring out a daily. All in all, competition was hotting up and *The Times of India* had to put its house in order, he said. That was the context for the changes suggested in content, design and, of course, the editorial structure.

The journalists acted disinterested and distracted for most part of the meeting. They paid little attention to what Samir Jain said. They frequently interrupted him as he spoke. While Samir Jain liked to think that he was outlining to them the big picture, the path for the organization, the journalists detained him with problems relating to day-to-day affairs of the company (including the condition of the toilets). Clearly, the meeting was not working as per plan.

Eventually, the journalists said no discussion on the changes was possible in the absence of the editor, Girilal Jain. These were policies pertaining to the editorial function and he ought to be present to decide the way forward. The meeting ended at that. The following day, the journalists forwarded their signed petition to Girilal Jain.

Girilal Jain did not formally take up the matter with Ashok Jain. For the time being, discussions on the changes came to an abrupt halt. It led the journalists to believe that they had triumphed. It was rumoured that the proposals had been withdrawn. The protesters had prevailed. It was believed that Girilal Jain, whose tenure was to end in July the following year, would now be given a three-year extension. That would put a stamp of finality on the surrender by Samir Jain.

Although Girilal Jain did stay on till 1988, the journalists' self-congratulation was misplaced. To begin with, Ashok Jain was unhappy at this development. He felt that this was a 'unionized' protest against his son. That was not acceptable, coming from journalists who held senior positions in his company. He conveyed his displeasure to Inder Malhotra. 'You should not have allowed such a collective memorandum,' he said.

He refused to be placated when Inder Malhotra reasoned that it had been a voluntary protest. Even if you do not force people to sign such papers, Ashok Jain maintained, '*jabar aa hi jaata hai* (they would have felt compelled)'.[13] After that, he made his son the joint managing director of the company.

Samir Jain, against whom the petition was targeted, responded firmly. The protest did little to change his mind. If anything, it seemed to have strengthened his resolve to implement the changes he had proposed. Initially, he appeared to be somewhat perturbed by this action of his journalists. Soon after the petition was received, Samir Jain called Gautam Adhikari. He had been one of the brains behind the reorganization plan and would play a key role in the group's transformation.

When Adhikari entered Samir Jain's office, he found the latter lying pensively on a couch. The lights were dimmed, as if he wanted to be by himself. He told Gautam not to talk to him but just to take a look at the note that the journalists had sent. 'He (Samir Jain) was more determined than ever to make the changes, "no matter what".'[14] He decided to axe the "dead wood" – the old guard – from the editorial. He decided to make Delhi his headquarters instead of Bombay. And he began looking to build his own loyal army.

It was not clear at this stage how supportive Ashok Jain was regarding these changes. It was one thing to resent the move against his son's proposals but quite another to back them and see them through. The journalists were inclined to believe that he was sympathetic to their cause. He had run his papers on a certain value system that was based on the supremacy of the editor. To dispense with that and have the proprietor suggest changes in content and layout would violate the value system that was in place.

Given their different working styles, there were undercurrents between father and son. 'Ashok Jain had initially been supportive of Giri and there were some bitter moments between father and son,' said a former executive director at BCCL who for obvious reasons did not want to be named. 'At home and in the office, they were poles apart. Samir had often walked out during heated conversations with the chairman. Nandita played an important role here,' he pointed out. 'She was her father's pet. She would go in and talk to him. She did it for her brother. She brokered peace,' he added. As it turned out, his father supported the changes. 'Samir was anxious to take over from Ashok Jain, who, at worst, restrained his zeal but never stopped him,' said Inder Malhotra. The elder Jain obviously saw the imperative of making his media business more profitable. Most of the other companies of the family empire were in decline. Either the sector in which they operated had fallen on troubled times, or they were beset with internal problems, which they were unable to resolve. By default, the media business emerged as the unlikely saviour for his family's business empire.

Most important, Ashok Jain realized that his son seemed to have a natural inclination for the media business compared to the other businesses which mainly dealt with commodities. He was determined to turn it around and make something of it. He had a cohesive game plan in place. It made sense to let him have his way. Once his father was convinced, there was no stopping Samir Jain.

If the media business had to be turned profitable, Samir Jain needed to challenge several long-held practices and belief systems of the industry. Treating newspapers as instruments of clout more than wealth-generating enterprises was only one of them. Another was to preserve the newspaper as an institution of democracy, relegating business and commercial interest to the background.

The most important hurdle in turning around the company would, however, be that leading newspapers saw themselves more as counterparts than rivals. The newspaper industry had been very much like a club of friendly publishing houses. Within this amicable, kind fraternity, even critical decisions including the pricing of space, were known to be taken collectively after mutual discussion.

If any of these houses had to chart their own trajectory of profitable growth, it would mean breaking away from this cosy arrangement which had been in place for decades. Shattering it was not going to be easy. What's more, proprietors had similar backgrounds and business interests. The affinity among the club members was thus even greater. They had business interests in manufacturing, construction, chemicals and jute, among others. There were occasional instances of proprietors related to one another through marriage.

In fact, *The Times of India*, along with the *Hindustan Times* and *The Indian Express*, were collectively referred to as the 'jute press', alluding to their common business interest. Violating the codes and rules of this collective, with the objective of making the business more successful and profitable, was bound to draw its ire and disapproval. It would require courage and patience.

Another interesting phenomenon in the newspaper industry at that time was that prominent English-language newspapers had carved out territories for themselves. They respected one another's domain, as it were. It was not a formal or structured arrangement and there were examples of one group challenging the other on its home territory. But perhaps as part of the overall socialist set-up, where licensing and regulation ruled over competition, the leading newspapers also let one another be.

Bennett, Coleman and Co. was dominant in western India with *The Times of India* having an unchallenged leadership of the Bombay market. The Birlas ruled Delhi with the resounding sales of the *Hindustan Times*. *The Indian Express* also had a substantial presence in Delhi. The Kasturi group had a strong hold over Chennai and large parts of south India through *The Hindu*. The East continued to swear by *The Statesman*, though *The Telegraph* had started to disturb the balance.

Clearly, if Samir Jain, or indeed the proprietor of any other leading publication, desired to transform his organization into a modern, competitive and profitable unit, he was up against the inertia of the industry. He would have to change the self-image of the media, unshackle it from its time warp and place it on the path of professionalism. There were the fraternal relations in the industry to contend with on the one hand, and internal resistance to change on the other. Samir Jain turned his attention first to the latter.

His proposals for the editorial side of his newspaper were part of a larger blueprint for change for the company as a whole. In fact, few appreciate that the changes on the marketing side were much more profound and far-reaching than those dealing with the editorial content. He covered the entire spectrum – from circulation to marketing to pricing and content. It turned out that the changes on the editorial side generated more attention and controversy owing to the sensitive nature of the subject.

'Samir Jain would often come and lecture us at the Times School of Journalism during those years. He was making statements that were shaking up the industry,' recalled Vinita Dawra Nangia[15] who later became the editor of the *Saturday Times*. 'He would talk about the newspaper and what it ought to be. He also insisted that journalists should learn about marketing. Journalists must cohabit with those who sell their product, he would say,' she added.

'He would take the team out for movies. Once we saw a Japanese film with him, and he asked us what we had thought of it. He also went on to explain what it was about. He interacted quite a lot with the first two batches that came out. The institute was then called the Times Research Foundation Institute (TRFI). It was probably set up to get the right sort of journalists into the newspaper. Samir Jain was trying all sorts of things to get his point of view expressed. He wanted change,' Nangia said.

Chandan Mitra recalled that Samir Jain's management philosophy was to create a corporate culture for Bennett, Coleman where the divide would be not between marketing and editorial but between the management and the rest. '"Editors and managers should be used interchangeably; senior journalists need not write," he would say. "The company does not expect them to write. If I need writers, I will outsource them; why give office facilities?" he would argue.'[16] Mitra joined *The Times* in April 1987. He fell out with Samir Jain in 1990 and quit in February that year.

A completely different view comes from someone who was closely associated with Samir Jain from the start. Vijay Gopal Jindal – a number-crunching trouble-shooter for the Jains – spent fourteen years in his first stint with the group and went on to be director (corporate).

When he spoke to me in October 2001, and again in December that year, he had quit the group, and set up a media and entertainment outfit, Karma Network. He was yet to take over as MD and vice chairman of Zee Networks.

Seated in his modest office in Mumbai, with a poster of the Jimmy Shergill–starrer movie *Haasil* (produced by Karma Network) behind him, he told me: 'The company was in urgent need of overhaul. Years of government control had made it bureaucratic. Samir Jain's impatience was evident. He was being pitted against ossified structures and systems. The malaise was across the organization.

There were rigid systems in the company, a legacy of the days when the government was in control. There was complacency born out of a secure position in an industry and economy with limited competition. There was a "take it or leave it" approach'.

Further, the organization worked in tight silos. 'There was a definite divide between not just the news side and the edit side, but also between managers and journalists. Producing a newspaper and marketing it were seen as distinct functions. There was little interaction among staff from the editorial, advertising, production and circulation departments, not to speak of the dichotomy within the editorial team. The result was that various wings of the organization often ended up working at cross purposes.'

In this state of affairs, it was impossible to steer an organization to achieve common objectives. Many things had to change. In fact, the journalists did have a point when they accused Samir Jain of trying to take control of the newspapers through his reorganization plans. He was indeed trying to take control. Because without that, there was no hope of his organization, a collection of disparate groups of people working in multiple directions, evolving into the focused, market-savvy and profitable group that he wanted. He had to break these watertight compartments for his newspapers to function as thriving, profitable enterprises.

Within the set-up, Samir Jain felt that the editor ought to behave like a CEO. He needed to take a 360-degree view of the entire business and not just handle the editorial content. The editor was in a position to demolish the silos and forge partnerships with other wings of the organization. He needed to take an integrated view of content, advertising and circulation and move the organization forward cohesively to grow and improve the bottom line.

Michael Fancher, who retired in 2008 after serving for twenty years as executive editor of *The Seattle Times*, and who was a leading advocate of the market-driven approach, had said, 'A successful editor must integrate the business and news sub-division and become a marketing expert.'[17]

Pradeep Guha recounted that Samir Jain was clear, bold and determined about the new direction that journalists needed to take. 'Samir Jain wanted a newspaper that would talk to its audience at the same level. Giri (Girilal Jain) was an editor in the Pope-like style, talking from the pulpit. He hardly left the department. News editors dealt with the desk, and chief reporters dealt with the reporters. But beyond that there was hardly any interaction. Samir wanted a different format,' Guha said.[18]

He wanted editors who could help him manage the affairs of the newspaper and not just stick to their ivory towers from where they wrote their moving editorials and lengthy opinion pieces. 'If he hired a senior journalist above the rank of an assistant editor, he believed that that person must be hands-on with issues facing the organization and not confined to writing. In fact, he ought to be as much a manager as a journalist,' pointed out Chandan Mitra. Samir Jain believed that a senior company executive must have 'line responsibility'. He must handle the editorial product and the nitty-gritty of overall management.

And in keeping with this conviction, an assistant editor (Partho Ghosh, then) was also made general manager (response). A resident editor of that period (Ajay Kumar) had interconnected responsibilities with then senior assistant editor Siddhartha Ray, and they were to coordinate the operations in Lucknow, Patna and Jaipur (LPJ). Chandan Mitra was appointed assistant general manager for LPJ. At a marketing meeting in Bombay, Samir Jain made sure that Partho Ghosh and Ajay Kumar shared the same room or sat together at meetings. Chandan Mitra was asked to accompany Ray to other towns and look into management issues. Everyone had their editorial responsibilities, of course.

Things began getting more and more difficult for the journalists, more so for the old guard dominating the newspapers. They were primarily oriented to write. They were completely out of their depth when it came to matters of business. But to mix the journalistic and the managerial roles was not just a skill question. They considered it moral sacrilege to combine the two roles. An editor could not be weighed down by considerations of business and bottom line. Any concern for the bottom line seemed to them an infringement of editorial freedom and a potential dilution of objectivity.

This approach irritated Samir Jain. A former company director, who did not want to be named, and who had supported Samir Jain through the change, obliquely mentioned that the reorganization also had something to do with personal ego. 'Samir believed that editors were a *hasti* outside; that they had stature and a certain amount of positioning and respect while managers didn't. "Why must they be larger than life?" he asked.'

'Samir carried the memory of those years when the editor was "untouchable". He thought the editors had to be shown their place,' recalled Baljit Kapoor. And the editors might not have helped matters either. Dileep Padgaonkar admitted: 'At first, Samir Jain was not at loggerheads with the journalists. He even made the effort to interact with them. But most editors had a patronizing attitude. Some were too hot to handle and the younger lot was plain cold towards him.[19]

'Most editors were in the traditional mould. They were deeply interested in politics, and vibed well with Ashok Jain who shared this interest. But Samir Jain was not interested in politics at all. Conversations with editors would dry up quickly. Most of the editors were nearly double his age,' Padgaonkar pointed out.

Samir Jain may have also been rattled by the fact that as the owner, he did not have all the control that he wanted. If he wanted a few items included in the paper, such as a medical column, it was resisted and shot down by the resident editor. This angered him and could partly be the reason for his counter-attack.

He started to point out mistakes in the editors' copy. He even made snide remarks about them. It is possible that journalists were touchy at times and exaggerated Samir Jain's aversion towards them. There is an infamous episode where at a lunch for the editors at The Times Group guest house, Samir Jain got Dileep Padgaonkar to mimic Girilal Jain in his presence. Some of the editors were not amused. They later cited this as reflecting Samir Jain's disrespect for editors.

Samir Jain may have been uncomfortable with the fact that the editors took little interest in the management of the company and that they were aloof from marketing and business functions. They were so preoccupied in interlocuting with the State that it was difficult to synergize their work with the rest of the company.

'In fact,' said one of the *TOI*'s former resident editors in Delhi, 'they led an almost schizophrenic existence' at a time when Samir Jain was trying to position *The Times* as a brand, something that had never been tried in Indian newspapers before. 'He wanted Bennett, Coleman to feature among the most sought after companies for jobs by management graduates in the country, and that was not going to happen without big-ticket change,' he added.

If Samir Jain showed contempt for some of his editors, they responded in almost equal measure. When the interviewer in the *Sunday*[20] article, Sumit Mitra, asked Girilal Jain whether he faced any problems of adjustment with so young a person as Samir Jain, he said: 'Why should there be any problem of adjustment? If there is a problem, it is not mine. Ashok (Jain) was young when I was dealing with the late S.P. Jain [Samir's grandfather]. The old man used to invite me for breakfast and dinner. Ashok used to sit there and listen to the discussion. I never approached any member of the family for any personal gain. So why should there be any problem of adjustment right now?'

During the same interview, Girilal Jain also gave a glimpse of how journalists viewed the business side of the company. It was completely contrary to what Samir Jain believed then. 'For one thing, *The Times of India* is highly profitable. So the question of viability does not really worry us,' he observed. 'We are number one in the richest city of India. All other Bombay newspapers put together do not sell as much as we do.'

In fact, Girilal Jain believed that the problem was inadequate editorial space in the newspaper. 'We have only forty-eight columns of editorial matter out of 176 columns (the rest is devoted to advertisements). This means that the scope for display and features is extremely limited,' he told Sumit Mitra.

He was also clear that the existing format of the paper, with its focus on news and views and the primacy of politics, 'will be more paying than an attempted entertainment'.

These views were divergent from those of the owner in many respects. Samir Jain's starting premise itself was that the company was far from profitable, especially given its leadership position in Bombay. Besides, contrary to his editor's view that editorial space should be enhanced, Samir Jain wanted a greater share of space for advertising to generate higher revenues. Finally, he was against the primacy accorded to politics in the newspaper, preferring to give more space and attention to citizen's local concerns, corporate news and entertainment.

With the editor and the owner completely at odds on the priorities of the business, only one of them could have prevailed. It turned out to be the owner.

Eventually, Samir Jain had his way. The corridors at the Times House were abuzz with stories whispered in sepulchral tones. Inder Malhotra, one of the strong opponents of the reorganization, put in his papers. Even at that point, Samir Jain asked Inder Malhotra to help him run the paper. But the latter turned down the proposal. 'As a journalist, my primary duty is to write,' he is believed to have said. That was, effectively, the last showdown between the two on this matter.

Girilal Jain stayed on. But the new structure envisaged by Samir Jain came into being. Among other changes, an executive editor was appointed. The newspaper had recast itself and the changed emphasis in content, approach and layout was visible. In 1989, Girilal Jain was politely told that given his failing health (which was true), the company did not want to strain him more.

Sunil Jain, however, has a different version regarding the run-up to his father's exit from *The Times of India*. 'My father was getting uncomfortable in the new environment particularly when the 150-year celebrations began. *The Times of India* had only two celebrities then – R.K. Laxman (the famed cartoonist) and Girilal Jain. Dad wanted to leave. But Ashok Jain did not want him to go during that year (1988) so as to avoid bad press. So my father agreed to stay on,' he said.

'He never wanted another extension. There was never a meeting (as rumoured) with (the then prime minister) Rajiv Gandhi asking the latter to intervene. Dad was far too arrogant for that,' Sunil Jain said.

The battle between Samir Jain and his journalists was a fairly unequal one and the protests ended in a whimper. 'The editorial cadre did not really resist Samir's moves. They may have ridiculed his ideas at first and protested a little. But that was all. When the outcome seemed inevitable, they just succumbed and fell in step... it was a walkover,' said N.P. Singh, a former advertising director at BCCL.[21] In hindsight, he suggested, the protesting editors brought this state of affairs upon themselves. 'Their reaction was largely impulsive. They never made the effort to understand the issues being raised by the owner. Nor did they make a concerted effort to explain their point to him. If they had done that, the outcome would perhaps have been a balanced one. Their protest was a knee-jerk reaction and once they were rebuffed, they had practically no follow-up action.'

The change was probably too abrupt for them to cope with. While the organization itself was in urgent need of reform, they also missed the changes taking place in the larger context. India was taking the first uncertain steps towards economic reform and opening up. A new middle class had started to emerge. Consumerism was beginning to rise. It was not easy to grasp such mega societal changes, and the journalists lost the plot.

Although they gave it the colour of editorial freedom under attack, the other wings of the organization had no such moral dilemmas about the change. A former head of marketing, who wished to remain anonymous, is blunt. 'I do not believe there was anything wrong with Samir's attempt to reorganize the power structure. This was the owner's call. One could go blue-faced arguing, but that was it. In the end, the owner is the boss and he proved as much. It is the publisher's right to decide the power structure. It is he who decides the profile of the paper. Editors have only delegated powers.... Samir was the publisher. It was as simple as that.'

Although the point about separate editors for news and views hogged a lot of attention, there were many other significant elements to the eight-page change plan proposed by Samir Jain. If anything, the editorial revamp was only a precursor to the more fundamental changes that took place over the next decade.

Samir Jain proposed that the Sunday editions of both *The Times of India* and *Navbharat Times* become independent and full-fledged publications by themselves. The practice until then was to treat the Sunday editions as a continuation of the weekday papers in content and texture, with a few light articles thrown in.

But he proposed a separate team led by an editor for the Sunday editions. There would be more feature articles and trend stories, along with designated weekend columns. The share of pure news reportage would be much less, with the Sunday team encouraged to write in a more engaging and interactive style. The emphasis on packaging, design and layout would also be more in the Sunday editions. This was modelled on international papers like *The Sunday Times*, London.

The Saturday editions too would have more feature articles. Although he did not propose it at this stage, the Saturday edition of *The Times of India* came up with an all-colour supplement, with articles on fashion, lifestyle, glamour, cooking and social trends, which evoked significant appeal among the emerging consumerist middle class. As for advertisers, they had never seen anything like this before in an English-language newspaper.

Another highlight of the eight-page document was on the need to impart a modern look to the newspaper. Newspapers at that time bore a dreary, monotonous look, with little attention to design and layout. Samir Jain proposed that professional teams be recruited to focus on design and layout in the newspapers.

All these suggestions transformed *The Times of India*. At a time when magazines were booming and television had just turned colour, these initiatives were critical for the survival of newspapers. Even among newspapers, new players like *The Telegraph* had already started out with the latest in design and packaging. Although there was initial resistance to these initiatives among the traditional newspapers, they followed suit.

It is significant that a large number of suggestions in the note had to do with recruitment and training. The newspaper industry paid little attention to these issues at that time. Although newspaper reputations were built around their journalists, there were no structured programmes or training initiatives to develop and groom people. They mostly learnt on the job. Samir Jain proposed the setting up of facilities for training and refresher course for the staff. In line with this, he scaled up the journalism school of the company, then part of the Times Research Foundation. Given the state of the profession at that time, these were progressive steps.

Newspapers were never known to be good pay masters. They were mostly unable to attract talent from other streams like management studies. Samir Jain outlined the need for better people practices. He suggested faster promotion channels. He emphasized the need for improving the salary and perquisite structure to be able to attract better talent. His change plan also favoured incentive systems that linked remuneration with performance. None of this was prevalent in the newspaper industry at that time.

He realized that if his papers had to expand and grow as he

envisaged, he would need talent to manage that growth. He needed people at all levels, including resident editors, to manage the editions in each city. While his initial point was merely that he wanted to recruit bright graduates from 'India and abroad', he aggressively pursued the talent search and recruitment. This applied both to the editorial side as well as marketing.

The need for new blood in the editorial team was first recognized by Ashok Jain. But he had been persuaded by some of his editors that talent was scarce in the country and the exercise was practically a non-starter. Once Samir Jain came into the picture and found himself at odds with many of the journalists, it was imperative to infuse new talent.

In late 1985, the subject was taken up once again with Ashok Jain. Samir Jain, together with Gautam Adhikari, made out a case for recruiting talented people as assistant editors to build the organization for the future. At the instance of Ashok Jain, both of them finalized a list of thirty people from among the leading newspapers in the country. Having got the go-ahead, they went about approaching these people personally. Starting with the summer of 1986, they began recruiting aggressively. Over the next two years, many of the talents in the shortlist had joined the company.

They included T.N. Ninan, Jug Suraiya, Chandan Mitra, Swapan Dasgupta, Arvind Das, Subir Roy, Praful Bidwai, Bachi Karkaria and Ajay Kumar. Most of them would play a critical role in the transformation at Bennett, Coleman over the next five years, and beyond.

Perhaps the most notable recruitment on the editorial side was of Dileep Padgaonkar, who came in as associate editor in September 1986. His association with *The Times of India* started in 1968. Just twenty-four then, he had sent in a piece to *The Times of India*. The legendary Sham Lal was the editor. He liked the piece. Dileep Padgaonkar next asked him for a job, and got it.

He was the Paris correspondent of *The Times of India* for the next five years, and then elevated to assistant editor. In 1978, he left *The Times of India* to join UNESCO. In 1986, he was done with this stint. That is when he ran into Gautam Adhikari in Paris.

Around that time, Ashok Jain was exploring the idea of setting up an international edition of *The Times of India* in New York. In May 1986, he asked Gautam Adhikari to visit New York along with Ramesh Chandra Jain, then the CEO of Times television. They were to stop by at Paris, and were asked to look up Dileep Padgaonkar. They offered him the job and he accepted.

'They hit it off right from the beginning. Dileep displayed class, intellect, global exposure and his collection of Hussain paintings,' said Adhikari. Dileep Padgaonkar was intellectually inclined to Leftist ideology and thought, but apolitical. Samir Jain brought him in. ('Gautam was Samir's right-hand man those days. He had a room right next to Samir's room. Samir had flanked Giri with Gautam on one side and Dileep on the other. Arun Shourie had been appointed executive editor but that was too short-lived; it didn't last. Giri saw to it that the experiment failed. One would've thought that Gautam would've taken over,' said a former assistant editor of the *TOI*, who did not want to be named.)

Two years later, Samir Jain elevated Dileep Padgaonkar to executive editor. This was done while Girilal Jain was still around. It marked the start of a new era.

'Samir Jain's thoughts annoyed traditional journalists. But he was less interested in influence and more in reach,' Dileep Padgaonkar told me.[22] "If you are not in this market, you have no mindshare and therefore no profitability," Samir Jain would say,' he added. 'Those who argued against this were not ready to look at what was happening around them, particularly in America. Much is made of the fact that he was close to the Sulzbergers of *The New York Times*. He was! He had met both father and son. He may have even learnt a few things but he wasn't going to swear by them. The key words in his dictionary are mindshare and profitability. The *NYT* model was not for him but for his editors and journalists,' he pointed out.

Jain felt that if there was no fit between the editorial and the business sides in the organization, there was no hope in hell that the company could grow, Padgaonkar noted. 'He therefore shifted the focus of the organization from the mandarins to the marketers. In other words, he began changing the focus of Bennett, Coleman from editorial-led to being marketing- and advertising-led,' he explained.

Under the new 'plan', new managers were brought in at every level. Changes on the managerial side were far more radical than on the editorial side. Samir Jain brought in people from industries other than publishing. If he wanted to create a corporate culture within the company, with an aggressive focus on marketing and branding, he had to choose the right people who would drive it.

Among the new recruits was Satish Mehta, a former marketing director of ITC, who joined the company in January 1987. He had also been chairman of the Tobacco Board and had run it like a profit centre. In 1986, he quit ITC and started his venture. Unfortunately, that business bombed.

He was on an early morning flight from Calcutta to Delhi, and was seated next to Bish (B.P.) Agarwal of ABC Consultants.[23] Agarwal asked about his plans. As the conversation progressed, Satish Mehta got two options from the man, whose firm was also into headhunting. He could either join Bennett, Coleman or Shaw Wallace which also had an opening at that time. Satish Mehta told him it would be the former. Agarwal asked him to call the Times House in Delhi the following morning. Soon after, Mehta met Samir Jain briefly and then went in to meet chairman Ashok Jain, who offered him the post of marketing director. 'You will be working with Samir, who is very market-oriented. Remember never to contradict him in public,' Ashok Jain advised Mehta.

When Mehta subsequently met Samir Jain again, the latter asked him whether he read newspapers. Mehta replied that he did not. Samir Jain reiterated the offer made by his father. Mehta joined. 'I remember I was quite impressed with Samir when I first met him,' he reminisced. 'He was well educated as opposed to most businessmen his age. He had certain fluency about him and he was outward-looking. He had a delightfully fresh approach and a stream of some very great ideas. He also had that wonderful ability... to imagine,'[24] he pointed out.

Another person who played a critical role in the transformation, N.P. Singh, was recruited a year later. He had spent twenty-five years with Hindustan Lever and TOMCO, and also managed Godfrey Philips. He was contacted first in early 1988 by Ram Tarneja, the then MD of The Times Group. He showed interest.

Samir Jain interacted with N.P. Singh over the next three months, including two luncheon meetings. He was brought on board in 1988. He was the first head of the advertising division of the company. Vijay Jindal who had joined in the early 1980s was brand manager of *The Economic Times* before being elevated to corporate director of *The Times of India*. Together with them, BCCL's lead management team had Pradeep Guha, P.R. Krishnamoorthy, Arun Arora, G. Krishnan and Pritish Nandy. This was the core team till 1994, and was at the heart of the transformation.

Samir Jain, Pritish Nandy and Gautam Adhikari comprised the 'troika' that had drafted the eight-page note. Ironically, for a man alleged to have disdain for journalists, it was a journalist who acted as the sounding board for Samir Jain through the years of change.

Gautam Adhikari, like Samir Jain, had grown up in Calcutta. They went to the same school (St Xavier's) though in different years. Gautam Adhikari's father, a banker, knew Ashok Jain. At a party at the Jain House in Calcutta, Gautam Adhikari met Samir Jain who was just out of college. But there was nothing significant about that interaction. They were to meet again fifteen years later.

In the meantime, Gautam Adhikari started his career with the State Bank of India and soon switched to journalism with *The Economic Times*, Calcutta. He did stints with *The Hindu* and *The Telegraph*, before joining the *ET*, Bombay, in 1982. He soon moved as assistant editor, *The Times of India*, Bombay. It was here, three years later, that he met Samir Jain in the stairway.

Samir Jain told Adhikari that he had liked some of the pieces he had written. He had sent him notes on some of his articles. He did not say more. A couple of months later, he got a call that the JMD (Samir Jain) wanted him to be transferred to Delhi. That call was made by Baljit Kapoor. 'Perhaps he wants to talk to you more often,' Kapoor joked.

A week later, Gautam Adhikari received a note from Girilal Jain transferring him to Ahmedabad as resident editor of *The Times of India*. Girilal Jain had obviously learnt of Samir Jain's interest in one of his assistant editors. He had acted swiftly.

Gautam Adhikari was reluctant to move to Ahmedabad. When he was still mulling over the developments, he got another call a few days later from Delhi. This time it was Samir Jain. He was livid. The order to transfer Gautam Adhikari to Ahmedabad had been passed in his absence.

The tug of war ended with Girilal Jain calling Gautam Adhikari over to his office in Delhi to inform him that he was being transferred to Delhi as Samir Jain's editorial advisor. He moved immediately. The day after his arrival, Samir Jain invited him home and introduced him to his family.

The search for talent was not confined to the top levels. Vijay Jindal and Bidyut Sarkar, who managed the Times Research Foundation, travelled across the country, including 'C' category cities, to sell journalism as a career option to youngsters. They specially targeted students in business schools and convinced them to join *The Times*.

These initiatives were greeted with scepticism – even derision – by some of the old guard. They scoffed at the idea of people from the consumer goods sector being called in to run a newspaper. One editor gave them the epithet – Samir's mannequins.

Clearly, in the mid-1980s, Samir Jain's obsessive determination was being underestimated. So was the scale of the change that the company was about to witness over the next decade.

By the mid-1990s, there was another round of acrimony between Samir Jain and his editors. This time, it was his chosen ones of a decade ago who could not keep up with him. But this round was reduced to being a subtext within the larger transformation that Samir Jain and The Times Group had unleashed across the media space of India.

In one of his pieces, Khushwant Singh asks rhetorically: 'Do you know who the editor of *The Times of India* is (today)?'[25] Well...if you do not, that is exactly what has happened to the quintessential, larger-than-life editor!

Dileep Padgaonkar, who had signalled the editorial transformation that occurred to the editorial head at *The Times of India*, was not fixated on the politics or the socio-dynamics of the nation, then. In fact, he had some very good marketing ideas to offer to the organization, making Samir Jain say that he (Padgaonkar) could make for a great marketing director of the *TOI*.

Over the years, the equation changed. Sometime in early 1994, when Padgaonkar was on leave, his name in the newspaper's print line was replaced with that of the late Dilip Mukherjee's, the then edit page editor. Vijay Jindal was appointed as acting editor.

In March 1994, Padgaonkar quit *The Times of India*. The reasons he gave were that the establishment was unable to retain or attract editorial talent in the group and that 'the newspaper should have a deep commitment to values that extend beyond the market and the consumer'.[26]

In an interview to *Sunday*, that month, he had also said, '...rather than have a marketing-led editorial, it is logical to have an editorial-led marketing.' He had asserted that his kind of journalism was rooted in certain ethical and intellectual choices and that he was finding it increasingly difficult to practise that kind of journalism at *The Times of India*.'[27]

When I asked him about that phase, he told me, 'What happened in 1994 was that the minute you have a give and take between the business side and the editorial side, the supremacy of the editor has to diminish...I subscribed to the philosophy that the group had to be strengthened. In the end, unless you are successful in the marketplace, there was no meaning. But my differences in 1994 stemmed from my belief that the newspaper ought not to vacate itself from the influence market, the government and the bureaucracy. The owners had to determine which market they were in. Our differences reached such a head that I decided to leave.'

In 1998, he came back to the group in a new role, as corporate director. 'I had decided that I would be successful in the new model where marketing reigned supreme, as well. If the name of the game is entrepreneurship, so be it...and let us see what happens, I told myself,' he said. 'I made that transition because I accepted that *The Times* was and is a proprietor's newspaper. It is not an editor's newspaper. I see nothing wrong with that,' he proffered.[28]

Padgaonkar continues to write for the paper.

## Load-shedding!

Apart from building his key newspaper brands, Samir Jain needed to take some tough decisions on consolidating the various publications within the company. These decisions brought focus, freed management time and benefited the bottom line. Most important, they sent a clear message that he meant business.

Core competence may not have been a fashionable term in the mid-1980s, certainly not in India; but it was being tried out elsewhere, notably by Jack Welch at General Electric (GE). His celebrated idea that a business must either be number one or number two in the industry or close down saw the GE group close and sell several businesses in the mid-1980s. Those were the 'Neutron Jack'[29] years.

It is not clear whether Samir Jain was influenced by these events on the global corporate map. But he was convinced that if certain publications or products had to be nurtured as brands, he would have to single-mindedly devote resources and time to them. So around 1986 he decided that he could not continue with loss-making publications of the company. He was not going to put up with feckless attempts at restoring their lost glory and he was determined that they ought to be shut down. It was a tough decision because many of these publications had enhanced the family's social standing. Some of the magazines had been started by his grandmother, Rama Jain. Other publications too had sentimental value for the family and its associates.

Rajnish Rikhy, a former general manager (response) at BCCL said: 'Samir Jain foresaw that generic magazines would not have value in the future and that magazines would need to develop core competencies to seek specific reader and advertiser attention. Niche magazines, he believed, would thereby have a greater chance of survival. In any case, magazines contributed less than 10 per cent of the company's advertising revenue. Even *Dharmyug*, which was selling in large numbers, did not contribute significantly to the bottom line. Samir Jain believed that investments of time, money and energy ought not to be wasted on the magazines.'[30]

Another reason behind closing down unviable publications was that of focus. If the group had to build brands and associate them with a certain value to the advertiser, it required focus, resources and time. Samir Jain was clear that the organization could not spread itself thin over numerous publications and hope to build distinct, powerful and profitable brands. A former director says: 'Samir Jain's idea was that the organization did not have much talent to look after loss-making publications as well. He felt that we had just enough talent to look after the English-language daily newspapers.'

There was also a basic disconnect between Samir Jain and the people running these magazines. 'Many of them were from the old block. For them, the publications they were managing were meant to provide good reading material and act as a discussion forum, with less orientation to returns. But Samir Jain insisted that he could not be giving 50 per cent of his time to publications that did not bring any money for the company,' Dileep Padgaonkar told me.

Samir Jain is believed to have said: 'If they cannot survive on their own, they should be allowed to go.' He realized that *The Times of India* and *The Economic Times* were two publications that could survive on their own. He decided to invest in them. He was charitable towards the *Navbharat Times* as well. 'Unlike his father, Samir was not tight-fisted,' said Baljit Kapoor. 'He was willing to spend to promote these two or three publications. But he was certainly not going to put his money into something that he knew from his gut would not work,' Kapoor added.

To make his point forcefully, Samir Jain decided that taking head-on some of the magazines that were close to the family would send a strong signal down the organization. So, at a meeting in Agra, where several old-time managers were present, he announced his intention to close down some magazines.

Everyone was stunned. The closure would involve layoffs. The group would have to handle protest and frustration, besides facing industry reaction to the move. But Samir Jain was determined. By 1993, most of the 'unviable' publications were shut down.

'Samir was very clear about how he wanted to grow. He was against expansion or diversification. He did not want too many brands. He had noticed that while *ET* and *TOI* made profits, the other publications were making losses. He decided to shut them down. This is in contrast to the expansion plans of the Express group of newspapers, which was spreading across the country,' Vijay Jindal pointed out.[31]

Samir Jain was happy with Delhi and Bombay, cities with affluent and influential markets. He had his eye on that which was relevant to him, which was profit, and what was reverent to him – the intelligentsia and policymakers. It was in these areas that he wanted to grow. And, that is exactly what he did.

'Folding up the loss-making publications was the most important decision Samir Jain took when he began making changes at Bennett, Coleman,' believed V.K. Gambhir,[32] a former internal auditor at BCCL.

'Increasing the selling price of these publications was no option. They would just have to go. The company could have taken the losses. But Samir Jain was focused. In a span of two years, everything was shut down one by one. All his loss-making publications went. It was a ruthless move that clearly spelt that Bennett, Coleman was becoming profit-oriented. These magazines had been making losses for a few years, and Ashokji was aware of this. But they had a sentimental value, and were therefore being continued,' he argued.

'The impact of this move perhaps was not reflected so much on the bottom line; these publications had a limited contribution. But it had a lightning effect on the organization,' noted Padgaonkar. 'It was a powerful signal. It laid the ground for change and the process of transformation as a whole acquired credibility in the eyes of employees. Once this was achieved, any change, no matter how challenging, became less difficult to implement,' he added.

It also demonstrated an interesting side to Samir Jain's personality, which would often be visible all through the transformation. The closure of loss-making publications showed that the company is unsentimental and ruthlessly business-like when it comes to the profitability of its products. 'Samir Jain is very hard on taking decisions. Once he decides, he makes sure that it is done. But he is equally quick at rescinding decisions, as well if he finds that their original objective is not being met,' Padgaonkar said.

The move came in for much criticism. But the management sent the message that it was leaving no room for nostalgia in business. The circulation and marketing teams in these newspapers were also clearly told about their objectives. There were, no doubt, problems of laying off staff, shutting down offices and coping with protests. But once these were done, the direction became clear.

How *Femina* and *Filmfare* survived was a matter of chance. By 1993, most of the magazines had been shut down. These two magazines were also heading for the chopping block when out of the blue, two young ladies, who had been promoted by *Femina* to represent India in international beauty contests, won their respective competitions. Sushmita Sen became Miss Universe and Aishwarya Rai became Miss World.

Head honchos at these magazines were convinced they could use this opportunity to breathe a fresh lease of life into these entertainment glossies and make them money-spinners. They also persuaded the management to let these two magazines be. And so, *Femina* and *Filmfare* survived and have arguably become launch pads for those aspiring to make a career in the fashion, film and glamour world.

## The Illustrated Weekly, *the Group's Legendary Magazine*

The *Weekly*, launched in January 1880, was initially meant to be a wrap-up of the week's news. In 1929, it was renamed *The Illustrated Weekly of India*. It had a remarkable run in the 1960s and 1970s. Between 1969 and 1978, the magazine was edited by its feisty editor Khushwant Singh. These nine years are believed to be among its best and most successful phases.

Singh, a former diplomat, ex-UN official, editor and writer ran the magazine with panache. At its peak, the *Weekly*'s circulation touched 3.39 lakhs in 1977. It was *the* English magazine in India. Singh left under controversial circumstances and M.V. Kamath took over as editor. He was followed by K.C. Khanna. But the magazine never recovered its lost glory.

By 1989, the *Weekly*'s circulation had dropped to 81,000 copies, a result of the changing landscape of the media industry.

The *Weekly*'s downfall coincided with the rise of *India Today*. The *Weekly* was feature-oriented while *India Today* was news-oriented. The latter caught the fancy of the news-oriented reader, who was looking for such a magazine to satiate his thirst for hard political news. Besides, technology spoilt the game for the *Weekly*. It was printed on rotogravure machines. *India Today* took a technological leap and also improved its visual appeal.

The *Weekly* was losing money and this did not fit into Samir Jain's framework. But it did not go down without a fight, led by Samir Jain himself.

In 1982, the company brought in a brilliant and flamboyant editor to manage all its magazines. Pritish Nandy, poet and writer, had been awarded the Padmashri at the age of twenty-five. Several collections of his poetry had been published by then, most notably *Of Gods and Olives* published by Writers' Workshop.

Nandy met Ashok Jain on board a flight from Bombay to Calcutta. He was planning to take up a Homi Bhabha fellowship. Impressed with Nandy, Ashok Jain offered him a job and appointed him publishing director of Bennett, Coleman. The MD of the company was an administrator and the publishing director was responsible for all publishing activities.

Nandy was not the typical journalist-editor of that time – sedate, serious-looking or sombre. He was flashy, loud, gregarious and pompous, by his own admission. He used to dress unconventionally during those days and spurned the regular company Ambassador car and drove to office in a jeep. Nandy[33] was very candid about that stint, pulling no punches.

'I was the most highly paid person in the Company – Rs 4,000 a month; and also the most unpopular man in the *TOI*. And, my name appeared on the masthead,' he began. 'My brief was to revive all of Bennett, Coleman's magazines, which were making losses of Rs 2 crore to 2.5 crore every year. Vimla Patil, the former editor of *Femina* was looking after them.

'The product was anachronistic in that time and age. It had lost its zest for life. I felt that the products would die unless they were urgently revived, particularly *Femina*. Magazines were savvy then. But the *TOI* magazines were outdated,' he said.

'At *The Times of India*, there were fiefdoms. There was no interface. In early 1983, we were also hit by labour trouble. We were selling barely about 13,000 copies a week which were fudged to show 25,000,' Nandy recalled.

'I told Ashok Jain that I will give the *Weekly* a dramatic makeover. I needed the legitimacy. Just then, a young man walked in and said, "It is a bloody good idea." Samir Jain was going to support me.

'Three weeks later, I redesigned the product. We had a cover on "The legacy of Mohandas Karamchand Gandhi" in our issue of 2 October 1983... The heavens fell on our heads. The *Weekly* had become aggressive. That now became the spirit of the magazine. They suggested we print 20,000 copies. But we sold more than 50,000. By the fourth issue, we were selling one lakh copies, and we flew,' he remembered. 'There was no idolatry at the *Weekly*. It was iconoclastic. I styled it as an editor's magazine, and brought in "Mindsport" and "Quiz Mountain". We started with sixty pages and went up to seventy two pages. It was still number two after *India Today*, but we had turned it around. I had had about forty hits – taking on the establishment. The nation was young. It was outraged. People wanted to know more and we gave them information. Journalism had an impact,' Nandy recalled with fervour.

'The fallout of the kind of stories we did was that politicians began filing cases and suits against the company. It would have cost the company only about Rs 10 lakh or so to fight them. But Samir decided the company was not going to support either me or the *Weekly* in fighting these cases. The bickerings between us began,' Nandy said.

At one stage, in 1990, the top brass believed that the *Weekly*'s 85,000 copies translated into a readership of two lakhs. It had its strengths and that they must try to extend the *Weekly*'s brand life. They also felt that it could attract ads from corporates and high quality advertisers like hotels and airlines.

The *Weekly*'s 1990 model was a unique format. The changes had come in around December 1989. The large format magazine remained in place with over sixty pages and a twenty-page broadsheet – both of which came in a plastic bag every week. They cost Rs 7. After a while, the magazine was inserted into the broadsheet. In its third phase, it was completely transformed into a broadsheet publication.

These changes had been forced on the *Weekly* due to technological handicaps, rather than market forces. The obsolete rotogravure process of printing was difficult, as it needed a thirty-day lead period for colour printing and a fortnight for black-and-white printing. Meanwhile, competition had intensified from entrants like *Sunday Observor*, *Sunday Mail*, *Saturday Times* and the Sunday edition of *The Economic Times*. That triggered the downfall and final collapse of the *Weekly*.

'One morning,' Nandy recalled, 'Samir suggested we close it down. That was my first spat with him. He had even decided to sell off the rotogravure machines so that we could not print the *Weekly*... We started making losses. We had to change its printing to offset and then to tabloid form. It began losing its identity. In 1991, I quit.

'Ashok Jain did not have much of a role to play by then. He really did not have a say in decision making. I could see that Samir was waging guerilla warfare,' Nandy reminisced.

Baljit Kapoor gave a pragmatic interpretation to the closure of the *Weekly*, as indeed the other publications. He said, 'At the *Weekly*, the circulation and the advertising revenue together were not even meeting the variable costs of newsprint, production, processing and distribution.

'Samir had announced that he would not finance his dying magazines. If they cannot survive on their own, they should be allowed to go, he used to say. Therefore, *The Illustrated Weekly* had to be killed.'

Vimla Patil, former editor of *Femina* (1973 to 1993) had a rather terse view: 'Nandy made journalism a vehicle for building his self-image. He had a close coterie consisting of film stars and artists. He had a clique of some politicians, actors and a few members of the entertainment industry. He got close to Nusli Wadia and the Ambanis. He used the *Weekly* to meet his personal ends and worked by the lowest common denominator. During that phase, it was his raj and he tried to rule through the magazine. We should have cared better for the *Weekly*. It might have survived.'[31]

FIVE

# The Price Matrix

*'All newspapers are run to make profits. Full stop.'*

Rupert Murdoch[1]

EVEN AS THE NON-CORE publications were being weeded out, major steps were being taken by the company in the area of space selling. The main marketing challenge was to secure the maximum amount of advertising revenue from each centimetre of space in the newspapers. That was central to the goal of boosting profitability. All other initiatives were to support that goal.

Samir Jain believed that though his newspapers were generating considerable value, they were allowing the value to accrue to advertisers. Some of this value had to be captured and retained by BCCL. While advertisers benefited a great deal from advertising through his newspapers, he was unable to get them to pay adequately for it.

This was understandable. Until then, the newspaper industry priced space on a cost-plus basis. Space was priced in a manner to cover costs and secure a profit margin of 10 per cent or so. It had no correlation with how much the advertiser benefited from that space. Nor was any attention paid to how much the advertiser would be willing to pay.

As such, pricing lacked dynamism. In any competitive business, pricing is a strategic weapon that can grow sales, boost profitability and expand the market. In the Indian newspaper industry at that time, the importance of pricing was hardly appreciated. Price was just a passive tag, increasing incrementally as per a time-tested formula. Its relationship to the value being derived by the advertiser was ignored.

Samir Jain was going to play the pricing game. He was convinced that space in his newspaper deserved a premium. One option before him was to simply jack up the prices. The argument could be that the prices had lagged behind the value derived by advertisers. This was a way to catch up. That was obviously not sustainable. A one-off increase may have been accepted by the market. Beyond that, hikes would be difficult to justify. Any major hikes would have to be accompanied by enhanced value for the advertiser.

The company could have milked its near-monopoly position in Bombay. But there was a limit to that too. Besides, Samir Jain perhaps realized that he could not get very far on the strength of only one or two editions. His other editions and publications also had to perform. He had to get them to move up and bring some balance in his portfolio.

His main focus was on Delhi where the *Hindustan Times* was far ahead of *The Times of India* in terms of circulation. He could not afford to price advertising space higher than the leader. There had to be other means to improve revenue from space in Delhi.

American educator, media critic and journalist, Ben Haig Bagdikian, had once noted that 'market-driven journalism gathers an audience not to inform it but to sell it to advertisers.'[2] Aggregating relevant audience for the newspaper through changes in the product was an important step. Advertisers may be willing to pay a certain premium on that account. Undertaking brand-building initiatives to attract younger readers would also happen. But that was some time away. For now, innovative ways had to be found to attract advertisers, boost the performance of all editions and improve returns per column centimetre.

There were some clear strengths that BCCL enjoyed in this respect. First, of course, was the leadership of *The Times of India* in Bombay which offered it considerable leeway to price space. The other advantage was that it had a multi-city presence. Besides Bombay, it was a major player in Delhi. It had editions of *The Times of India* in Lucknow, Jaipur, Patna, Bangalore and Ahmedabad. In contrast, most rival newspapers were mostly confined to one part of the country.

The third important feature was that it offered a range of publications. The closure had been effected mainly in magazines so that the focus on newspapers could be enhanced. BCCL, besides its multi-city editions, had a financial newspaper in the form of *The Economic Times*. It had multilingual offerings too. The *Navbharat Times* in Hindi was a major player in the north, particularly Delhi. *Maharashtra Times* had a presence in western India.

While the range and diversity of the company's portfolio was a source of strength, the flip side was that performance of these newspapers was very uneven. In certain cities, they were either leaders or had at least a significant presence in terms of circulation. In some areas, they were laggards. In many such cases, performance had not improved for years. The numbers were either static or dwindling. Advertiser interest in these editions was negligible.

For example, in 1985, *The Times of India* had a combined national circulation of 5.95 lakh copies. Of this, Bombay alone contributed over three lakhs. Besides being the leader in the financial capital, with over 70 per cent plus market share, it accounted for more than half the national circulation of the newspaper.

In Delhi, the *TOI* sold about 2.15 lakh copies. In most other markets, its performance was indifferent. In Ahmedabad and Lucknow, it did about 25,000 copies each. In Bangalore, its circulation was about 18,000 copies. In Jaipur, *The Times of India* sold just about 12,000 copies. The numbers in Lucknow, Patna and Jaipur were too low to attract any significant advertiser interest.

The *Navbharat Times* also presented a mixed picture. It topped sales in Delhi, doing a little over three lakh copies daily. This was more than Delhi's most-read English daily, the *Hindustan Times*, whose daily circulation then was 2.7 lakh copies. But the Bombay edition of *Navbharat Times'* sold much less; about 98,500 copies a day. It was an active player in the LPJ (Lucknow, Patna and Jaipur) markets.

*The Economic Times* sold about 81,000 copies daily in 1985. Its nearest competitor, *The Financial Express* (from the Indian Express group) was selling less than half that number. *Maharashtra Times* was selling about 1.9 lakh copies that year in Bombay. But it had practically no presence beyond that city.

When BCCL studied the entire configuration of its papers, it was a mixed bag. It had two English newspapers, one Hindi newspaper, one in Marathi, a Hindi eveninger, and several weeklies, fortnightlies and magazines. The company had a wide network of publications in north and west India. But barring Bombay, it was not the leader in any market.

Each market and city had a different story. In Delhi, the *Hindustan Times* was the player number one. People had been reading it for years. Newspaper choices tend to be sticky. It is not easy to get people to switch to another newspaper. The company would achieve that in certain markets. But that was in the next phase, and still a few years away. For now, it had to accept its number two position in Delhi.

In Ahmedabad, there was no major competing English language newspaper. But people there preferred a Gujarati daily. In Lucknow, Patna and Jaipur again *The Times of India* did not sell enough because people mostly preferred Hindi newspapers. In Bangalore, where there was a sizeable section of the English-reading population, the *Deccan Herald* held sway.

*The Economic Times*, though the leader in its segment, did not have a high circulation. The market for English-language newspapers was limited by the number of people who were comfortable with the language. Similarly, business publications were constrained. Interest in equity markets was still confined to a small section of people and the private corporate sector was evolving. For newspaper readers, politics and administration generally took precedence over economics.

Samir Jain looked at this total picture. It was highly skewed. All his newspapers were working more or less in isolation. Space in each newspaper was being sold separately, by individual teams, at rates that each publication could command on its own. Although there were some combo rates offered by the publications across editions, there was no concerted effort to synergize across markets and publications.

He decided to make all his newspaper publications work for one another. Advertisers buying space in one newspaper could, for a concessional extra charge, obtain space in another edition or in another newspaper of the group. An advertiser putting out an ad in, say, *The Times of India*'s Bombay edition could pay a little extra and get space in *The Times of India*'s Lucknow edition. Taking that forward, he could even secure space in *The Economic Times*, Bombay, for an additional charge.

Rather than approach the advertiser as stand-alone entities, Samir Jain bound his publications together into a bouquet, as it were, and presented that to the advertiser. As it turned out, this was a path-breaking innovation in selling space in newspapers. While shoring up the fortunes of the company, it transformed the way newspapers in India did business. When first launched, its caption was prophetic: Mastermind.

William Randolph Hearst (1863–1951), the legendary American newspaper publisher, who built the largest newspaper chain in the US and whose pugilistic, controversial streak also led him to be discredited following charges of yellow journalism, is believed to have once said, 'If you make a product good enough, even though you live in the depths of the forest, the public will make a path to your door, says the philosopher. But if you want the public in sufficient numbers, you better construct a highway. Advertising is that highway.'[3]

Mastermind was BCCL's grand highway.

It was a matrix of rates, suggesting numerous permutations and combinations to the advertiser. For example, a display advertisement in the Bombay edition of *The Times of India* cost the advertiser Rs 125 per column centimetre if he bought space in the edition on a stand-alone basis. The same advertisement, if combined with Delhi and Ahmedabad editions, was offered a rate of Rs 230 per column centimetre (Rs 118 for Bombay + Rs 85 for Delhi + Rs 27 for Ahmedabad). If the advertiser added Jaipur, Patna and Bangalore editions in the plan, he would need to pay only an additional Rs 6 each per column centimetre for these three editions.

Similarly, for *Navbharat Times*, advertisers were paying Rs 180 in all for a column centimetre in the Delhi, Lucknow, Patna and Jaipur editions. Now, with Mastermind, they needed to pay only Rs 10 more per column centimetre to advertise in the Bombay edition as well.

It was easy to dismiss Mastermind as another 'rate card'. Newspapers at that time would bring out charts that listed out prices for space. These would include discounts here and there for multiple insertions of an advertisement or other bulk purchases. Although Mastermind too was a collection of advertising rates, Samir Jain was clear that it would not be another rate card. The difference was that there would be a sound basis for the pricing of the combinations. The rates would be backed by business logic.

'Mastermind was fundamentally a compromise of aggression,

on the one hand and caution, on the other,' said Pradeep Guha while explaining its concept. 'It looks like a marketing tool. But it is essentially a balance. In trying to make money, we ensured that we did not lose what we already had. The system had enough safety nets built into it,'[4] he elaborated.

At the end of the day, any package in Mastermind would have to improve overall value for the advertiser. There had to be a certain character and theme to the rates it laid down. For the advertiser, Mastermind had to bring in a better response to the advertisement, promote the product or business he was advertising and offer bigger bang for the buck. Without that, it would only be a random mix and match of rates, of limited value to the advertiser.

Rather, it was positioned as a tool which would help the media planner to mastermind his advertisements and insertions in newspapers across the country. It would enable the advertiser to achieve maximum impact and relevant response for his advertisement.

This meant that designing Mastermind was a major challenge. It had to take several parameters, including intangible ones, into consideration. The characteristics and needs of each market had to be taken into account while deciding the price for space in that market. The design of Mastermind would have to be sensitive to the diverse profiles of advertisers, their choices and preferences, what would make sense to whom, at what rate would buying space make sense for them, and so on. It also had to consider the reader profile in each city, for each publication. On the basis of these and other criteria, it was possible to make some assessment of whether a certain combo would prove effective for the advertiser at that price point.

While keeping in mind the interests of the advertiser, the company also had to look at its own position in various markets while creating Mastermind. The objective was to boost sales across publications and markets and this had to be balanced with the needs of advertisers. It would have been easy to pile the burden onto the stronger editions and thus lift the weaker ones. But the company was clear that weaker editions had to benefit without harming the stronger ones, thus improving profitability overall.

Further, Mastermind could not have a free run as far as pricing was concerned. BCCL had to assess its competitive position in each market before arriving at the rates. In cities where advertisers had other attractive options, including in the regional-language space, the price had to be accordingly competitive. It needed a sharp understanding of markets, advertiser behaviour and the company's relative strengths in each market. Indeed, there is an art and a science of strategic pricing applicable across product categories. In this case, it was just that the newspaper industry was trying it out for the first time.

Samir Jain had set up a corporate team of eight to nine people to work on the numbers and the detailing. He himself spent a great deal of time studying the split rates, assessing their implications for the advertiser and trying to harmonize the matrix. Vijay Jindal, who worked closely with him, remembers Samir Jain's passion in developing Mastermind. He was obsessed with the fact that he had to get it right. He was like a management trainee. He studied pharmaceutical companies and the airline industry and anything else that he could get his hands on. He paid great attention to detail. 'During the making of Mastermind, he was eclectic; there was an alchemy in his mind,' Jindal recalled.[5]

'Every day, we would make ten to twelve prototypes of Mastermind and tweak them. We would sample them and find faults. There was no technology in computers then. And, we wanted to bring about a certain amount of transparency in our pricing. There were mistakes. So, we manually tweaked them. We did this hit and trial for about two months. Finally, it worked out. Samir Jain was thrilled,' Jindal said.

The corporate unit did plenty of data crunching and analysis. Multiple teams worked on various facets of Mastermind. They listed publications by profitability, studied advertising patterns, analysed reader profiles, examined the competitive position of the company's publications in key markets and worked out the implications for the bottom line. The overall package had to be designed in a way that met BCCL's objectives while retaining its allure for advertisers.

Multiple editions and languages was not the only source of complexity. The overall space for advertising comprised several subcategories. Each had to have a relevant price depending on its customer segment. There was, for example, a set of column centimetre rates for financials, legal notices, public notices and tenders. This customer segment, comprising corporates and government departments, could afford higher rates. They were charged more.

The retail market, on the other hand, was charged moderately. Cinema and theatre owners were offered even lower rates. The company was thus able to use price as an effective lever in the competitive game.

There was resistance in the financials category. Advertising space was offered to them at a premium. Advertisers questioned the logic of this. If they used the space to insert an ad for a public issue, they had to pay more than if they used the same space to advertise their product. 'What I put into the space that I have bought is my business,' was their argument.

At the end of all the detailing and resistance, Mastermind was cleverly done. BCCL had identified the two strong editions – *The Times of India*, Bombay, and *Navbharat Times*, Delhi. Practically all the other editions, including four each of *The Economic Times* and *Navbharat Times*, needed support in one way or the other. Mastermind was designed in such a way that the two strong editions were made the 'hubs'.

Broadly, it offered three slabs of rates – a basic rate, a repeat rate and a super-concessional rate. Advertisers who wanted to buy space in a single edition were charged the basic rate. Those who wanted to use two or more editions of a daily were entitled to the repeat rate, which was lower than the basic rate. Finally, advertisers who bought space in all editions of a single publication, or in all publications from a single centre, could avail of super-concessional rates.

This was flexible enough to cover diverse advertiser requirements, while enabling the company to undertake tactical warfare in key markets. Advertisers who wanted to focus only on a select area or market could avail of super-concessional rates by buying space in all publications in that market. Others who wanted a national coverage were similarly entitled to super-concessional rates, if they bought space in all editions of a publication.

The idea was to try and persuade advertisers in Bombay, who had an operation in the west to buy space in *The Times of India*'s Ahmedabad edition. Similarly, if the advertiser had an operation in the north, he was offered space in Delhi as well. Then the company started offering him Marathi readers through *Maharashtra Times* and for a little extra, the Hindi-speaking readers through *Navbharat Times*. *The Economic Times* was an added attraction, with the promise of reaching out to readers in corporate houses, government and the bureaucracy.

But it was in Delhi where the story unfolded in the most interesting manner. An advertiser in Delhi could have a coveted space in *The Times of India*, Bombay, at a discounted (or super-concessional) rate if he chose to also advertise in *The Times of India*, Delhi. That was a tempting proposition for advertisers seeking a national coverage. It also enabled advertisers in this category to secure space in other editions of the paper, such as Lucknow and Jaipur, at nominal rates. Alternatively, the Delhi advertiser, if he chose all company dailies in Delhi, had the advantage of securing space in *Navbharat Times* at an attractive rate alongside. Either way, *The Times of India* in Delhi became an attractive proposition.

Media planners, who as a matter of routine had never looked beyond the *Hindustan Times* in Delhi, started to evaluate the *TOI* package as an option. Vibha Desai, who was the executive director of O&M when I met her in July 2001, recalled: 'Mastermind made a huge impact. It was a consolidation of rates. At an incremental rate, you could put out ads in XYZ editions. This was the key to the financial battle. The battleground was Delhi.'[6]

There were many facets that contributed to the success of Mastermind. First, it became extremely attractive to advertisers who were seeking a wider audience for their communication. The number of people who wanted multi-city coverage was growing. As businesses evolved and distribution networks spread beyond the metros, companies were interested in reaching their communication beyond the metro markets. Every time they launched a new consumer product, they wanted to make an impact beyond Delhi or Bombay and cover Bangalore, Lucknow and Jaipur.

The opportunity to advertise across languages and reader profiles through the *Navbharat Times* and *Maharashtra Times* was an added advantage. At a later stage, *The Economic Times* came into its own, offering a distinct set of readers in the combo, making Mastermind even more tempting.

Apart from companies, certain sections of individual advertisers also wanted to cover more than one location. Matrimonial advertisers, for example, wanted a wider reach. Mastermind provided a convenient, one-stop shop for all such advertisers. They did not have to negotiate with individual city offices. The prospect of a discounted combo rate for some of the emerging cities was undoubtedly an attraction. The more space you bought, the less you paid for every incremental column centimetre. It served to increase the overall pie of business for BCCL. For many advertisers who were undecided about including Jaipur or Lucknow in their media plan, the availability of such a package was a clinching factor.

For the company, this was a masterstroke. The most obvious benefit was that the power of the stronger editions could be used to lift the fortunes of the weaker ones. The Bombay edition of *The Times of India* could cross-subsidize the edition in Ahmedabad, for example. Over time, these smaller editions would come on the radar of advertisers. 'The idea behind Mastermind was to provide crutches to the weaker brands till they could stand on their own legs. And then withdraw the crutches systematically,' said Rajnish Rikhy,[7] former general manager (response) at BCCL.

It was not just to help the weaker markets. The focus of Mastermind was to give a boost to *The Times of India*, Delhi, in its battle against the *Hindustan Times*. Tied to its Bombay edition, the Delhi edition suddenly became an attractive proposition for advertisers in Delhi.

Mastermind enabled the company to leverage its multiple offerings across markets. This was a distinct competitive advantage. Rivals were mostly strong in a particular market or region, with practically no presence in the rest of the country. They did not have the reach and diversity to match this move. The Times Group had a virtual free run on this account.

This move also helped align the organization towards a common goal. While the sales teams continued to sell space in individual publications, they soon moved to selling entire Mastermind packages to media agencies and their clients. That led to synergy among the field teams.

An important benefit of this move was that it created excitement in the market. There was something new and innovative and it soon became a talking point. It got media agencies and advertisers to revise their approach and assess various permutations and combinations of rates to see how they could benefit from this package. For a market stuck in its conventional ways for years, this brought dynamism. The Times Group, at the centre of this shake-up, benefited immensely as a brand and a game changer.

In fact, the impact of Mastermind was felt within the first two years of its launch. The packages triggered more ads. The group continued to build on it and received a boost when *The Economic Times* started to do well and many more editions of the paper were launched in the early 1990s. 'Media planners and marketing people among advertisers started selling Mastermind more than *TOI* itself,' noted Bashab Sarkar, who was also with O&M in 2001. 'The trends of cost efficiency and economies of scale were attractive, and they were bought in.'[8]

There are a few interesting stories of how Samir Jain hit upon the idea of Mastermind. Although Samir Jain had been thinking about the skewed performance of his businesses and the need to leverage the stronger editions, the idea surfaced in a strange way. Vijay Jindal recounted that during a casual conversation among the top brass, one of the managers narrated how he and a friend had recently been served a glass of Royal Challenge whisky free at a bar after he bought the first drink.

This was the 1980s, and the concept of 'buy one get one free' or 'happy hours' in bars was still some years away for Indian consumers. While most people in the group reacted to the experience at a superficial level, it set Samir Jain thinking. He is believed to have enquired: 'Does that mean that people will continue to fall for something that comes for free?'

That is how the idea for Mastermind, one of The Times Group's most striking strategies, was born, Jindal said. The concept of the 'happy hours' appealed to Jain and he wondered if he could boost the sales and advertising revenues of his publications by offering freebies to his subscribers. The fact that many of the newly launched editions of *The Times of India* in north India were not doing well was weighing on his mind. This offered a way forward. This chance conversation may have sparked off the idea of linking together publications.

But like his other new initiatives, launching Mastermind meant overcoming resistance from several quarters. To start with, his people were doubtful whether it would work. The organization was conditioned to sell space in a particular fashion. There were existing packages and combos on offer. But these were simple combinations. For example, advertisers were entitled to a discount if they inserted the same advertisement multiple times in a single newspaper. Such offers were mainly confined to the Delhi and Bombay editions where there was already a pull from advertisers. Mastermind would require the sales team to get interested in new markets. They would also have to explain the logic behind the package rates offered under Mastermind.

The major reason for the resistance, though, was that Samir Jain wanted to kick it off in an audacious manner. He wanted to sell a combo of *The Times of India* and *Navbharat Times* in Delhi. This was unheard of: the leading English daily being packaged with a Hindi publication.

The sales team, including its members at the top, was convinced this was not going to work. They had thus far sold advertising space in their respective publications separately. They saw no synergy at all between the two publications. The reader profile of the two newspapers was completely different. Few advertisers would be looking to address readers across such a wide spectrum. There would be no takers for this combo. They anticipated that for many advertisers who were addressing the readership of *The Times of India*, the readers of *Navbharat Times* would be irrelevant. Similarly, those advertising in the latter would be out of place in the English daily. This was going against the group's basic premise of aggregating relevant audiences for the advertiser.

Pradeep Guha was then a resourceful senior manager and candid enough to publicly categorize the two papers. Guha's point was that, in Mumbai, *The Times of India* was read by the elite while the *Navbharat Times* was read by the migrant labour and local rickshaw pullers. Scandalized staffers looked aghast as Samir Jain heard this out quietly even though this must have hurt his pride. There was a time when Samir Jain saw The *Times of India* as number one, *NBT* as number two, and *ET* as number three in the Bennett, Coleman empire. The issue died out in Bombay. But Samir Jain persisted and they went ahead with the combo in Delhi.

Samir Jain had a different logic. Most of those in his team who opposed the move were based in Bombay. The *Navbharat Times* in Bombay was read mostly by migrants from Bihar and UP. Many of them were engaged in petty trade and low-skill jobs. In Bombay, the readership profile of *Navbharat Times* was indeed very different from that of *The Times of India*.

In Delhi, it was a different story. Samir Jain argued that the Delhi edition of *Navbharat Times* was the paper of the Hindi elite – of parliamentarians, rich businessmen and traders and agriculturists of north India, the 'cow belt' and the 'coal belt'. The advertisers of *The Times of India* would be interested to reach out to these sections of readers of *Navbharat Times*.

'For Samir Jain, *Navbharat Times* enjoyed the status that language publications had for the Bengali intelligentia, or at least that was the correlation he was seeking,' said Nataranjan Bohidar[9] who was brought in as brand manager during the 1988 sesquicentennial celebrations of the group. It was perhaps his intention to accord *Navbharat Times* the status that the *Ananda Bazar Patrika* had in Calcutta.

He had decided to embark on this initiative based more on his gut feeling about the market and not on the basis of any market research or data. 'He seemed to be driven by a pride in his products that bordered on obsession. He trusted his personal individualistic insights of his products and the market to such a dangerous extent that he eschewed the traditional industry-standardized or sanitized research completely,' Bohidar noted.

But this was not going to be a cakewalk. His sales team found *Navbharat Times* infra dig and felt that to combine it with *The Times of India* would wreck the latter's image. Yet, Samir Jain did not give in to the combined wisdom of his senior staff. He had already visualized the process and seen it through in his head till its logical end and had obviously felt that it would click.

With the success of *The Times of India*–*Navbharat Times* combo, the group developed the courage to move ahead. But those who saw Mastermind as merely a package of bulk discounts and combo concessions missed the point. The main point of the exercise was to use pricing as a strategic tool. Instead of a passive, almost inert, approach to pricing, Samir Jain wanted to base it on changing market realities and advertisers' ability and willingness to pay.

This was obviously a risky approach. Once the industry entered this paradigm, it would mean that prices could move either way. Every time competition intensified or demand for advertising space dropped, prices would have to be slashed to adjust to the market reality. Newspapers would have to charge less, irrespective of what happened to cost during that time.

But Samir Jain was committed to this approach of price as a strategic tool. That, rather than cost-plus pricing, is the way of competitive business, with all its attendant risks. Except that in socialist India, where government licensing and controls rather than competition governed the fate of industries, cost-plus pricing was the norm in most sectors. Given that the newspaper industry too was in a comfort zone, with all players in a friendly club, cost-plus pricing could have survived a little longer. But Samir Jain was keen to change the rules. He was stirring things up.

As such, Mastermind was a basic framework which presented the relative prices of space across markets and publications. The prices in this matrix were supposed to bear a correlation with value, not with cost. Accordingly, while prices in certain markets had been reduced to reflect their lower value for the advertiser, they were jacked up steeply in other markets.

So, following Mastermind, space in the Jaipur, Bangalore and Patna editions could be obtained at an addition of only Rs 5 each per column centimetre. That was supposed to reflect the lower value of these editions. But at the same time, the price of space in the Bombay edition deserved to go up to reflect the higher value. In the event, the hike that Samir Jain decided on was no ordinary one. The price of space in the Bombay edition of *The Times of India* went up a whopping 68 per cent at one go, from Rs 125 to

Rs 210 per column centimetre. Mastermind would be applicable, but at these revised rates. Similarly, the price of space in *Navbharat Times*, Delhi, went up 40 per cent. In the Delhi edition of *The Times of India*, rates were hiked 31 per cent to Rs 125. *The Economic Times* became more expensive by 28 per cent at Rs 150 per column centimetre in September 1987.

'Mastermind was not just a rate card,' reasoned Satish Mehta.[10] 'It was a vehicle designed to get higher profits for the company. Once he got Mastermind in place, Samir Jain was able to raise prices.' He did not stop at one round of hikes. In the five years starting 1987, The Times Group hiked its advertising rates thrice. Not just the quantum but the frequency of hikes also went up.

By December 1988, the advertiser had to pay Rs 290 for a column centimetre in the *TOI*'s Bombay edition. This went up to Rs 410 per column centimetre the year after, an increase of 314 per cent over three years. Similarly, the cost of space in *The Times of India*, Delhi, and *Navbharat Times* went up 163 per cent in three years. In *The Economic Times*, Delhi, advertising rates increased 178 per cent during 1987–90. It did not stop at that. The group imposed a 20 per cent surcharge on saleable price to 'offset a hike in newsprint prices' in 1988. By 1990, the column centimetre rate in *The Times of India*, Bombay, had scaled up from Rs 500, to Rs 700 in 1992 and to Rs 1,111 in 1995. The rate of increase may have slowed, but it continued to be high nevertheless.

The advertising industry, and their clients, protested against the hikes. Earlier, the practice in the industry was to limit the hikes to 4–5 per cent. They were normally announced with prior approval of advertising agencies. Newspapers had to cite reasons for a hike, such as an increase in newsprint costs, or offer excuses like rents and salaries having gone up. They had to inform agencies in advance and give them appropriate time to prepare and adjust. But the

*Times* did none of these. It just announced the hike one morning, as it were. It maintained that it had arrived at the conclusion that many of its products were delivering considerably high value and charging very little in return.

Before any of this happened, Samir Jain had to explain the logic to people within his organization. When he was going in for the first round of hikes, he had to overcome scepticism and resistance in the company. The team in charge of selling space in Bombay was contacted. They were obviously perturbed by such a substantial hike. There were serious concerns that this could lead a sharp fall in demand for space. Eventually, they agreed reluctantly. Dr Ram Tarneja took time getting convinced. 'You are going too steep,' he is believed to have said. He wondered if this would scare away advertisers.

But Samir Jain worked closely with the field team through all this. In one of the sessions, he said ad rates had nothing to do with cost. They had to do with the value of the product or service. They were directly in proportion to the value offered to the advertiser. 'If my paper delivers 75 per cent of Bombay's readership to product owners, it should be valued as such. That is very high value. Why should I be embarrassed and why should I look for excuses? I should charge a fair value for what I deliver and what the market is prepared to pay,' he said.[11]

Over time, his field team started to appreciate his point of view. During the sesquicentennial celebrations in Bombay, Samir Jain got the trigger he was looking for to convince his people. As part of the celebrations, there was an art auction being conducted by Sotheby's. Paintings were being auctioned on the ship, INS *Jawahar*. That was where an Indian painting – a Hussain – was sold for the first time for over Rs 10 lakh.

Besides the euphoria it created, it was also an eye-opener for Samir Jain's team. The internal obstacle was overcome. They now believed it was possible to demand a better price for space and that they were not doing anything outrageous. The following day, the hikes were announced. After one round of rate hikes, Samir Jain apparently told his managers: 'If the price of consumer goods keeps rising incrementally, we are justified in asking for a better price for our space.' The increase in rates was a 'rationalization', not a hike, he argued.[12]

These explanations aside, he seemed to have gauged a potential in the market which others had missed. The Indian economy was on a new growth trajectory in the range of 5–5.5 per cent. This increased growth was largely on the back of increased consumption spending, financed by high government deficit. New players had entered the consumer goods space. New products were being launched. Perhaps advertising space, especially in a pan-India English publication, was more prized than newspapers realized.

As it turned out, the advertising agencies reconciled to the hikes. As far as they were concerned, it could be argued that they gave in because with the hike, their commissions, normally based on the client's advertising budget, would go up. But the fact remains that their clients, the corporates paying for that space, considered it worthwhile to bear the burden of higher rates. Their ads were obviously having a positive impact on the business to the extent that even at the higher rates, buying space made business sense.

Besides, there was a certain basis to the hike. In evaluating these moves, it is important to note that these were not random, knee-jerk hikes in price. They were not uniform or across the board increases. There seemed to be a logic or rationale, at least within the group, for the price in each location or segment.

'One year, staffers suggested a 10 per cent hike for the following year. Samir Jain threw a fit at that,' recalled N.P. Singh. 'He was not hiking these rates for a lark. He could stand by each and every hike he had made. It was based on how much a market would be able to pay for space in the publications.'[13] For example, though the rates for the Bombay edition had been hiked, the rates for Delhi were kept relatively low. This was done to milk the advertiser in Bombay, while not letting it affect *TOI*'s equation in Delhi where the *Hindustan Times* was the leader.

Until 1985, the ad rates for *The Times of India*, Bombay, and *Hindustan Times*, Delhi, were similar. Perhaps the underlying logic was that both were market leaders and space should cost more or less the same in both. But Samir Jain believed this was unfair. *The Times of India*, being the leader in Bombay, was in a position to deliver much more value than the leader in Delhi.

Accordingly, in 1990, after the series of rate hikes, space in *TOI*, Bombay, became much more expensive than in *Hindustan Times*, Delhi. In fact, it was *Navbharat Times*, Delhi, that was now pitched against *HT* Delhi, as far as ad rates were concerned. The then *Navbharat Times* executive editor maintained that the *NBT* was Delhi's number one newspaper, not the *Hindustan Times*. It took courage to pitch a Hindi daily against the leading English newspaper, especially for one who spoke in terms of value to the advertiser. But The Times Group seemed to get away with it.

The hikes cannot be seen in isolation. They were accompanied by several changes in the quality of the offering. Weekend supplements in colour and on glossy paper served as attractive platforms for the advertiser. The layout, design and get-up of the newspapers were improved. Advertisers, especially the major ones, could see that the group had a strong orientation to maximize the value for them. As a signal, for example, the space-selling department was renamed 'Response'. This was to signify that the role of this team was to generate response for the advertiser, rather than just sell him space.

The Response team was also strengthened in terms of resources and people to serve advertisers better. A senior official was recruited as director of response. From being at the periphery of the organization, subservient to editorial content and journalists, Response was accorded pride of place in the organization. Its offices were refurbished. These intangibles improved the experience for the advertiser as well.

The group was open to experimenting and collaborated with advertisers to find ways to give better exposure to their ads in the newspaper. Certain competitors would be particular about not allowing advertising to impact the layout of news content beyond a point. The front page was treated as sacrosanct. The Times Group was relatively open on these issues. The advertiser often got primacy over others.

Besides, the group also sliced the market and its advertising space, depending on the potential and the paying power of the advertiser. It sold each segment in a different manner. For example, the appointments ads were a potential money-spinner. So The Times Group strengthened these pages and even levied an additional surcharge for this section. Rates for international advertisement were also pegged high. Gulf ads were offered at a special rate. Matrimonial and classified sections were strengthened.

Much later, it created special editorial supplements around lifestyle, education, city affairs and so on. These provided cost-effective options for advertisers. There was also a close fit between the products and services they advertised, and the profile of the supplement. Overall, there was a calibrated, nuanced approach to the business of space selling, rather than a one-size-fits-all swipe at the market.

In many ways, *The Times* was a more attractive package for the advertiser. Vibha Desai noted: 'In 1986-87, what did the advertiser want? He looked forward to colour, better reproduction and professionalism. The Times Group read the market well. It rightly predicted that the *Hindustan Times* would not be able to replicate it.'[14]

Despite the hike in rates, the amount of advertising space in The Times Group's publications went up, not down. The number of columns for advertising went up 10 per cent in *TOI* during 1988. *Navbharat Times* also increased the number of advertisement columns. This, in many ways, vindicated Samir Jain's position on hiking the rates.

The immediate impact on the financial performance was highly positive. Turnover went up 32 per cent in a year, from Rs 140.33 crore in 1987-88 to Rs 185.84 crore the following year. Profit after tax shot up from Rs 1.66 crore to 8.55 crore, a whopping 415 per cent growth in a year. The following year, net profit doubled to Rs 17.48 crore while turnover increased to Rs 228.26 crore.

Samir Jain was helped by the fact that the competitors' response to his bold moves was slow and tepid. The *Hindustan Times* came up with colour options for advertisers only in 1989-90, which was too late. 'It was like an overgrown schoolboy who did not know how to present himself,' recalled a top ad agency executive. Competitors may have also lagged behind in professionalism and service standards. *HT*, for instance, had a somewhat conceited and pedantic approach to space selling due to its dominance of the market.

'At first, competition did nothing at all,' recalled Rajnish Rikhy. 'In 1991-92, they began reacting. *HT* had an April model for its rate hikes and *The Hindu* had a September–October model, a once-a-year model. But in the 1990s, *HT* began hiking rates close on our heels.' To that extent, the rate hikes initiated by The Times Group benefited the rest of the industry. It helped the group and the industry capture some of the value they were creating for the advertiser.

But it was not just about skimming off some of the gains. Samir Jain was looking to establish his newspapers as brands with a distinct personality and consistent experience. He wanted these brands to be able to command pricing power in the market, rather than be restricted by a cost plus formula.

His bold and intrepid moves to hike rates had gone through. For this to be sustainable, he had to work in diverse ways to build the brands of his newspapers. These efforts would, of course, cover the content and production of his newspapers. But brand building would also extend to events and initiatives beyond the news pages. This was a first for any newspaper in India, and endeared the newspaper to the youth in the urban centres.

SIX

# Lights! Camera! Action!

*'Any damn fool can put on a deal, but it takes genius, faith and perseverance to create a brand.'*

David Ogilvy, the 'Father of Advertising'.[1]

ONCE THE PATH THAT its journey into the twenty-first century would take had been identified and clearly stated – being relevant and top of the mind – The Times Group began putting in place one of the cornerstones of its success story—consistent and relentless brand building. Under the new dispensation, the newspaper was hailed a 'product' and the product would now metamorphose into a 'brand'.

In a country dominated by regional newspapers, the idea was to stand out and be counted across the nation. This process began in connection with the preparation for celebrating the 150th anniversary of the founding of *The Times of India* and involved the inputs, resources and energies of a large army of participants. Events had to be planned, permissions had to be sought, large-scale arrangements had to be made and enough was to be invested in the process in terms of the number of man-hours spent on making it spectacular.

It was decided that there would be a grand celebration at *The Times of India* running for a year, starting from November 1988 to November 1989. Its magnitude and impact would be such that it would permeate every bit of mind space possible and offer its consumers and patrons a rare, hitherto unfelt experience.

Termed or branded the 'Sesquicentennial', these celebrations rode on a new slogan, 'Good times, sad times, changing times', and were showcased in both Delhi and Bombay. They brought a certain savvy and the much-needed pizzazz into the 'staid' newspaper industry. No publication or newspaper house had ever tried this at such a level and the onslaught got all the attention it was trying to attract.

Samir Jain's lively sister, Nandita, whose aesthetic tastes and love for art and beauty infused *The Times*' workplaces with a breath of fresh air, spearheaded the project. Insiders at *The Times* remember her and her enthusiasm with affection and nostalgia. She was vivacious, friendly, understanding and humane and she ensured that the events, especially the ones on art and culture, were executed extremely well.

A few persons put their innate strengths behind making this dream come true. Pradeep Guha and Pritish Nandy partnered with Nandita Jain, discussing and sorting out the blueprint for this massive brand-building exercise and ensuring that things got under way. Guha was head of advertising (which had been rechristened 'Response') and Nandy had been brought in as group editor and publishing director and was in charge of running the magazines including *The Illustrated Weekly of India*, *Evening News* and *The Independent*.

'The Sesquicentennial, for all practical purposes, was an opportunity seized with remarkable gusto by Nandita. She had several ideas of how to turn around the brand image of *The Times of India*. The approach was to make the Old Lady begin donning mini-skirts now,' recalled Pradeep Guha. 'As it is, the company was shedding its old leadership for the new and the young, and the

"Sesqui" (light-heartedly sometimes called "Sexycentennial") was in line with that theme,'[2] he added.

'We held several workshops to figure out and discuss the many issues that were to be sorted out, both in Bombay and in Delhi, but more so in the former. We started these preparations about a year before the deadline. Specialists were selected to handle niche areas. Sabina Sehgal Saikia would handle all classical music events. She thought about them, planned them and supervised them; and we worked on getting sponsorships,' Guha noted.

Nataranjan Bohidar coordinated most of the activities that were to be held in Delhi. Guha was handling everything outside of Delhi. There was enough follow-up and monitoring to do. With the Bruce Springsteen event in Delhi, the team found out that his Human Rights Concert was already on. It spoke to the organizers about adding Delhi to their list of destinations. That is how it worked out.

'We set about conceiving the sort of events that could help *The Times of India* showcase its legacy and reassert its unassailable sweep over the city's readership,' Guha remarked. The celebrations were also about reinvention, about the future. And the focus was on elite areas – art, culture, sport and history.

Nandita Jain was a great connoisseur of art and was responsible for a lot of the physical artwork displays that mark the offices of *The Times* in Delhi and Bombay. She had travelled to the Shekhawati region in Rajasthan looking for artwork and sculptures to buy for the Response office in Bombay, and the Delhi office too benefited from her inputs.

The celebrations began on 3 November 1988, with the release of a commemorative postage stamp in Bombay by the then prime minister Rajiv Gandhi, who also released a Sesquicentennial volume of books. It is a coveted collection. One of these was master cartoonist R.K. Laxman's *The Eloquent Brush*. His most famous mascot, the 'Common Man', too was honoured on the stamp.

Seven other books collating the best of *The Times* included: *Forefront*, *Viewpoint*, *Centrepiece*, *Feedback*, *Past Times*, *Flashback* and *Brand New*. Four Sesquicentennial magazines on culture, society, economy and sport were also offered to discerning readers.

*The Times* backed this up with concerts held in both the metropolitan cities with Bruce Springsteen, Tracy Chapman, Peter Gabriel and Sting coming to the one in Delhi, and 'Europe', a rock concert, being held in Bombay. The financial capital also saw a jazz performance by the American guitarist Charlie Lee Byrd.

The Human Rights Concert in Delhi also showcased the talents of the Senegalese singer and percussionist Youssou N'Dour, who is known to have helped develop a style of popular music known in the Senegalese language Serer as 'mbalax'. At that time, he was perceived as the inheritor of Bob Marley's mantle. In other words, enough effort went into planning the concerts and bringing in musicians that most Indians had not seen live or in concert.

Dance exponent Astad Deboo performed at the inauguration – a fusion of the traditional and modern dance forms. An Yves Saint Laurent fashion show was held against the backdrop of the historic Gateway of India in Bombay. Nearly twenty festivals of Indian classical music, under the umbrella of the theme 'Unusual Ragas' and a festival of Indian classical dance were also held. The team also localized some of these events.

In Ahmedabad, it held a twenty-four-hour relay music festival called Sampoorna Ratri with one performer taking over from the other. In Lucknow, the team organized a mehfil. In Calcutta, the events were held at places along the Hoogli River. 'The idea was for *The Times of India* to have a breakthrough look and feel; and make these events very experiential and expose visitors to something novel, unique and impressionable,' Guha pointed out.

Then came the focus on art. The Gothic Victoria Terminus station, designed by English architectural engineer Frederick William Stevens in 1887-88, and built over a period of ten years, was transformed into a rare art gallery owing to the Timeless Art exhibition that was held there. Especially dressed up and illuminated for the occasion, the Terminus building, headquarters of the erstwhile

Great Indian Peninsular Railways, with its characteristic pointed arches, ribbed vaults and flying buttresses, was also in the spotlight.

Imagine converting one of the busiest railway terminuses in the country (renamed the Chatrapati Shivaji Terminus in 1996, and commonly known as CST or VT) into an art gallery with huge canvases and striking sculptures dotting the place. That brought the focus on both the architectural grandeur of the Terminus and on the art it was showcasing. No commuter (almost 2.8 million people are said to use this station everyday) had ever encountered this sort of a cultural bonanza ever.

'The bus stop outside VT was painted by Manjit Bawa himself; I may still have a photograph of that,' reminisced Guha. 'The story inside VT was even more phenomenal. We opened the exhibition at 12.40 a.m. after the last train left and closed before the first train was to embark on its trip at 4.40 a.m. It was a midnight drama. The paintings hung on for a week and created a huge buzz. Having feasted their eyes on the work, the invitees would walk across to the J.J. School of Art and party on its lawns,' he added.

'There was no concept of event management, in India, then. We later realized that the Sesqui had been what one would term the first major full-blown professionally managed event, on such a large scale,' he said. It not only covered several areas and regions in the country; it also showcased the power of brand building at its finest. The first event management institute was launched a year and a half after the Sesquicentennial and event management as a business took off.

*The Times*' focus on art also made it involve Sotheby's of London into auctioning rare Indian art aboard the naval training ship, INS *Jawahar*. This particular event showcased the work of thirty-five individuals including Nalini Malani, Manjit Bawa, Manu Parekh, Tyeb Mehta, N.S. Bendre, Bhupen Khakhar, Vivian Sundaram, K.G. Subramanyam, Nilima Sheikh, D.L.N. Reddy, Himmat Shaw, Ravinder Reddy, Mrinalini Mukherjee, Pushpamala N., Gieve Patel, Alex Mathew and Madhvi Parekh, 'catapulting them into the international arena', according to a BCCL publication.[3] The lavish, well-attended auction, besides bringing the artists into the limelight also saw the then Maharashtra chief minister, Sharad Pawar, announcing that the government would donate a plot of land to the Bombay Arts Society.

Theatre too found space in this smorgasbord of activities with actor, director playwright Satyadev Dubey's plays being held. A cafe theatre was held at The Oberois where visitors could have their lunch while savouring the plays. Sport was catered to as well, with tournaments being held in cricket, golf, polo and snooker.

And finally, there were the seminars including a National Editorial Seminar, an International Editorial Seminar, a Marketing and Technology Seminar, held by the American Newspaper Publishers Association, and The Grand Debate.

The Sesquicentennial truly brought the might of *The Times* network on display and began reinforcing the 'idea that was *The Times of India*'. It also ushered in intangibles such as customer perception and managed to convey the 'personality' of the product besides repositioning the papers and the company with long-term perspectives.

And no matter what *The Times* did other than engage in the business of news, it was aware that each and every event had to contribute to strengthening this perception of the *TOI* brand. Hence, the makeovers to the Femina Miss India pageants and the effort put into making the Filmfare Awards Night a special experience. Both these events have been successfully 'branded'.

'We always kept the final goal in mind when we began these turnarounds,' explained Guha. 'We were very sure of what our vision was and how we were going to achieve that. Take the Femina Miss India contest, for example. While everyone saw a Miss India, I was already envisaging a Miss World and a Miss Universe. The scale was bigger, more far-reaching, and we got there,' he noted.

The company was aware that every initiative, no matter where it emanates from, has to fulfil its purpose, which is to contribute to its health and growth. And successive initiatives have paid off for *The Times*. Brand building isn't something that can be done overnight, in most cases, and *The Times* has been at it for a very long time. Its attempts to remain in public memory have been consistent, and its initiatives have been multifarious, numerous, diverse.

One such initiative has been to use the magazines under the umbrella of the group as a sampling platform for FMCG companies to promote their consumer goods. The sampling of products with magazines turned out to be a win-win idea for every partner in this experiment. *Filmfare*, the magazine used in this venture, earned more revenue, the reader got a free gift and the products of the advertising companies got an inexpensive delivery system.

Warren Buffett is believed to have once said, 'Your premium brand had better be delivering something special, or it's not going to get the business.'[4] Even the launch of the all-colour newspaper on 18 March 2003 was a way of reiterating the position that the brand was taking, acknowledging the importance of variety and colour in our lives. This move improved the *TOI* readership by 33 per cent and helped its growth.

On 17 March that year, passers-by on 'Delhi's Fleet Street' – Bahadur Shah Zafar Marg – had to halt for a minute and take in the large, colourful, zesty mural painting, in comic-book graphics, of Krishna and the Gopis celebrating Holi on the façade of the Times building. The message being sent across so loudly was that *The Times* was young, hip and trendy – far from its image as a 165-year-old grand dame of Indian newspapers.

It was a bit of a shock. To some passers-by, the façade may have seemed garish, as it previously had been very serene: it was always painted white. This was a move that could have gone either way but the decision had been taken and there was a certain amount of conviction about declaring itself 'all-colour' in this manner, and as time was to prove, readers still remember the façade and of course what it was trying to convey.

'The idea is to constantly be at it, no matter what; try every avenue, make the attempts, learn and move on,' said a young brand manager at *TOI* while discussing brand building at *The Times*. 'I must agree here that some of these initiatives have not worked but that has not and will not deter the team from trying new things,' he added. (Would you say that this group is then in a constant state of manthan, I remember asking him. 'That's exactly it,' he said. 'We are in a constant state of manthan.')

Take, as a case in point, the move by *Navbharat Times* to experiment; moving away from a Hindi that was too complex for the layman to a new language – Hinglish. Puritans might have turned their nose up at this but, for a larger segment of the reading population, it was a welcome move. And today, we see that this new language is being widely used by the electronic media as it is easy to understand and far less cumbersome.

City-centric life supplements, such as Bombay Times and Delhi Times, with their unabashed focus on the good life and its connoisseurs too, say something about the *TOI* brand. Begun in 1994, these supplements brought exposure to haute couture, fine dining, art and high living. While catering to the glitterati, they began stoking aspirations among the lesser mortals. Over time, these supplements seem to have become almost stand-alone papers, sometimes more preferred than the main edition.

The creation of these strong brands too was strategic. They slowly but carefully built their image and catered to that one common need in all human beings – desire: the desire to be; the desire to have, to possess; wanting to do, to say and to share, among other things. On the other hand, the advertising was carefully managed, and big, prestigious advertisers lured with adequate initiatives (discounts and packages) to buy space in these editions to encourage the others to follow suit, which they did.

Relentless efforts have continued through the years, and they spring up almost unexpectedly. The annual budget issue of the newspapers, presented with elan and humour, illustrates this point. The budget editions of *The Economic Times*, with their morphed images of the finance minister in 2002 and 2003 attracted much comment and attention. It was a radically bold move, almost irreverent. Readers and policymakers must have gasped at the sight of the two flagship newspapers of the group exploding in a gargantuan mass of neon-tipped fireworks on its pages, particularly on a subject as grave as the 'budget'. (The finance minister in 2003, in fact, wanted the original artwork for his personal collection.) This practice of 'having a blast' while working on the budget editions has since been emulated by some of its competitors.

The budget editions of both *The Times of India* and *The Economic Times* seek to demystify the annual budget exercise. Apart from expert analyses and opinions, these editions carry reports from the perspective of the readers, thereby decoding complex subjects and pointing out the impact that the budget would actually have on the common man's life.

The budget edition is not the only one. The group has systematically looked at routine, but important, events to make the brand stand out. For example, general elections are routinely covered by all publications, have high reader interest but offer little scope for differentiation. During the 2004 general elections, a team of editors from *ET* was assigned to the *TOI* to revamp and liven up its pages. Jaideep Bose, Arindam Sengupta, Shankar Raghuraman and Abheek Burman were a part of this special unit. They decided to cover the run-up to the elections from the day the Election Commission (EC) announced the dates.

It was on a Sunday afternoon that the EC announced the dates. The sort of stories that had to be carried had already been planned. The page was to be entitled 'Noise, Voice, Choice', or something to that effect. They kept working on it. It was 11.45 p.m. and the printing team was raising hell. They wanted the page – and the edition – to be released.

Just then, Jaideep Bose called his colleagues to say, 'Change the title of the page. Call it "Dance of Democracy".' That raised eyebrows at first, but with time, the campaign clicked. No prizes for guessing whose suggestion this was. (Samir Jain used to 'suggest' names for supplements and special pages in his papers.) The 'Dance of Democracy' covered the tamasha of electoral politics, in a tongue-in-cheek manner. It was a satirical take on the political circus of the country and touched a chord with every reader who looked at this whole process with a certain amount of indifference and disdain. The brand too got its value. It was perceived as innovative and audacious, something that rings a bell with the youth and the upwardly mobile class.

Getting a grip on the intangibles is something The Times Group is good at. In its own words, ideas such as this one are 'in line with the overall philosophy of the group – creative and intellectual disruption.'[5] But one does perceive the singular theme in all such ventures as lengthening the life of the brand and protecting and improving its reputation.

Take, for instance, 'The Speaking Tree'. It is a bona fide concept. Why not delve into the spiritual as a harbinger of 'news'? But when it was first launched, some people scoffed at it. There were enough discourses on philosophy and the realm of the soul in the outside world. Yet *The Times* went ahead with this and offered it to its readership – both catering to a latent demand for such wisdom and also in the process creating more demand. This idea too has been emulated by the group's rival publications and contemporaries. 'The Speaking Tree' has gone on to be so successful that it has emerged as a separate supplement. ('The Speaking Tree' in *TOI* and 'Cosmic Uplink' in *ET* are Samir Jain's pet ideas.)

The USP of *The Times of India*'s DNA may lie in its ability for ceaseless innovation. In keeping with its theme of staying relevant to its readers, the group also launched a 'Speednews' campaign. This would be a new edition, designed for those who are hard-pressed for time, eager consumers of capsule editions, which summarized events with their crisp stories.

The paper also realized that to be in the reckoning in any region, it had to dominate the pulse and the choice of its city dwellers. Therefore, it increased its focus on local coverage by increasing the number of pages in its newspapers, highlighting local events and happenings. There was no better way to capture the attention of say a south Bombayite or a west Delhiite or an east Calcuttan and so on and so forth.

This campaign was launched in Delhi, Calcutta, Hyderabad, Bombay, Pune, Bangalore and Lucknow. In the first three cities, where there was pressure from a close competitor, the idea was to wrest the mantle by conveying that the *TOI* did know the city and its inhabitants well enough and that it cared about their needs. In the others, the campaign celebrated the spirit of the particular city by focusing its coverage on the most enterprising professionals of the region. This was a sure way of co-opting new readers.

Taking this a step further, and to cater to the natural interest of every resident in his locality and its happenings, *The Times* launched hyper-local initiatives called Pluses. These are pull-outs, normally restricted to specific localities, and spanning a 3–4 kilometre radius. These super-focused supplements put the spotlight on the common interests, tastes and needs of those living around the same area and were also meant to encourage better community interaction and social welfare activities.

One of the *TOI*'s most well-known campaigns, executed brilliantly, was called 'A Day in the life of India', which showcases India and Indians as they are – self-absorbed but well-meaning, fearful and moral, yet laden with the most outrageous contradictions. It takes potshots at the spuriousness of political life and of the unpredictability and shallowness of politicians. It also captures the journey of a 100-rupee note as it makes way from 'briber' to 'bribee'. Such campaigns established *The Times of India* as a newspaper that had its finger on the pulse of the nation and also as one which was audacious – a provocateur.

To build a buzz around the brand, *The Times* plunged into events held by and for the advertising community. It associated itself with the Abby Awards (given away for creative excellence in advertising), the Emvies (introduced to honour a measurable and significant contribution in the field of media) and the Effies (an effectiveness award, with the participation of clients and academicians as well).

Besides such advertising club events, The Times Group also became the official representative of the Cannes advertising awards in India. All these initiatives and a strong presence in the Indian Advertising Festival helped boost the brand's aura on an international platform as well.

Then, there were the high-octane annual parties by the city-centric supplements such as the Bombay Times Party, attended by the glitterati and sought after by wannabes, and covered extensively. Such festivities reinforce the idea of *The Times* as a well-heeled, stylish, glamorous entity, thereby stoking aspirations and generating a feeling of kinship with the brand.

These numerous forays have helped *The Times of India* establish and maintain its brand image and its domination over the Indian media landscape. And no matter how much they have been emulated or copied by competitors, *The Times* does seem to grab and enjoy the first-mover advantage.

I shall now leave you with one of the most enduring stories of brand building at *The Times*. This could very well be the perfect blend of trade and art, of commerce and concern; and of marketing initiative and social intervention.

The 'Newspapers In Education' (NIE) programme, launched in 1985, was a method of brand building, founded on the ground that children and young adults also needed to be updated on current affairs, global events and other relevant happenings. But the product had to be reinvented and redone to suit their interests and tastes.

It took off under Nandita Jain's tutelage, and may have been inspired by what she had seen in some American newspapers during one of her visits to the US. She discussed doing something similar in India with the senior management, and the project was approved for execution.

The launch pad for this enterprise was Delhi. But across the country, almost 400,000 students from nearly 2,000 schools were brought under its ambit. A sixteen-page customized edition was brought out with content that was acceptable to schools and useful for children. Career-related news was in focus. And students contributing to the edition were accepted as cub reporters and therefore co-opted.

By catching children young in school and by introducing them to a product customized for them, *The Times of India* was able to develop a new constituency. Children in most public schools get individual copies of the paper with articles and special stories of their interest. Clearly, there was a concerted effort behind this initiative. Considering that newspaper reading tends to become a habit that is difficult to shed, this ensured a long-term loyal readership for the paper.

During a telephonic conversation in February 2013, from Bangalore, one of NIE's earliest programme coordinators, Maya Menon, spoke about its journey.

Menon was teaching at a public school in Delhi when she chanced to see an ad in *The Times of India* sometime in 1985 seeking applicants to handle this project. Excited with the prospect of exploring new things in education, she went ahead and applied, and subsequently met Nandita Jain. The late Sabina Sehgal Saikia (well-known food critic of *The Times of India*, who fell victim to the 26/11 terrorist attack on The Taj hotel in Mumbai) was also present besides Ruma Singh, who was heading the project.

Delhi was a market Menon worked on for two years. It was a part-time job. Initially, about fifty schools in the city were covered and a subscription of about ten thousand copies picked up. In time, it was decided to cover two hundred schools over the next two years. The programme kept expanding.

But her real challenge was in Bangalore when she moved there in 1988 after having formally joined the *TOI*, and began setting up NIE, there. 'The *TOI* was trailing at number four in the city then. Its circulation was about 14,000. When I set up the programme, I didn't know whether it would work here, but by the time I left in 1995, sixty schools across Bangalore were actively subscribing to the newspaper as a learning tool. And one-fifth of *TOI* Bangalore city's subscription (one in every five newspapers sold) was coming from NIE,' she said.

'The process really is to approach newspapers meaningfully and link them up with learning. Newspapers are not just healthy diversions in school. They had to become teaching tools. With this in mind, we worked on multiple things: we brought out a media education handbook. We brought out monthly worksheets and planners. We organized quiz competitions and play fests, and we held events. We were a team of four. We had a limited budget. No one was breathing targets down our neck. We were fairly insulated from the rest of the organization. We reported to the branch head. But we had a lot of space to innovate and create something fresh,' she recalled.

I asked her if NIE was more a marketing function than an editorial one. It was covered under the Times Publishing House, not BCCL. 'We were aware that we were performing a marketing role and establishing a young, loyal readership for the newspaper. That is true,' she said candidly. 'But there was a genuine attempt to provide educational service as well; an effort to build reading ability, bring about an awareness about the community and develop qualities of citizenship in our young,' she pointed out.

The newspaper kept at its promotional activities too. For about two years, it printed five-rupee and two-rupee coupons in the *TOI* which students subscribing to it could collect and redeem for classified ads on Teachers' Day. The newspaper brought out an entire pull-out of those ads one year.

Over the years, several other newspapers have followed suit. *The Hindu*, *Deccan Herald* and *The Indian Express* have their NIE projects. 'But they copied it. The *TOI* had pioneered it, and it had done that at an interesting time,' stressed Menon. 'I was asked about the programme and about how to get it going. I didn't want them to replicate us, and I told them so. But they didn't trust their own judgement to do something on their own,' she pointed out.

The programme has since taken off in Bombay, Pune, Hyderabad and Ahmedabad. In Bombay, it was started half-heartedly and didn't do very well. It was shut down and restarted later. That might have had something to do with the fact that *The Times of India* saw itself as the market leader in the financial capital and really didn't feel the need for the initiative. Also, some people even within the organization saw it as a side service, something not too important in terms of achieving the larger business objectives.

'But imagine the huge readership NIE has been able to build over the last twenty-five years. All those children who were brought under this umbrella then must be CEOs, top managers and senior executives today. And they must be reading *The Times of India,*' Menon concluded, validating once again Benjamin Franklin's dictum: 'An investment in knowledge pays the best interest.'[6]

## SEVEN

# The Pink Panther

WHILE *THE TIMES OF INDIA* created turbulence in the media world, *The Economic Times* was undergoing a makeover of its own. This was a relatively quiet affair. It did not stir passions or controversies the way the *TOI* did. But it was no less significant than what was being done in the rest of the company.

*The Economic Times* went through a complete overhaul of content. Its design, layout and even the colour were changed in a way that made it unrecognizable from its earlier version. Its cover price went up to one extreme and then down to another. It attracted new readers and created a loyal and robust market for business dailies. All this happened in a span of less than five years.

These initiatives were relatively less controversial, perhaps because the *ET* was not seen as a mainstream newspaper in the sense of a general newspaper like *The Times of India* or *Hindustan Times*. From the start, it had been geared to a niche segment of readers and advertisers. Issues of editorial freedom and public interest were not at the forefront in its case.

In that sense, the resistance was much less and the teams leading the changes had a relatively free run. Its transformation was more a story of imagination, creativity and innovation than of overcoming resistance to change. At the same time, the changes in this case were far more dramatic and that much faster.

In the story of the transformation of The Times Group, the success of *The Economic Times* makes for a rich marketing case study. The product, while continuing to be a business and economic daily, was put through a complete overhaul. Its customer base expanded significantly while the positioning was upscale. Price was used deftly to grow the market, while keeping the product 'aspirational'. This was backed by strategic advertising for the brand. Before all that, an A-team was put in place to drive the transformation.

*The Economic Times* had been launched in Bombay in 1961. This was the time when Shanti Prasad Jain was rapidly expanding BCCL's portfolio. The country had completed nearly a decade of state-led economic development. Private entrepreneurship was mostly confined to small business and trade. The private corporate sector played a relatively small part in the overall economy and was dominated by family-owned businesses. The primary role in the economy was performed by the government through its planning machinery and public enterprises.

Much of the economic debate was about using public policy and government companies to promote balanced regional growth and alleviate poverty, while creating basic infrastructure. The consumer goods sector was ignored and discouraged, in the assumption that the country would be better off channelizing resources to sectors like capital goods, metals and minerals and irrigation that were deemed more critical for long-term growth.

It was largely a closed economy, with focus on import substitution. Exports were either discouraged or completely disallowed. Interaction with economies overseas was mostly seen as detrimental to the domestic economy. This was not peculiar to India; the immediate post-colonial economic and political discourse favoured this approach.

The fact was that in such a context, the options for an economic or financial daily were limited. It was a bold initiative to go in for one. Perhaps having an economic daily added to the prestige of the company and the owners. Besides, Bennett, Coleman and Co. Limited was in an expansion mode and being an uncharted area, economic reporting would have been seen as an opportunity.

As it turned out, Bombay saw the birth of not one but two financial newspapers in 1961. The other was *The Financial Express*, launched by the Indian Express group under the patronage of its feisty owner, Ramnath Goenka.

The first editor of *The Economic Times* was P.S. Hariharan. The paper started with a modest circulation of 11,000 copies. Hariharan was succeeded by Dr D.K. Rangnekar in 1964, who was the editor for over a decade. During this period, the circulation of the paper went up to about 60,000 copies. He had introduced lighter stories and increased the paper's political coverage. The idea was to make the paper more readable.

Although *The Economic Times* had created a base of loyal readers for itself, it was circumscribed by its content. The tone of the paper was bland. It was a newspaper of record. It reported government policy announcements at length, often verbatim. It provided a platform for economists and policymakers to discuss important, but dense issues such as poverty, income distribution, inflation and food security.

Its possibilities were limited. Economics and business were closely intertwined with government and policy. Government prescriptions and control were becoming more detailed and complex by the day. Maintaining transparency in the face of such controls was also a challenge. An economic newspaper that tracked these developments and interpreted them for the reader was performing an invaluable role.

But its readership was limited to mainly economists and people from academia. The *ET*'s orientation was very GNP-focused. There was little interest beyond this. Economic literacy was confined to a small section of people in the country. Politics was primary. It was driving economics too to a very large extent.

Despite these obvious constraints, it was decided to expand the reach of *The Economic Times*. After remaining a single-edition paper for almost thirteen years, *The Economic Times* was launched in Delhi in 1974. Two years later, a Calcutta edition saw the light of day.

Rangnekar left in 1979 and went on to edit *Business Standard*, another economic and business daily, launched by the Ananda Bazar Patrika group in 1974. Dr Hannan Ezekiel took over from him and Manu Shroff from Dr Ezekiel.

'At this time, *The Economic Times* was not considered a dynamic paper. It was sedate, verbose and staid. It stuck to the core themes of economics and policymaking, centred on the bureaucracy and government,' reminisced N.P. Singh. 'It was,' he said, 'an esoteric paper widely read by economists'. When the RBI's credit policy was announced, *ET* would have the authentic account. Every bill passed by the government would be faithfully represented. The paper would report official data and statistics on every conceivable economic parameter.

Not much changed for almost a decade after Rangnekar, as far as the paper's content and focus were concerned. Speaking about *The Economic Times* of those years, Gautam Adhikari, a former executive editor of The *Times of India*, said the *ET*'s format 'had this five-year-plan look'. In terms of content as well as layout, design and texture, it was stuffy. For it to become really influential, it had to be distinguished from the other financial dailies.

In the meantime though, something interesting started to happen in the marketplace. During the decade of the 1980s, the circulation of *The Economic Times* started to climb. Its sales in 1980 were 61,000-plus copies. Three years later, the figure was over 65,000. This reached nearly 81,000 by 1985. The same year, it added an edition in Bangalore. By 1987, its circulation reached 87,688 copies.

Although this rate of growth was nothing much to write home about, *ET*'s circulation was reaching critical mass. Along the way, the company had created some hype around *The Economic Times* by celebrating its twenty-fifth anniversary in 1986. The paper had inched up to a level where it was becoming consequential. Besides, its readership was always believed to be significantly higher than its circulation, given that it was read mostly in offices and academic institutions. At this level, it had the potential to be on the radar of advertisers.

While BCCL was closing down its non-core publications, *The Economic Times* had clearly been identified as a newspaper that would survive and receive management focus. It offered opportunities for synergy with the other publications. It was an important part of the Mastermind package, an added inducement that provided advertisers access to corporate readers and the bureaucracy.

Now, with circulation nearing the 90,000 mark, the management took notice. 'Gradually, we felt that we must develop a constituency for the paper among advertisers and readers,' said N.P. Singh. The foundation for *ET*'s growth would be laid soon after. 'Samir Jain wanted the paper to be very corporate-focused. He wanted the paper to explore and write about brands that were active. He wanted it to focus on the needs and requirements of a much larger sector,' noted Pradeep Guha. 'He wanted a new approach, a new outlook and a new thrust for *ET*,' he added.

Almost the very first thing that Samir Jain did in this regard was to recruit an editor. This time again, he was looking for – and found – a person who could take a 360-degree view of the brand. While being sound in the editorial function, he needed to be sensitive to the dimensions of marketing and circulation. Within the editorial function too it was important to unshackle from the past and chart a new course. Without that, a makeover would amount to nothing.

Samir Jain chose T.N. Ninan for the job. He had served as business editor of *India Today* and, later, had been elevated to executive editor of the magazine. He had had a successful, though somewhat stormy, stint at the India Today group. Earlier, he had worked for an Amrita Bazar Patrika group magazine, called *New*

*Delhi*, edited by Khushwant Singh. This was a fortnightly, an ambitious venture from the group, modelled on the American *New Yorker*. It was priced at Rs 5 in 1978. Though the magazine was short-lived, Ninan's writings were noticed. Among those who followed his pieces with keenness was his future employer at *India Today*, Aroon Purie.

'Aroon has a penchant for bringing on board people with clear thinking, original writing styles, integrity and devotion to duty,' said cartoonist Ajit Ninan,[1] who was T.N. Ninan's colleague at the magazine. (He is with *The Times of India* now.) 'Aroon has a soft corner for the serious worker, who would walk the extra mile to put in his best and who was above office politics. So, he decided to get T.N. Ninan on board, and made him business editor,' he pointed out.

'Ninan functioned superbly as business editor. Aroon was so impressed by him that he gave him out-of-turn powers. The other editors played dirty and went away on mass leave, leaving Ninan to handle the show. But even during the crisis, he was brilliant. He would write political stories and edits with flourish, covering areas such as Punjab at the height of terrorism, among other hard-core political events,' Ajit Ninan recalled.

T.N. Ninan's efforts did not go unnoticed. Aroon Purie elevated him to executive editor ahead of several senior editors. This had never happened before. A business editor had never overnight become the executive editor at *India Today*. Ninan was effectively the number two, after the managing editor. There was uproar among the senior editorial staff.

This was the time when BCCL made him the offer to be the executive editor of *The Economic Times*. The prospect of recasting the country's number one economic and business daily was exciting – more so, when he would have a virtually free hand in accomplishing the task.

T.N. Ninan joined *The Economic Times* in 1987. From the start, he got cracking. He was allowed to choose people from across the industry and build his own team. He was in a position to offer them attractive hikes in salaries. The organization and its offices were also spruced up. There was a certain freshness, and space for a new work ethic. A blueprint for change was prepared. Ninan was promised that he would get all the resources he needed to effect the change. He would have a free hand on content. To Samir Jain's credit, he kept that promise. 'Ninan came in strong and with a huge mandate. He had all the authority that he needed. Samir Jain and he would discuss issues a lot, and we sometimes saw Ninan being a little dismissive of the owner's suggestions, saying, "That isn't good enough" or "this won't work" or "why don't we try that instead",' recalled Priya Ranjan Dash,[2] managing editor of the *Financial Chronicle*, who was then with *ET*.

'The team knew then that the company was playing with a strong balance sheet,' recalled Paran Balakrishnan,[3] who worked with Ninan at *ET*. 'Samir Jain was not spreading himself thin. Having closed many of the non-core publications, he had only a few brands to focus on. There was clarity and commitment to the objective. We had the space to imagine and innovate.'

At that stage, *The Economic Times* had an annual revenue of about Rs 10 crore. It was a paper with ten pages. Ninan brought in a fresh and wholesome approach to *ET*. He took into account the readers' need for analytical, vibrant and thought-provoking content. He also captured their keenness to be exposed to newer arenas, both professional and personal.

There was plenty of innovation in the way the team went about revamping the content of the paper. At first, it expanded the meaning of business and finance. From relying on government press releases and official briefings as its staple content, it started to report on subjects like management, marketing and advertising, consumer issues and personal finance, property and investments. Many of these were to become 'mainstream' subjects in later years. But they were hardly prominent in the economic and business newspapers of that time. The bigger leap of faith, though, was including fresh themes that had little to do with economics and business.

*The Economic Times* introduced its readers to science and technology. There was a weekly page devoted to book reviews and publishing. Art and culture got a page as well—Artscape. Articles on theatre were made a regular feature. This was a complete departure from the earlier flavour of *The Economic Times*.

Underlying all the changes was a sharp and acute understanding of the reader. The paper was now taking a holistic view of its reader. It saw the reader as a multidimensional personality, not just a consumer of staid economic policy reports. It is in this that it scored over its rivals.

As an insider puts it, from being a *business* paper, *The Economic Times* became a *businessman's* paper. The paper could anticipate that its readers, besides reading about economy and business, would also be interested in themes like management and industrial relations. Art and theatre would be an integral part of their lifestyle. Real estate and car finance would be of interest to them and they would have a healthy curiosity in science and technology. They would look for ways to 'combat stress'. By the same logic, subjects like intellectual property rights and diplomacy were discussed at length in the columns of *The Economic Times*. The number of pages was increased regularly.

In the early 1990s, the paper, on a normal day, would have articles on the advertising industry with interviews of people who mattered in the sector. There would be articles on leisure, sports and on themes of 'winning'. During the week, it carried a separate page called 'mid-week review'.

At the same time, it did not give up its core content. There was a banking page, for example, where public sector banks and global banks, among others, were written about extensively. Similarly, there were special pages on 'taxation and finance'. Commodities were covered at length. One section would be devoted to metals, for instance. With growing interest in equity markets, the 'Investor's Guide' spread across several pages was a crowd-puller.

Further, the paper was sensitive to the fact that this category of readers would still need a summary of political developments. So it did not shy away from including sections of political news, analysis and debate in an economic and business paper. It was careful not to report politics in the conventional way of a general newspaper. Instead, it was more interpretative and compact, pointing out the interconnections for a business reader. In fact, it got S.P. Singh, then editor of *Navbharat Times* and an astute political commentator, to write a column 'Poli-Talk' in *The Economic Times*. Talk about pushing the boundaries! Political columnists like Tavleen Singh were roped in. N. Ram of *The Hindu* contributed regularly.

Through another smart move, the paper was able to attract a completely different profile of readers. This smart move was upgrading the stock pages of the newspaper. The stock markets had yet to evolve into modern, regulated entities with sound processes. They were controlled in a perverse way, with the controller of capital issues even approving the price at which a public issue could be offered.

Full-fledged reforms and regulation in the stock exchanges would come a few years hence. But the late 1980s saw a surge in interest in equity among small investors. On the one hand, the markets had boomed on the back of select economic reforms. At the same time, the emergence of Reliance Industries, which relied on small investors, increased participation in the stock markets.

Awake to this change, *ET* completely redesigned its stock pages. In the era before business channels and the Internet, investors relied on newspapers the following morning for the latest stock prices. As participation in the equity market grew, the interest in the stock pages went up. Customers with a completely new profile started to buy *The Economic Times* only for its stock pages.

The suggestion to strengthen the stock pages came from Satish Mehta, BCCL's then marketing director. The coverage of stock prices was made more comprehensive. The listed price of all companies was carried on the pages, gauging that many of the small retail investors would be interested in the smaller stocks.

Several relevant sections were added to spruce up the value from these pages. The paper began to list stocks with the highest turnover, or ones that had shown the highest growth or loss during the previous day. All this was available to readers at a glance, and it was worth their while for traders and small investors to buy the paper as a reference for their stock market actions.

There was a 360-degree approach to revamping the paper. While content had gone in for a complete makeover, it was complemented with changes in the look and feel of the paper. All the matter was laid out in fresh new fonts and reader-friendly designs.

The paper was divided into different sections, with each page having its distinct character and focus. It started to pay attention to details like enhancing the visual impact through pictures and blurbs. The writing style was interactive and lively. Under the new *ET* format, stories were written elaborately, informatively and tightly.

At that time, it was normal for newspapers to use filler news items here and there. These would be small, inconsequential bits and pieces. There was no attention to standardization, and pages would look radically different each day depending on the news flow. On days when the news flow was light, many pages would be a mishmash of items, big and small, without any symmetry or character.

In *ET*, care was taken to ensure that nothing redundant or irrelevant was carried on the pages with the idea of just filling up space. It required a certain discipline on the part of journalists and the news desk to adhere to the rules of layout. Reports and articles had to stick to a word limit so that all the items on a page came together to impart a clean and ordered look. The paper also experimented regularly with headlines, using clever turns of phrase. There was energy and excitement on the pages of what had been a bland and boring fact sheet of a newspaper.

Providing the finish to all this was a change in the colour of the newspaper. From the conventional white, it switched to a tasteful salmon pink in 1989-90. This idea was probably borrowed from *Financial Times*, London, which had switched to pink during the Great Depression in Europe to reassure readers that business would soon be in the pink. That colour came to be associated with business papers. Now, *The Economic Times* was able to proclaim itself as the first Indian paper to go pink.

This gave it a certain novelty and exclusivity in the Indian market. This had never been done before. And this new *ET* found many takers. 'Going colour was a great move at the *ET*. It was a novel attempt. The Indian reader and the advertiser had never seen a pink paper in India before. And that attracted a lot of subscribers,' noted N.P. Singh. 'Pink looked good under the armpit. It gave people a badge of honour of sorts,' he added.

This happened rather cheekily. Around 1990, the Ambanis, a business family growing in clout and importance, were set to enter the media business with the *Business and Political Observer*[4] (the original 'BPO' of another generation!). One of the features of the high-profile product would be that it would come in pink. There was also a rumour that *Financial Times*, London, would be launched in India. In 1993, Times Publishing House (TPH) registered the 'Financial Times' title with the registrar of newspapers for India (RNI) under the Press and Registration of Books Act (PRB Act), thereby owning this title in the country. Chances of the Financial Times Limited publishing an edition of the UK-based *FT* in India were stalled.

Although pink newsprint cost an extra $25 per tonne at that time, the company decided to go in for the 'pink edge'. Even as the launch of *BPO* was being contemplated (*BPO*'s gestation took too long and the project was delayed), BCCL went ahead and launched *The Economic Times* in pink. To start with, a four-page mini-issue was circulated in pink with the Bombay edition of *The Times of India*. Many of the changes in *ET* may have been modelled on the *Financial Times*, London. But the team had the bandwidth and capability to see them through here. It was practically the rebirth of the paper. Incidentally, *BPO* had had a similar agenda. It was to be a forty-page newspaper with highly specialized sections, pages and segments. And it was to be pink.

The content makeover of *The Economic Times* went in tandem with profound changes in Indian economy and society. The early estimates of the 'Indian Middle Class' may have been exaggerated. But this category of population was growing fast in the late 1980s. Although government finances were in the dock, a wave of consumerism had been unleashed. Private enterprise had started to emerge. The consumer goods sector was no longer the pariah it once used to be. There were some initiatives towards relaxing imports. By the end of that decade and by the beginning of the 1990s, the country and its social class was in the middle of a palpable transition.

The consumer boom had taken off post-1986. The multinationals were in with their 'exotic' brands. Fancy products, attractive labels and hitherto unknown gadgets and services were being introduced into the Indian market. In general, profit was less and less a bad word. The country was on the threshold of a satellite television revolution. There was a marked openness to computers and technology. The political discourse may have been dominated by caste and communal issues. But there was another enclave that was modern, positive and looking to prepare for the twenty-first century.

Business publications were in fashion. *Business India* had been the pioneer in this segment and it continued to rule, though *Business Today* posed a challenge. In the newspaper space, the Ambanis' decision to launch *BPO* created a flutter. They justified the hype with high-profile recruitments and premium salaries. Insiders believe that the aggression and speed demonstrated by BCCL in revamping *ET* was prompted partly by the impending threat from *BPO*. But the Ambanis seem not to have got their act together in time, and it turned out to be a damp squib.

At the time the consumer boom was unfolding, *The Economic Times* had attained a sizeable presence. But being a business paper, still catering to a niche audience, it was not top of mind for advertisers. Television had become visible post-1982, when it went colour just before the Asian Games. But this was much before satellite television and print was very much the reigning medium as far as advertisers were concerned. In the late 1980s, about 75 per cent of the total advertising expenditure would go to print. Radio and cinema would together get about 10 per cent. Outdoor advertising such as hoardings received another 10 per cent. The remaining 5 per cent went to television.

Companies in fast moving consumer goods would go in for magazines and fortnightlies for their product launches. Television would get some allocation from advertisers owing to its audio-visual effect and to reinforce the print campaigns. The top ten advertiser companies used a combination of dailies and magazines and television. But print was on top of their priority list.

However, *The Economic Times* was not on that list. During those days, if media planners thought of undertaking an advertising campaign in Delhi, they would go for *Hindustan Times*, *The Times of India*, *India Today* and *Business India*. They would also consider buying space in a Hindi paper. But they were not really looking at *The Economic Times*. While the demand for advertising space was going up and advertisers were willing to pay more, *ET* did not have any notable share of the spoils. It was here that the move to launch supplements proved vital.

Besides the far-reaching changes in content, *The Economic Times* made supplement reading a great success and a veritable pleasure. Each supplement was launched to cater to a specific market segment. The quality of the paper used for these supplements was superior. The pull-outs were glossy, trendy and stylish and their content and language, gripping and engaging.

The first feature section to be launched was 'Corporate Dossier' on Fridays. Initially, it was a one-page pull-out with articles on corporate strategy, management and best practices. But the first big thing that happened in the supplements' space was 'ET Esquire'. This was meant to be the Saturday section of the newspaper.

The company realized that for *ET* to be attractive to advertisers, it had to address two major handicaps. It was read in the office, not subscribed to at home. And it was read primarily by men. ET Esquire and the supplements that followed sought to overcome these handicaps.

Samir Jain decided to go in for colour. If newspapers abroad could be in colour, why not *The Economic Times,* he reasoned. Underlying this initiative was that colour advertising was going away to television and magazines.

Said Paran Balakrishnan, ET Esquire's first editor: 'The Saturday section was aimed at expanding the reach of the paper. Before this, *ET* only went to offices. Nearly 70–80 per cent was delivered there. People did not buy and read it very much. It was also felt that the paper ought to have a stronger Saturday section.

'*ET* was also primarily a paper read by men and we wanted to encourage women to begin reading it,' he added.[5] So, ET Esquire was begun as a four-page supplement. Samir Jain insisted that the supplement be printed on art paper. The editorial cadre obviously liked that, but was unsure whether the management would stick to this decision to use art paper for good. It did not want to face a situation later when this paper would be withdrawn from use and the supplement printed on regular paper. That happened some years down the line when using art paper became very expensive, but by then the supplement culture had taken root.

ET Esquire was introduced to a pleasantly surprised readership in August 1989. This was a supplement of lifestyle stories, aimed at the well-to-do professionals, businessman and upper-middle corporate executives. It contained material that could be read at leisure over the weekend, and interest the family as well.

Significantly, it started with a 50:50 ad:edit ratio, which meant equal space to articles and advertisements. Until then, newspapers generally devoted more space to editorial matter. ET Esquire's first lead story was about clubs in Delhi. A later issue had a story on expatriates living in the city. Its approach was fresh and invigorating.

This was also a novel way of bringing newer and fresher subjects, complementing the overall approach that *ET* had adopted towards content. There were columns on sports, which was unusual for a business paper. Here again, conventional subjects were approached in a manner that would suit the taste of the reader.

'We invited Rishi Narain to write for us on golf; Michael Ferreira wrote on billiards. There was a design column and a travel column, which was run every alternate week. There were stories inside, and the fourth page was reserved for book extracts and book reviews,' Balakrishnan recalled.

ET Esquire was received well. From the advertising point of view, it was a winner practically from the start. Glossy paper in colour, tastefully done, premium feel and designed to hold the attention of the consuming classes – the combination was irresistible. It was pitched to advertisers as an alternative to magazines. And within a few months, it began making money.

In fact, Balakrishnan remembers that 'it made a lot of money in the first year itself.' The editorial and the marketing teams worked together and not against each other to achieve a certain target. While the editorial team concentrated on upgrading content in the paper to make it appealing to a wider readership and expand its base, the marketing and advertising teams thought of ways to improve sales.

'Incidentally, the marketing department at the group had first objected to the supplement coming out on Saturdays. They had based their argument on some ORG survey that had then been done in Jaipur, which had indicated that no one read the paper on Saturdays as there were no stock pages on those days. They later turned around and said after a few years that Saturday was a better day as people had more disposable time to read during the weekends,' he noted with a chuckle.

The success of ET Esquire set the ball rolling for more such supplements to be introduced into the market. Brand Equity, another supplement, which was launched soon after became a bigger marketing success. It was to be an editorial product with authentic articles on developments in the advertising and marketing space. Of course, it would also have a strong market orientation with an eye on the advertiser. *A&M*, the magazine launched by Srikant Khandekar, had done quite well for itself by devoting its attention to marketing and advertising.

While advertising and marketing were growing in the country alongside the consumer boom and merited a stand-alone supplement, there was also a tactical reason for this move. Advertising agencies were powerful. In any media plan, advertisers relied on their agencies to decide which publication ought to get how much of the ad budget. It made business sense to keep them in good humour. While BCCL had overruled the advertising agencies and increased rates unilaterally, it was also taking care of them by dedicating an entire supplement to their interviews and campaigns.

But there was another, perhaps more important, factor that led to Brand Equity. With the success of Saturday Times as a supplement for *The Times of India*, Samir Jain was probably convinced that supplements were the way to go.

Brand Equity was to be sectionalized and was initially a two-page colour pull-out; soon after, two more pages were added to it. This supplement was structured to focus on four areas – advertising, marketing, media and research. The name first suggested for it was 'Market Pulse'. It was meant to be an editorial-driven product. The journalists at *ET* liked the idea and work began in real earnest towards its launch.

Sanjoy Narayan, who went on to edit *Business Today* before becoming the editor-in-chief of the *Hindustan Times*, was Brand Equity's first editor. He was in Bombay working with *Business World*. He had just completed a year. Before that, he had worked at *ET* in Calcutta for six years. When T.N. Ninan contacted him, asking whether he would like to join the team, Narayan agreed.

'Ninan had this aura around him. When he invited you to join his team, it felt great and you could just not say no. Besides, he had already brought together a great team for the paper. And it seemed as if great things were about to happen there,' said a former Brand Equity team member. Anand P. Raman was features editor. P.G. Mathai was *ET*'s resident editor in Delhi. T.C.A. Srinivas Raghavan and A.K. Bhattacharya had also joined the team. Sadanand Menon was editor of the Artsscape and Design pages.

Narayan had two people working on Brand Equity with him – Aditi Chatterjee and M. Shankar. In Bombay, the section was headed by Nandini Laxman, who worked at Rediffusion and then with *Business Standard* Weekend. And Jyoti Mani Thapa was to design the product.

Dummies of the supplement were made. Everything was put together for the launch, including the masthead, and the team was waiting to release the edition slated for the first week of September 1990, a Wednesday, when there was a call from Bombay. It was Ninan. He was told that everything was ready with the supplement and that page 1 was going. Ninan asked Narayan to 'hold everything'. He had been in a meeting with Samir Jain in Bombay. Jain wanted a change in the supplement's name. It was to be called Brand Equity instead of Market Pulse.

A new masthead was to be made. The art department got back to work. The journalists' team saw the attention to detail that the management was devoting to these supplements. They also looked up the meaning of the words – Brand, Brand Worth and Brand Equity.

Within a week after the change of name, Brand Equity was launched on a Wednesday in September. The paper used for this supplement was cream in colour. Samir Jain felt strongly about using colour in his publications. He did not want the colour to be heavy. Rather, he wanted it to be visually pleasing and different from other supplements to give Brand Equity an edge.

For the first time, hype was created around the launch of a

supplement. There were hoardings in the city announcing that such a pull-out was on its way. The supplement's first lead story was on Pepsi Foods and on Cheetos, a pure business story. The piece had a nit-picking kind of approach. It asked – has Pepsi got its strategy right. This has now become the standard approach. One questions all the time nowadays. It was not so direct and bold then.

For all its emphasis on advertising, Brand Equity was an editorial-driven product. It was a pioneering effort. It had qualitatively exhaustive stuff with lots of facts and did not initially look at the advertising world. There was no pressure on journalists to do any specific stories. There were suggestions from Ninan about write-ups but no direct orders/commands from the management. Ninan managed everything. He was in touch with the owners and with his team.

Incidentally, Brand Equity, for all the effort and hype surrounding it, did not do very well initially because the advertising rates on its pages were high and the market was not willing to pay so much. Subsequently, the rates were lowered and that is when things began really moving. In fact, ironically, the ads began moving slowly from ET Esquire to Brand Equity, and the former was shut down, to be relaunched later.

This is typical of The Times Group. It could come up with a product, launch it with hype and push it aggressively. Subsequently, if the venture stopped making money for the company, it would be withdrawn. This was done with *The Independent* and with Saturday Times. The Times Group is unsentimental and ruthlessly business-like when it comes to the profitability of its products.

To go back to Brand Equity and *ET*, this supplement may not have found early success also because *The Times* may have underestimated the loyalty of business readers to *Business India*. Vibha Desai said, '*Business India* and *Business Today* were already fighting it out for the marketing and corporate segment. When Brand Equity joined the race, it did not calculate that it would be pitted against them as well. It was not a runaway success until

BCCL decided to scale down its ad rates. That was one sure way of ensuring that this section began looking attractive.'

Eventually, Brand Equity became a grand success. Besides attracting advertising, it would be used as an important lever in the company's bold experiment on newspaper pricing.

As the changes in *ET* began getting noticed, its profile started improving. The average daily sales of the paper in 1990 had crossed 100,000. It now had five editions, with the fifth one launched in Ahmedabad that year. Bombay was the leading centre with a circulation close to 40,000. But Delhi too was doing well at about 33,000. Calcutta contributed about 14,000 while Bangalore did a little less than 12,000 copies.

There were also some brand-building initiatives. After celebrating *The Economic Times*' twenty-fifth anniversary in 1986, BCCL followed it up with the thirtieth anniversary celebrations in 1991. Besides supporting the changes in *ET*'s content, Samir Jain had tried to boost the paper's fortunes by making it part of Mastermind. To that extent, it was working on course. Yet it was felt that *The Economic Times* had far greater potential. This time, the potential was sought to be realized by playing on the cover price of the newspaper.

This was a significant first step. Until now, the company had refrained from using the cover price of the paper to impact the bottom line. Its efforts were directed mainly at the pricing of space. The changes in its editorial product and price innovations like Mastermind were meant to enhance the value of advertising space in the paper. The cover price had not figured in any strategy.

The appetite for business news was clearly growing. In particular, there was a shift in the attitude of a section of the English readership. Readers were showing a keen interest in being updated on financial news. Their awareness of business and economic conditions had increased. The stock market had become buoyant. And there was more disposable income among the middle- and upper-class segments in the country.

BCCL had also noticed that in keeping with this change, publishing houses across the board had launched separate business sections in their publications. Some had even come up with new products. The hunger for business news and financial analysis on stocks and shares was growing.

Under Ninan's editorship, the paper had already been largely upgraded. It had enlarged its news coverage. It had improved its presentation of stock market data. Its economic features had become more qualitative and analytical. And it was evident that it had laid special emphasis on bringing out its supplements. As a result, its circulation was moving north through 1991 and it seemed as if it would continue to go that way for a while.

Samir Jain felt he could recover more from the reader. BCCL's marketing director, Satish Mehta, played a crucial role here by working up the strategy. The company made its first move by hiking the cover price of *The Economic Times* from Rs 1.80 to Rs 2.50. Thereafter, just as it had done with advertising rates, it continued to hike the cover price almost every six months. The price would be hiked by fifty paise to a rupee each time.

By 1991, the price of *ET* had gone up to Rs 5.50 in Bombay. The purpose of the hikes was not just to recover the increased cost of the paper, but also to position it as a premium brand over competitors. Surprisingly, sales of the paper went up from nearly 100,000 copies in 1990 to 120,000 copies in the second half of 1991, the period when the prices were being hiked. During January–June 1992 period, of course, sales had increased to 160,000 copies.

Samir Jain thought he could slowly take the cover price of *ET* to Rs 10 because he had decided that Rs 10 was the right price for the paper. However, *ET*'s cover price stabilized finally at a princely Rs 5.

'At that price, when we announced it, there was a sensation,' recalled N.P. Singh. 'There was no paper at that price in India then and *ET* was charging that price every day of the week. So, suddenly a paper that had cost Rs 40–50 a month began costing Rs 150. It was a huge hike. But again, that built up people's aspirational levels. They said a paper at that price must be really good,' he added.

The company felt that a higher cover price for *The Economic Times* could be absorbed because buyers rarely paid for it from their own pocket. 'Many people continued to read *ET* because their companies paid the cost of the paper,' said Singh. 'Yet others would borrow or steal a copy.' *ET* had a sizeable subscription base among those in government, the bureaucracy and the corporate sector. They had no problems shelling out more from the official account.

Having gone that far, the company now decided to reverse course. It chose to drop the price of the paper, but only for one day of the week. There is an interesting story on how this came about. One morning, Samir Jain told Satish Mehta that he had seen long queues outside the Zoo in Calcutta on Mondays because entry was free on that day. He is believed to have asked Mehta whether the combination of zero price and high consumer interest could be applied to the newspaper business as well. Mehta went on to put together a plan for 'high quality, low price'.

The reaction of senior managers in Bombay was gauged. Most of them found it too risky and unrealistic. Hence, it was decided to use the Delhi market to test the experiment. The logic behind the move was that the number of people interested in business and economic news was growing rapidly. Through change in content and design, *ET* and the rival dailies that followed its trail, had been able to kindle interest among new sets of readers who had so far kept away from economic and business papers.

Priced at Rs 5, *The Economic Times* had become aspirational. A large section of potential readers desired it but were unable to afford it. The National Readership Survey data showed that *ET*'s readership per copy was five as against the 3.3 for general newspapers. This meant that there was a latent set of readers who were reading the paper at work, but perhaps unwilling to pay Rs 5 for it.

There was also a mindset issue: the practice was for families to subscribe to a general newspaper at home while the business daily like *The Economic Times* was meant to be read at the office. This mindset had to be changed. The potential readers had to be given a taste of the paper by making it affordable on one day of the week.

There was no fixed method to decide what the price ought to be. There were three options: Rs 2, Rs 2.50 and Rs 3. Finally, it was decided to offer *ET* at an 'invitation price' of Rs 2 on Wednesdays. The term was coined by Satish Mehta.

This was not going to be easy to implement. First, of course, there had to be a large enough number of new buyers who would see value for money at two rupees. Without that, the paper would merely end up losing revenue on Wednesdays. Besides, there was bound to be uneven demand for the paper during the week. The production and finance teams had to be brought on board.

The biggest hitch, of course, was convincing the hawkers who distributed the paper. In addition to uneven demand, they ran the risk of losing commissions which are normally linked to the cover price of the paper. 'The entire concept was quite maverick and had to be explained in detail for acceptance,' said Mehta, about the invitation price process.

The company addressed this concern by simultaneously revising the price of the paper on others days of the week from Rs 4.50 (the price of *ET* Delhi at that time) to Rs 4.90. The assumption was that with the corporate sector and government being major subscribers, they would continue to buy at the higher price. That would compensate the hawkers for any loss in commission on Wednesdays.

In deciding the cover price, both for Wednesdays as well as for other days, all other considerations had to be balanced as well. For one, after all the cover price modifications, the total monthly bill of the paper would have to remain unchanged. This was to ensure that corporate and government buyers would be in a position to buy the paper without a hitch.

Further, the invitation price had to be less than half of the weekday price. It was assessed that at that level, it became attractive for new buyers. It also had to be less than half the normal price of comparable brands. That was necessary to pull new readers including those subscribing on personal account.

At the same time, the company had to ensure that at the invitation price, the paper should cost the vendor at least twenty paise more than its scrap value. Without that, vendors would make money from procuring huge numbers of the paper and disposing them as scrap, creating a 'non-reader hump' in the circulation.

The next point to be decided was the day of the week when the invitation price would be offered. The company decided that they should offer the lower price on the day the paper was perceived to be at its best. The choice was between Monday, when *ET* came with Investors Guide, Saturday, when it came with ET Esquire and Wednesday, when Brand Equity was offered as a supplement. Wednesday was chosen as the day for the invitation price as it was perceived that the paper was at its best on that day. It would have a higher appeal among the new buyers, persuading them to subscribe on other days of the week as well.

Besides, Samir Jain wanted more and more people in the advertising and marketing fraternity to read *The Economic Times* and also savour Brand Equity. Wednesday was the obvious choice for offering the paper at an attractive price. At the same time, advertisement rates in the paper were raised by 15 per cent on Wednesday, on the ground that circulation would be much higher.

The invitation price was launched on 1 March 1992, barely two years after BCCL had started hiking the cover price. The response was euphoric among readers. 'It was like opening a small door to a hungry crowd,' pointed out Singh. 'What a fantastic and clever idea! What a manoeuvre in the dynamics of the market and consumer behaviour! How you could buy it...but only once a week! How unaffordable and thereby so very attractive,' he exulted.

Persuading the new buyers was not much of a challenge. Besides the quality of the paper, it was a perception game. 'Nobody ever said that we are not getting value for money because they felt that its real price ought to be Rs 5. Readers were grateful to get it at Rs 2,' Singh believed.

The distributors, after initial reluctance, came around to the new arrangement. Trade earned huge margins on the higher price of Rs 4.90 during other days (and later, on the weekend price of Rs 10). They had a 25–30 per cent commission. Eventually, it was a win-win situation for everyone.

As the differential pricing had initially been applied only to the Delhi edition of *The Economic Times*, it was rolled out in the other cities only after assessing its success. Within six weeks of its launch, sales of *ET*, Delhi, moved up from 51,000 copies to 87,000 copies on Wednesdays. The highest purchase order for the *ET* that year was 93,700 copies on 22 April, a Wednesday. What's more, the sample offer on Wednesdays led some of the new readers to become regular subscribers of the paper. The circulation in Delhi on other days of the week also climbed from about 50,000 copies to 60,000.

Clearly, the invitation price had made the desired impact. In fact, the results in Delhi had been stupendous. For the Calcutta edition, the group went a step further. The invitation price would apply for two days in a week – Mondays and Wednesdays. This was a 'double header'. This too worked.

Across all markets, there was a positive reaction. The sales of *The Economic Times* in Bombay went up from 58,200 copies before May 1992 to 76,000 copies by 10 June 1992. In Ahmedabad, it rose from 9,500 copies to 13,000 copies barely six weeks after launch. By 24 June, it had touched 13,500. In Bangalore, the *ET* used to sell on an average 19,500 copies on Wednesdays, prior to the introduction of invitation pricing. A month after the invitation price was introduced, *ET*'s sales touched 27,000 copies on 22 June. Similarly, in Calcutta, where average Wednesday sales were 31,800 copies before 1 May, they went up to 36,700 on 3 June

(Monday) and up to 40,500 on 22 June (Wednesday). 'We had made a breakthrough,' Satish Mehta asserted.

By all accounts, the *ET* experiment is unmatched in newspaper publishing for its sheer novelty, finesse in execution and the scale of its impact. The Times Group first worked on the product to make it premium and relevant. Thereafter it increased prices to impart a measure of aspirational value to the brand. Finally, it surprised the market by offering a window to a wider section of customers by lowering the price on select days of the week.

Circulation first jumped by over one lakh copies on the days when the invitation price was offered. The group then started pricing the paper cleverly on other days as well. From November 1993, the invitation price was extended to alternate weekdays – Mondays, Wednesdays and Fridays. The idea was that readers would find it difficult to ask their hawker to remember to drop the paper only on alternate days. With this, they would rather buy the paper on all days of the week.

As the next step, by March 1994, the paper was priced at Rs 2.00 from Monday to Friday. The price of the weekend editions was hiked to Rs 10. Incidentally, this was the premium that Samir Jain had always sought for the paper.

As a result of such strategies, the circulation of *ET* grew from 190,000 to 290,000, a growth of about 53 per cent, in six months. This was the highest growth recorded in the history of *The Economic Times* until then. By the end of 1994, *ET* was selling around 360,000 copies. Increased volumes for the newspaper began leading to specific gains in advertising revenue and also enhancing the strategic corporate strength.

*The Economic Times*' cause was helped a great deal by disruptive changes in the external environment. In the latter half of 1991, the Indian government was on the brink of default and went in for big-ticket economic reforms. These reforms, by drastically reducing the role of the government, encouraging private enterprise and welcoming foreign investment, had implications far beyond the economy. While politics continued to be important, economics started to occupy centre stage of public discourse, at least in urban areas.

*The Economic Times*, perhaps more than other business newspapers, could capture this opportunity. It addressed people's curiosity about economic and business issues by presenting facts and perspectives shorn of jargon. It made economic news accessible to a larger audience. The invitation price coincided with this sudden spurt in middle-class India's curiosity for economic and financial issues.

The boom in stock markets, followed by scams, and a general openness to economic reform, may have catalysed the success of the invitation price experiment. Yet again, the company seemed to have its finger on the pulse of the newspaper market.

Two months after the launch of invitation pricing, T.N. Ninan, the man instrumental for having built up the product, quit. Swaminathan S. Anklesaria Aiyer took over from him in May 1992.

Ninan's colleagues and teammates accord the master a grand salute. They concede that the *ET* makeover was entirely his doing. 'One must see the total transformation that Ninan brought about at *ET*. This was not just in modernization and in technology; he changed the profile of its employees and their mindset. He improved *ET*'s network and laid the foundations of *ET*'s future successes,' said Paran Balakrishnan.

'Look at how much *ET* improved between the time Ninan joined in 1987 and when he left four-and-a-half years later,' he added. *The Economic Times* was a Rs 15 crore brand when T.N. Ninan came in. It had become a Rs 100 crore brand by the time he left.

EIGHT

# DELHI...NOW!

HAVING A STRONG CITADEL in Bombay was one thing but cracking a tough, new market in an adopted city another. For Samir Jain, Delhi was indeed that. This was a city that thrived on a generous dose of politics and power play; its lexicon sprinkled liberally with words such as *chai-paani, chaltaa hai* and *jugaad;* a city of bureaucrats and administrators; the land of the post-Partition refugee, the petty trader and the migrant worker who could cut myriad corners, to survive. The *Hindustan Times* (*HT*) had a solid grip on this city.

Taking it on became Samir Jain's most formidable external challenge. In the mid-1980s, *The Times of India* was a much smaller paper compared to the *HT* in Delhi. While the latter had a circulation of 2.5 lakh copies, the Delhi edition of *TOI* managed just about one lakh copies a day.

*HT*'s dominance of the market was complete. In the eyes of Delhi, *The Times of India* was the 'Bombaywala' newspaper. *HT*, on the other hand, was ingrained in the ethos of middle-class Delhi. It had Congress leanings. It had a huge constituency in the form of local traders and shopkeepers. The paper was in complete sync with the preferences of its readership. Its language was one which its readers understood and identified with. Almost by instinct, it covered issues that were close to their heart. Its presentation and layout, though bland and unimaginative, was one they had grown up with. There was a close fit born out of years of association. *HT* was a habit.

Talking about what he termed the 'pre–Samir Jain' period, Baljit Kapoor recalled, 'At the Delhi office, the target was: "How do we overtake *HT*?"' *The Times* had tried to increase its circulation by attracting new readers because old-timers continued to subscribe to *HT*. It devised a Personal Contact Campaign (PCC) and allowed readers to sample its product. It supplied them with free copies for a week and when they were keen to shift, it offered them complimentary copies for thirty days. Every device had been tested and tried.

*HT* had no pretensions of offering cutting-edge news content. Its leadership in the Delhi market came mainly from its advertisements. A large section of its readers, particularly the traders and shopkeepers, bought the paper primarily for the advertisements it carried. The paper had far more advertisements than any other newspaper in the city could hope to offer, across a range of subjects that none could match. It did especially well in retail and individual ads, besides the usual government notices and corporate spreads. *HT* was ensconced in its own virtuous cycle: more ads offered readers more opportunity to strike deals, which generated more readers and which in turn made it more attractive for advertisers.

The paper had been the leader in Delhi for almost three decades. A degree of complacency and laid-back attitude was inevitable, both in its advertising team as well as the editorial. The paper often found itself short of space to accommodate the regular flow of advertisements. In this situation, it was hard not to be arrogant. While there were papers other than *TOI* available in Delhi, no one came close to being *HT*'s competitor.

Owned by the venerable Birla family, *HT* was part of the 'jute press' like *TOI*. The fact that rival newspapers at the time operated like a friendly club (they were contemporaries, not rivals) and rarely threatened one another's position made *HT* practically unassailable. It was in a position to charge a significant premium for space from advertisers.

Samir Jain's focus, from the start, had been on making BCCL more profitable. The thrust, therefore, was on obtaining more returns from the flagship edition in Bombay. He was doing that successfully through innovations in pricing of space. He had also leveraged the Bombay edition to improve the fortunes of his other editions, by linking them up through Mastermind. But at some point, he would have to battle it out in Delhi.

To be sure, Delhi was always on his mind. His move to offer a combo of *Navbharat Times* and *TOI* to advertisers in Delhi was a way to wean them away from *HT*. Mastermind had also helped in that endeavour; a Delhi-Bombay space combo of *The Times of India* had become attractive for the Delhi advertiser. But the rates for *TOI*, Delhi, were still well below those of *HT*.

Samir Jain's argument that value was not necessarily linked to circulation and that advertisers ought to pay for the former rather than the latter was a psychological offensive against *HT* Delhi. His emphasis on 'relevant market share', against the sheer number of subscribers, was meant to downplay the importance of circulation, an area where *HT*, Delhi, was way ahead of the pack. But after all that, it was now time for Samir Jain to fight on the circulation front against *HT* in Delhi.

It was not going to be easy. *TOI* had been trying to compete with *HT* even before Samir Jain came on the scene. It had introduced a large number of pages for matrimonial and classified advertisements. It had also brought out a few supplements. But none of that had worked.

*HT* enjoyed tremendous mind space among readers of English dailies in Delhi. To dent its position meant first getting noticed as a brand. For that, Samir Jain had to undertake multiple initiatives that would create excitement in the market and compel people to sit up and take notice of a paper other than *HT*. In attracting the attention of the Delhi readers, it was important that Samir Jain build a distinct image for his paper. His could not be another *HT*. That would have meant that the market would remain in inertia.

Before embarking on any changes in the product or the rate deals, Samir Jain decided to fight the battle of perception. He decided to seed the idea among advertisers and readers that his paper was positively distinct from *HT*. His pitch was that his paper was a 'premium product'. While the *HT* catered to the trader and shop keeper classes, *TOI* was supposed to be for the yuppies and the professional. That is what he sought to convey. He did back it up with concrete changes in the product. But the battle in the mind had begun much before that.

He was helped by the fact that during the early to mid 1980s, several professionals from the marketing and advertising fields had moved from Bombay to Delhi. They had been used to reading *TOI* in Bombay. In Delhi, they continued to patronize the same paper.

Besides being an articulate section, they were also the ones who decided the media plans for companies. They assumed that if they were reading this paper, their kind of people in Delhi would be reading it as well. In designing their media plan, they were looking for a paper to access the elite in Delhi. *TOI* appeared to be a natural choice over *HT*. A premium position for *TOI*, claimed by Samir Jain, came to be accepted.

'In taking this route of a premium positioning, Samir Jain understood the weaknesses of the advertising industry as well as that of the *HT*,' pointed out Bashab Sarkar, who was then with O&M. A premium position was something the *HT* could never lay claim to. Its mass appeal was its strength and it was content to remain in that slot. Even if it chose to, it did not have the speed, flexibility or orientation to transform itself and vie for a premium space.

As for the advertising fraternity, Samir Jain understood them perfectly. 'They had a frog-in-the-well kind of approach, these media planners,' Sarkar said. Samir Jain knew what exactly they were looking for from a newspaper in Delhi and strove to create that product. 'Therefore, you see his emphasis towards product upgradation from a marketing and advertising perspective,' he pointed out. 'This helped boost the *TOI* position in Delhi immensely.'

Samir Jain brought gloss and colour into his publications. The paper also began giving a lot of coverage to celebrities. It also featured the advertising and marketing world and the people who mattered in these sectors, prominently on its pages. And yes, it did begin to look different from the other newspapers that existed in the city during those years. It created 'premiumness' around itself, and this gold dust, which is so essential in media planning and marketing, clicked for it.

That provided an initial momentum to the newspaper. Thereafter, Samir Jain used multiple routes to attack *HT*. Realizing that *HT* had a loyal readership in Delhi and that it is generally difficult to get people to switch newspapers, he began by entering markets around Delhi across north India. That required stronger distribution, investment in facilities and tighter deadlines. But it enabled him to get a foothold in the region.

Next, he could see that higher advertising was boosting the circulation of *HT*. It was clear that *TOI* needed more and more ads. Not for the revenue that these ads would bring, but for the additional readership that they would attract. So he went the whole hog trying to attract more advertisements.

He created new supplements which made his paper attractive for readers as well as advertisers. Bringing in new kinds of content, different from the traditional 'news', had the same effect. He also priced space strategically – nominal rates at first to attract advertisers and hiking them once he reached critical mass. Advertising content was stepped up at the cost of rival papers and also by attracting fresh advertisers.

One of the most effective routes was the launch of a slew of supplements. These were built around specific themes like job appointments, education and local lifestyle and leisure. These supplements, with reasonably good content, proved to be a major draw among advertisers in these specific areas. They could now get a focused audience for their ads. The ad rates in these supplements were, in many cases, lower than for the main paper. *The Times of India* became far more attractive for these advertisers in Delhi.

Samir Jain's most decisive blow against *HT* was a sharp reduction in the cover price of the newspaper. The lower price, along with growing nuclear families and other changing demographics, helped expand the market and eventually enabled *TOI* to narrow the gap with its rival.

At a more fundamental level, this was a battle between a hungry, energetic innovation machine and a laid-back, conservative and somewhat conceited market leader. Not only did *TOI* narrow the circulation gap with the leader, it also induced *HT* to transform and reinvent itself, thereby changing the newspaper landscape in Delhi.

Samir Jain played the role of the challenger to the hilt. He was constantly trying to shake up the market, come up with something new and exciting and instigating stuff that would get his paper noticed. The 'Humpty Tumpty' controversy between the two papers, which broke out in early 1988, was a sign of things to come.

*HT* had circulated a letter on 31 January 1988 informing readers and advertisers that due to a rise in newsprint cost, it was hiking its advertisement rates from April that year. It had also said that although it had to stop printing some pages of some of its supplements, it would continue to print a twenty-page newspaper and sometimes a twenty-four-page paper.

But on 7 and 8 April 1988, *HT* published a sixteen-page paper instead of a twenty-page paper. Cause for concern? Samir Jain thought so. *HT*'s letter and the fact that it did not print the scheduled number of pages on two consecutive days were discussed at the Times House by its senior management. Strong opinions were expressed. Baljit Kapoor was one who resisted the idea of taking *HT* head on. Kapoor owed allegiance to that section of the newspaper industry which supported moderation and restraint in the business. Yet others like marketing director Satish Mehta, the former ITC marketing chief with the killer instinct, went along with Samir Jain. Following the discussions, it was decided that the *TOI* would pull up *HT* for its 'lapse'.

A cartoon was designed and carried on page 3 of *TOI*, Delhi, on 8 and 9 April. It showed an egg-shaped character, Humpty Dumpty (from the popular nursery rhyme) taking a mighty fall from a high wall. There was also a graph line that indicated that Humpty's fall had been great and precipitous. The report was labelled 'TOI-Ad News' and carried a caption in bold print. It read: 'Humpty Tumpty has a great fall.' Humpty Tumpty was an allusion to *HT* – *Hindustan Times*. The pun was fully intended.

After the cartoon appeared, all hell broke loose at *HT*. Its management was livid. Tongue-in-cheek advertising is common today in the age of the cola, telecom, airlines and FMCG wars. But that was not the case in the 1980s in the Indian media. *TOI*'s behaviour seemed unprecedented. This was not how counterparts behaved with each other. They had always maintained a facade of civility. Therefore, 'Humpty Tumpty' became a flashpoint.

Samir Jain had brought the latent war between *TOI* and *HT* into the open. He had used his newspaper to caricaturize *HT* and that evoked strong reactions from within and outside the media. *HT* took the matter up seriously. It demanded that *TOI* apologize to it 'unconditionally within a week' on its front page. Failing this, it warned, it would take the matter to the Press Council of India. *TOI* did not react to this threat. Perhaps it did not care. Perhaps this is what it wanted. It had sounded the bugle loud and clear and was in combat mode.

*HT* took the matter to the Press Council. The papers crossed swords. Two distinguished lawyers – Mr Asoke Sen for *HT* and Dr L.M. Singhvi for *TOI* – took the field in a keenly watched battle of wits. It was important for both newspapers to win. They had egos to massage. And then, there was the image factor and the readers' perception of their papers. Also, the entire advertising-marketing industry was watching their every move.

Both the papers contested their respective cases with aplomb. *HT*'s case was straightforward. Their counsel maintained that the *The Times of India* cartoon violated the accepted standards of journalistic conduct and ethics and was against good public taste. He further said that the cartoon was clearly meant to ridicule *HT* and lower its image and credibility in the eyes of its constituents and the general public. He added that the cartoon was defamatory in character and that *TOI* had not made any bona fide enquiries from *HT* asking as to why it had been unable to bring out twenty-page editions before coming out with the 'malicious' cartoons.

The *TOI*'s case was not to be that straight or easy. It had very clearly hit its competition below the belt. Nevertheless, *TOI*'s counsel argued that 'Humpty Tumpty' was not meant to malign or ridicule *HT*. He added that the cartoon had not adversely affected *HT*'s circulation, revenue or reputation. He asserted that *The Times* was justified in publishing the cartoon advertisement as it 'genuinely' believed that it had a duty to the public to ensure that the conditions on the basis of which the advertisement rates of the *HT* were to be raised would be adhered to.

To drive his argument home, he also said that cartoons have their own language and vocabulary and that they must be seen in good humour, just like *TOI* had done in the past. Dr Singhvi referred to how *TOI* had been called 'The Old Lady of Bori Bunder'. To that, he said, 'The *TOI* never took umbrage, but took it in its stride'. He also pressed for the newspapers' right to humour and said that humorous depictions of situations should be viewed in right earnest. Moreover, Singhvi pointed out that the Press Council was not the forum for *HT* to approach in such matters. This, he said, was because the Council was concerned with only maintaining journalistic ethics and preserving the freedom of the press.

The Press Council first took up the legal objection raised by Dr Singhvi regarding the jurisdiction of the Council. It concluded that it was indeed within its purview to take up the *HT*'s complaint. It also decided that *TOI* had acted without care and caution, and that it had indulged in black humour. In a judgment delivered in June 1989, it announced that *TOI* had erred in publishing the 'mala fide' cartoon. It also said that newspaper businesses were not merely industries to be run for the benefit of their proprietors. It asked newspapers to avoid stiff commercial competition and instead serve their basic purpose. It denounced the emerging trend of moneymaking among Indian newspaper owners, and concluded that such 'unhealthy trends must be checked and discouraged'.[1]

The council also had something to say to the *TOI*'s then editor Dileep Padgaonkar, whose judgement in allowing the said cartoon to be published in the newspaper was questioned. Padgaonkar had said that he had allowed the cartoon to be published because he did not find anything objectionable about it. But the Council decided that the editor had erred in his judgement and that he should have exercised his right to disallow such cartoons from being carried in the paper. Eventually, *TOI* was castigated for having allowed the 'lapse'.

This was but the beginning of *TOI*'s strife with *Hindustan Times*. Although the official verdict was against *The Times of India*, it brought immense benefit to the brand. In the advertising and marketing arena, it acquired a new image: that of being young, irreverent and spunky! Perhaps *The Times of India* had decided to throw away its old-lady look and was donning a more aggressive and youthful appearance.

Apart from taking on the leader publicly and projecting itself as young and irreverent, *TOI* had been working on its product as well.

An innovative move to counter *HT* and also boost profitability was to bring out regular supplements with the newspaper. These supplements expanded the range of subjects covered in the newspaper. They also enabled the paper to experiment with new writing styles and layouts, distinct from the main newspaper.

But the main purpose of these supplements was to attract more advertisements. In particular, where the supplement was built around a specific theme with a distinct set of readers in mind, it saved advertisers the clutter of the main newspaper. The advertisers could now communicate with their target audience of readers in a focused manner.

The first of these supplements was Saturday Times. It was launched in May 1986. It was produced by a new crop of journalists, some of them fresh out of The Times School of Journalism. These journalists worked in close cooperation with the marketing and advertising team of the paper.

Saturday Times carried soft feature articles, against the dry, hard news that was the staple of the main paper. Its USP, though, was that it was in colour. This was the first time something had gone all-colour in Indian newspapers. It was produced on high-quality, glossy paper. This was clearly aimed at attracting new advertisers, besides pulling them in from magazines.

The concept of an all-colour glossy shocked many in the lofty editorial cadre of the paper. They thought it vulgar. The subjects covered were also unusual – fashion, food, lifestyle and society. Even where Saturday Times did articles on serious issues like the fate of the victims of the Bhopal gas leak, the treatment and approach was different. The coverage was more in the nature of feature articles. Mainstream newspaper journalists did not consider this serious journalism. They saw Saturday Times as the 'management's paper'.

The groundwork for this supplement was done by Samir Jain's sister, Nandita. She was bright and proactive. It was she who had hired talented young journalists from The Times School of

Journalism, with her eye on launching something like Saturday Times.

The supplement's positioning was clear from the start. 'We were told quite categorically that Saturday Times was about happy things. We were asked to "put a smile on the reader's face",' recalled Vinita Dawra Nangia,[2] who studied at The Times School of Journalism and later became editor of Saturday Times.

'Once one of the editors did a story on suicide with the photograph of a woman's bleeding wrist on the cover page of Saturday Times. There was a hue and cry. Such photos were an absolute no-no for ST. We were instructed in no uncertain terms that gory pictures were not to be carried at all in the supplement,' Nangia remembered. 'You could carry pictures of non-vegetarian recipes but not of raw meat. There was a very clear line between what was acceptable and non-acceptable,' she said.

Saturday Times had to be suave, elegant and sleek. It was not just to be read but to be looked at like a coffee table book. Therefore, design was integral to the making of this product. 'People were bored reading so much on politics. They wanted other stories. And Samir Jain decided that the newspaper ought to foray into the world of magazines and make them redundant,' Nangia noted.

When ST was launched, both the market and rival newspapers reacted lethargically to the product. They scoffed at it as a gimmick. But soon enough, it started to impact the market. While engaging a new category of readers, mostly the young, it also caught the eye of advertisers. 'It was a trendsetter. It caught the imagination of the readers,' recalled Mannika Chopra, its first editor. 'Themes like health, fitness, sports, science, technology, beauty and fashion had never before been offered in a newspaper.'[3]

Besides, the younger generation was attracted by the glossy and colourful offering. It was not stacked with heavy prose, column after column, like in a newspaper. It flowed from one end to another and blended well. Its style was quite different. It was liberal, or even explicit, compared to the fare being offered by the media at that time. For youngsters, the content, language and approach were up their street.

It caused occasional discomfort at the Times House, though. 'I remember Mr Padgaonkar once saying that Saturday Times embarrassed him when people told him that they had to hide it from their children. Once we did a story on lingerie and I carried a picture of women, front bare, and called it Booby Traps. Mr Padgaonkar said – smart headline but try to avoid this,' said Nangia.

For BCCL internally, Saturday Times served to narrow the gap somewhat between the editorial and marketing. These were hermetically sealed segments and viewed each other as adversaries. Saturday Times ploughed through all this and ushered in a new working relationship.

On the advertisement front, Saturday Times was a hit practically from the start. 'ST was a product that took advertisers by surprise,' recalled Vibha Desai, who was then with O&M. 'The colour quality and the reproduction of the paper were top class. They had used imported paper for the first time, and advertisers reacted positively,' she noted.

The euphoria about Saturday Times lasted for as long as a year. It was a major weapon for *TOI* in its war against *HT* and for a while there was no counter-offensive. At the end of a year, *HT* tried to hit back by starting a whole new debate: does anyone read the colour supplements at all? This was meant to dissuade advertisers from buying space in the glossy. 'But BCCL had done its spadework rather well,' said Desai. 'They had all their data right. And several ad agencies felt that after dealing with the bureaucracy of the *HT*, it was all very welcome approaching a professional team at *TOI*,' she noted.

And indeed, *TOI* was quite professional about it. Both Samir Jain and Nandita Jain took special interest in Saturday Times. Samir Jain would drop in at the editorial desk at times and inquire about the lead story and even suggest changes. 'He would always be right in his assessment, and he never made an out-of-context remark,' Nangia recalled.

The success of Saturday Times prompted *HT* to follow up with its own supplement called Metropolitan. But it met with limited success. 'The *HT* supplement never stood a chance against *TOI*, then,' affirmed Bashab Sarkar. '*HT* had lifestyle supplements but it never got them right,' he added. For one, it was not easy. Nandita Jain was the one who ensured synergy between the Saturday Times' editorial content with the paper's marketing objectives. 'The thing about Nandita was that she was able to balance advertising and editorial. Her brief was to get the editorial in with the marketing. She meshed advertisements with editorials, and it worked out well,' Chopra remembered.

The team worked continuously to keep Saturday Times vibrant and lively. With time, ST started to have one page each on fashion, interiors and travel in the early 1990s. It got fashion designers to write for the paper. Fashion peaked in the early 1990s. That was when Saturday Times also peaked.

Saturday Times lasted for a little over a decade. Then, it made way for another of *TOI* supplements, Delhi Times. Perhaps *TOI* decided that Delhi Times was the more appropriate offering and that it no longer made sense to continue with Saturday Times, despite the success it had achieved over the past decade. Yet again, the group displayed ruthlessness and pragmatism when it came to closing down publications.

'When Delhi Times was launched, I was told, "when a parent has two children, he takes from the stronger to give to the weaker." So, fashion, food and society – our core areas – were given away to Delhi Times. That did not leave Saturday Times with much,' Nangia recounted.

When it was time to kill Saturday Times, there was one set of managers who suggested that the supplement be retained, with glossy pages replaced by regular newsprint. But Pradeep Guha was clear. His view, which eventually prevailed, was that the product would not be downgraded. Saturday Times had been a pioneer in its field. It had served its purpose. It was time to give it a decent burial.

Perhaps Saturday Times proved that even a marketing-led product could create a readership of its own in a world of 'hard news' papers. The supplement further signified that readers' interest, especially of the younger lot, was shifting from traditional news to softer and lighter articles.

After Saturday Times, BCCL launched another colour supplement. This was called Travel Times, and it had an equally successful run and was acknowledged as a top-quality product by both peers in the newspaper sector and by the advertising and travel industries.

Its first editor, Madhu Suri,[4] was working for *Indrama*, a magazine run by Sita Travels, when she was contacted and offered a job at *TOI*. The production of Travel Times had earlier been contracted to Anurag Mathur. But that changed when the management decided to bring some in-house expertise. Much effort was being put into getting these supplements going, at that time.

'When I joined in 1986, the idea of supplements had already taken off at *TOI*,' said Suri. 'Some niche marketing was being undertaken with automobile supplements as well. The economy was opening up. Things were changing,' she noted. 'Travel Times was meant to attract a particular segment of our readers, the travellers. It was Nandita's idea. She had so much foresight and enthusiasm, and a pulse on what would work. Those were exciting times,' Suri recalled.

'We were a small team but quite determined about what we were doing. We would sit for hours working not only on the content of the supplement but also on its layout, its format, font; the presentation; the logo; just about everything,' she elaborated. 'We'd be there working all the way up to 2 or 3 a.m., and Nandita would be around too. She didn't have to be. But she was so involved with the product,' Suri noted.

The editorial department of the main paper was far away from this world. 'It even held a somewhat disparaging view of journalists who were so kicked about working on these supplements. But the company was putting a lot of focus on them,' she pointed out. Travel Times was an experiment, and a successful one. Now, almost every newspaper has these pull-outs and they've become extremely niche and localized.

Travel Times, printed on glazed newsprint, was launched in the fourth quarter of 1987 and distributed free of cost to readers of *TOI* in Bombay and Delhi. In Delhi, the company printed 110,000 copies of the supplement, and 130,000 copies in Bombay, and it went with the metro edition (the city run) of both these cities. The eight-page niche, monthly product, part black-and-white and part colour, was distributed on the last Friday of every month.

Before launching any new product BCCL invariably makes a thorough study of its commercial viability. The products, while having to make sense to the reader, have to also click with advertisers and marketers. 'Travel Times was created with both readers and advertisers in mind. And advertising was kept in balance with 70 per cent space accorded for content and the remaining for ads,' said Suri.

'There was adequate advertising support for it from the travel, tourism, aviation and hospitality sectors, with the Ministry of Tourism, the India Tourism Development Corporation (ITDC) and some overseas tourism boards such as the Singapore and Mauritius Tourism Boards, supporting it. The state governments of Uttar Pradesh, Himachal Pradesh, Jammu and Kashmir, and Madhya Pradesh also bought advertising space in it,' Suri added.

'Hotels such as the ITC Welcome group, the Oberoi's and the Taj, and airlines such as Lufthansa, British Airways, Japan Airlines and Indian Airlines supported it too. Other advertisers including automobile and camera companies also advertised regularly,' she elaborated, when I asked her how it was planned.

Suri pointed out that 'advertising volumes would go up in certain issues like the special issue taken out on the TAAI (Travel Agents Association of India) convention in Kathmandu. This was a special issue dedicated to Nepal wherein additional advertising was generated from hotels, tour operators and other clients from Nepal. And an additional 2,500 copies were printed and personally delivered to all the Indian and international delegates attending the conference. Similarly special issues were done on Himachal Pradesh and Gujarat, which had additional revenues coming in from the state tourism departments, hotels and other tourism related clients.'

I asked her how it was received. We were at a coffee shop in Friends Colony in south Delhi. The sun was just about making its appearance on a cold, winter morning. Her eyes mirrored a smile. 'We got absolutely thrilling feedback. It was great, encouraging and exciting, both for content and for design,' she said.

'The content of Travel Times was unique. It took travel writing out of the ambit of the staid destination "seeing" to almost "experiencing" the place through its different facets: the food, culture, and shopping,' Suri pointed out. These are a given today. But at that time, it was a pioneering effort, she indicated. Travel Times tapped writers such as Bill Aitken and Hugh and Colleen Gantzer. Their language and style were refreshing. They did some wonderful stories. Therefore, the supplement had an exotic flavour, she pointed out.

Thematic travel was also introduced for the first time with this supplement. There were stories such as 'A wine tour of France', 'A cheese tour of Amsterdam', 'the Sun God trail in India', and a tour of the Kangra paintings, among myriad other themes on this line. 'Above all, the focus was on presentation, which was crisp, user-friendly and creative,' she reminisced.

Travel Times also addressed different segments of travellers. It wrote for the leisure traveller, the niche traveller, the well-heeled traveller, the first-time traveller, the pilgrim traveller, the family traveller and the solo traveller. It also focused on the group traveller and of course the business traveller.

'We were paying great attention to detail. And that worked,' Suri said. The supplement entered the market with great aplomb. Its design and editorial concept, the entire package, made quite a splash. 'We got wonderful feedback on all these parameters. And to validate that we were on the right track, Travel Times won two awards, both by the TAAI, between 1987 and 1989, at their annual conventions in Kathmandu and Srinagar,' she added.

'The designing of this product was also done in-house. And although none of us had any formal training on design, we had come up with something attractive and classy.... It was so distinct, and it had truly captured the spirit of travel,' Suri recalled. In fact, the Travel Times team got a call from *HT* asking them for the name and contact number of the designer.

The supplement also got written about. *The Hindu* talked about it in an article referring to the pioneering and exciting effort that the supplement was making to bring travel journalism to India. 'One of the international publications also wrote about us,' said Suri, trying to remember which one it was.

So, what happened to it? Why was it discontinued, I asked her. She reflected a bit and said, 'After a while, it was clear that we were getting only niche advertising revenue. There was a shortfall in the number of ads that we had anticipated because advertisers had a choice and they chose to go with Saturday Times.'

So, for some time, the Travel Times supplement went to *The Economic Times*, and became a travel page there every Sunday. Then, it was relaunched as a glossy. This was sometime in 1997. It also went out with the Bangalore edition of *TOI*. Its masthead was redesigned as well. There were some sponsors but the market was still not ready for two supplements at the same time. 'Saturday Times and Travel Times were in that sense, clashing,' Suri noted. 'And advertisers kept favouring Saturday Times,' she added.

There was no trouble from *TOI's* competitors. 'They were really slow in responding. They did not know how to react,' Suri pointed out. 'Our own calculations of how much advertising revenue a product would generate weren't being met. It did break even at a point but wasn't able to sustain that. It had to be redone. And that was tried,' she said. That is the other thing with BCCL. Experiments are initiated at all times and are dispassionately given up if they fail to elicit the desired response.

I asked Suri about Samir Jain's involvement with the supplement, and she said, 'He wasn't too actively involved with this particular product. He was busy taking marketing decisions. But he had such an incisive sense of what the audience, the reader, was ready for. He may have taken many of his cues from the West but he has been able to apply them to the Indian market and see his initiatives through. In that sense, he has revolutionized the industry and become a trendsetter.

'The Jains also succeeded in taking the newspaper industry into the commercial realm. This wasn't a very happy shift for journalists because there was sacredness associated with the editorial. So, there were undercurrents of discomfort and resentment. But over the years, it all seems to have worked out,' Suri noted.

Around this time, BCCL also took a conscious call that it would enhance local content in the newspaper. It was obvious that the tastes and profiles of readers across markets were widely divergent. While a healthy interest in national politics, sports and cinema was a binding factor, people in each city cared about different things. Delhi, for example, was far more interested in politics. As the capital, it had a sizeable bureaucracy and this had a bearing on the culture and preferences of the English-speaking middle class in the city. Bombay was more interested in commerce and economy. In later years, Bangalore with its software success had an entirely different orientation. It made sense to go local.

This was perhaps one of the strengths of *HT* in Delhi. It had a strong local orientation in the way it prioritized news. It appeared that residents of the city valued the fact that the newspaper took up issues of the neighbourhood and community. If *TOI* had to do well in Delhi, it had to similarly touch people's lives here by identifying with their day-to-day challenges and concerns. So whether it was civic issues, crime or education, the *TOI* decided to inject a generous dose of local reportage.

But in its local focus, it also went beyond the local issues normally covered by papers. It treated facets like shopping, leisure, eating out and fashion as components of 'local culture'. These were, so far, ignored by mainstream newspapers. But with a growing middle class and the opening up of the economy, BCCL foresaw that these aspects would assume as much importance, if not more, in middle-class lifestyles as traditional issues like civic failure and local taxes.

The most tempting reason for local sensitivity was that it would pull in local advertising. 'The perspective of the owners/managers is clear: theirs is never an editorial activity. It is purely market-oriented,' noted Umesh Anand,[5] the first editor of Delhi Times.

It made sense to the advertiser as well. The thinking, as A.N. Sen, one of *TOI's* former resident editors in Delhi put it,[6] was: Why should Nathu Sweets (an eateries chain in Delhi) advertise in the main paper when there is a local section? It would also benefit from paying a different and much lower rate to advertise in this section than if it were to advertise in the main paper. The more local the paper got... the more it stood to gain from retail advertising.

Around 1993, it decided to go in for a local supplement. While the city pages in the main paper would continue to focus on local crime and civic matters, the supplement would cater to the lifestyle dimension. The idea of Delhi Times took off when Vineet Jain, the managing director of The Times Group, said that the main paper was far too serious for him and that he needed something lighter for the youth.

Gautam Adhikari was the executive editor of *TOI* then. Reporters covering the city beats were asked to make a special add-on for the local supplement, which would be directed at the younger readers. It would be the metro section. This add-on was to be produced by the reporting department of the paper.

The limerick in the book *Tickle the Public*[7] by British writer and editor Mathew Engel in many ways sums up the philosophy behind Delhi Times:

Tickle the public, make them grin,
The more you tickle, the more you'll win;
Teach the public, you'll never get rich,
You'll live like a beggar and die in a ditch.

Delhi Times was a novel product, reporting on light and off-beat subjects. It started by covering local issues like health and education in more interesting ways. While the usual reportage was stuck in a conventional format, Delhi Times looked at the city from the point of view of the citizen and consumer. At one level, it was a shopper's guide telling all about discount sales. There was also a bit of fashion thrown in. It had a regular column on cars, a pioneering effort at a time when Maruti was just about the only car company around and a few international makers were on the verge of launching their products. The tone was light, the language crisp and lively, with interesting headlines.

These subjects were not considered to be news until then. It seemed as if such news had no value. But as it turned out, the middle class had tremendous appetite for these aspects of the city. They were hooked.

Delhi Times began as a four-page edition, twice a week. It went through various transformations. It introduced the 'Page Three' concept in India. Fashion and cinema started to get more and more attention. Celebrity was in and it took precedence over local and cultural issues, which was the original mandate of Delhi Times. But it had evolved into a formidable brand of its own.

'Interestingly, the response to Delhi Times from the journalist community was good,' recalled Umesh Anand. 'It captured a lot of mind space with its clever headlines and it was funny and provocative. It also proved the *TOI*'s argument that having a metro section was mandatory,' he added.

But it was on the advertising side that the response was stupendous. A senior marketing manager at *HT* acknowledged (off the record, of course): 'Delhi Times was a brilliant move. It just swooped on all the small advertisers and carried them away from us. *TOI*, Delhi, began getting independent ads after Delhi Times. That made the product viable and it hit competition big time. We actually struggled as retail advertising made that shift from us to Delhi Times. You can see the fallout. Most major newspapers now have their retail segment sorted out. We all have local supplements.'

Delhi Times put immense pressure on rival newspapers. To hold on to local ads, they needed to bring out their own local supplements. This meant printing more pages. Further, the ads in these supplements had to be sold at a lower rate, proving a double whammy. While this put *HT* under pressure and forced it to bring out its own city supplement, it was the smaller newspapers which were squeezed out of the local game and made space for *TOI* in Delhi.

'People may have scoffed at Delhi Times in the beginning. But as one can see, glamour is not really a problem; it is not that bad after all,' said Anand. Bombay Times enjoyed similar success. It began as a weekly and then was brought out twice a week – on Tuesdays and Fridays. Then, it came out thrice a week before becoming a full-blown, self-sustaining seven-day phenomenon, with its own loyal clientele.

In fact, the famous 'Page Three' in Delhi Times and Bombay Times had an interesting genesis. 'I wanted a lot of interesting content in the paper as I was trying to establish the product, but Page

One and Page Eight were not easily available for it as there were enough advertisements on these pages. Pages Two and Four were black-and-white. And I wanted one full page that could carry most of the interesting, attractive stories. The first right-hand page (where attention is due to go) that was available under the circumstances was the third page, which was the first opening page. We decided to go with that,' Pradeep Guha explained.

The page was branded. 'We wrote "Page 3" with a certain amount of intent on it. We filled it up with exciting, eyeball-grabbing content; we brought in celebrities and entertainment on the page; we made it vibrant and colourful and, of course, we had enough advertising. That is how the Page Three concept was born, led more by a machine configuration than by anything else,' he remarked.

With the success of Saturday Times and Delhi Times, the group had a formula that worked. Choose a specific theme, assemble content around it and attract advertisers who offer products or services around that theme. It was luxury and lifestyle brands in the case of Saturday Times. Delhi Times was built around the theme of local.

The group replicated the formula with Education Times. It created content around courses, educational institutions and career opportunities. This enabled the newspaper to attract youngsters. This segment was least interested in the political and policy fare that was the staple of newspapers. But with these themes, the paper was able to connect with them. This also served a platform for the education industry to advertise and reach out to this audience.

BCCL was aware that *HT* drew part of its circulation strength from its advertising. Many bought the paper mainly to access its ads while paying cursory attention to news and other editorial content. So it went the whole hog trying to attract advertisements. One of the first initiatives was to collate all the classified ads from group publications in English from across the country and print these free in the Sunday issue of *TOI's* Delhi edition. On the one hand, this provided more bang for the buck for the advertiser. But more important, it created the positive loop whereby more advertisements attracted more readers leading in turn to more ads. Within three months, the Delhi edition of the *TOI* had edged out *HT* in this respect.

Media watcher Sushil Pandit pointed out[8] that *HT*'s domination over most advertisement segments was near-total, and that the *TOI* had a tough time trying to make a breakthrough. The 'obituary columns', where friends and families of the deceased put out information notices, were a fascinating battleground for the two papers.

'*HT* had ruled the obituaries segment from time immemorial in Delhi. *TOI* would send condolence cards to the families of the deceased. That is how desperate the situation was for *TOI*,' he claimed. 'Well, of course, it was perfectly legitimate for newspapers to try and become part of the life of the people in the city where they were published. But *TOI* had to do this as part of a strategy,' he quipped.

To make inroads into *HT*'s dominating position in this area, *TOI* began a free obituaries column, noted Pandit. They had obviously realized that a busy obituaries column attracted sizeable readership. They worked on this segment over a long time and only gradually, by the mid-to-late 1990s, did they find themselves in a more comfortable position. 'The battle for the obituaries market between *TOI* and *HT* was a long-drawn-out one. In fact, no segment was left untouched. The tussle was stiff,' he said ruefully.

Prior to this, *TOI* had done an interesting branding effort with the appointments pages or the recruitment ads. The recruitment ads segment has multiple positives. The ads by themselves are potential money-spinners. Recruiters are willing to pay a premium for the right audience. Besides, these ads have a positive rub-off on circulation. They are of interest to a wide variety of readers, from fresh job seekers to those seeking to switch or upgrade jobs. Recruitment ads are often a window to the latest moves by a corporate or an institution. They lead to interesting conversations among peers. All in all, they bring additional readership.

*TOI* decided to focus on this segment of the market. To begin with, it had an appointments page once or twice a week. By and by, the number of pages went up to four a week. The paper packaged all the appointments pages under a brand, Ascent. It made Ascent a separate pull-out from the newspaper, once a week. The number of pages in Ascent went up from four to eight, to sixteen, and occasionally even twenty-four pages.

To achieve scale, *TOI* started inviting job ads at a hefty discount. At this stage, the objective was not so much to earn revenue but to build a flow of job ads for the paper. It had to become a credible platform where job seekers could expect to find ads and recruiters could be assured of suitable response.

For a while, the paper lost money bringing out Ascent owing to the low rates charged from recruiters. But it persisted. The aim was to wean away ads from rival newspapers, or at any rate, to emerge as an additional option for recruiters. It was aware that once a critical mass of advertisements was reached, it would enter the virtuous cycle similar to its rival. Of course, it had the deep pockets – and the appetite for risk-taking – to try this out.

Soon, ads began to flow to Ascent. With the software boom, a huge market was created for the appointments pages. The paper was in a position to capitalize on the opportunity. Over time, it introduced colour in Ascent. Once Ascent had established itself as a brand among recruiters and job seekers, the paper jacked up rates and even started charging a premium on these ads.

The success of Ascent led *HT* to come up with HT Horizons where it packaged its recruitment ads. A former senior marketing manager at *HT* – who had categorically told me, 'I will tell you everything you want to know. But don't quote me. I don't want to get caught in the battle between these two,' – pointed out that a similar brand for recruitment ads had been created and launched by *HT* much before Ascent. It was called HT Enhance. 'But the product was not marketed enough. *TOI*, on the other hand, went the whole hog with Ascent, and just see the difference,' he said, shrugging his shoulders.

Much of the success, whether it was Delhi Times or Ascent, was also on account of the aggressive field team BCCL had. These brands were not just created and forgotten. The field teams would proactively reach out to advertisers and readers, creating awareness and inducing purchase. There was a focused effort to build these brands in the minds of advertisers and readers.

At one level, it may seem that BCCL created a series of supplements and backed them with clever marketing. While that is true, there was a complete thought process that provided cohesion and direction to these supplements and other content changes in the paper.

For years, newspapers had placed the Establishment at the centre of their news coverage, opinion and analysis. Most reportage was about the actions and pronouncements of government. They were heavy in reporting on political postures and controversies. On the corporate side, primacy was given to announcements by companies and proclamations by CEOs. This did not necessarily imply that papers were pro-establishment or that they held the brief for those in authority. It just meant that papers were preoccupied with government, establishment and authority. This preoccupation, or rather obsession with the Establishment, cut across papers of all hues, languages and regions. The 'anti-establishment' media was as much about the actions and pronouncements of authority, as was the 'pro-establishment media'.

Samir Jain's idea was to break away from this practice of putting the Establishment at the centre of news coverage and analysis. Rather, he wanted to put the citizen and the customer at the centre of newspaper coverage. This meant, for example, featuring less of politics and politicians. Even where their pronouncements and rhetoric had to be reported, it had to be from the point of view of the citizen or reader.

'He looked at the public platform – the alternative establishment, which the British media had termed "disestablishment",' remarked Vijay Jindal. Similarly, in reporting changes in government policy, it was imperative to eliminate all jargon and explain to the reader the context and relevance of that policy to him or her. It was about empowering the reader over according primacy to government or authority.

It was, undoubtedly, a profound shift. It was indeed the case that the media devoted the bulk of its space to politics, politicians and their rhetoric. While figures of authority, including politicians, received their share of criticism in the media, this was mainly on the editorial pages. For the most part, they could be assured that newspapers would painstakingly report their speeches and rhetoric, as uttered by them, in the morning newspaper. Government could similarly take newspapers for granted when it came to highlighting some of their 'achievements and initiatives'.

Samir Jain sought to change all this and create a new hierarchy of news. The basis of news selection had to change. He believed that developments which news desks had, almost by habit, come to consider as news may no longer deserve the same space and exposure. Rather, these developments would have to make way for other, more relevant themes in his papers.

For example, a citizens' initiative or a national sports development may now be more deserving of the front page than the pronouncement by a politician against his local rival. A certain criteria for prioritizing news had been embedded among journalists, and indeed among readers. Some subjects were seen to be automatically making news. Others, by the same token, were never deserving of being called news. He was trying to flip the pyramid.

It was no longer just about news that was 'important to know'.

Instead, it was also about news that was 'useful to know', even news that was 'fun to know'. For example, he put much more focus on coverage of local issues. He felt that neighbourhood and city issues touch people at least as much as, if not more than, a shoot-out or accident in another part of the country.

At the same time, there was a conscious effort to lighten content while making the paper more vibrant. Led by the marketing team, the paper went about creating a feel-good effect in its columns, especially in the lifestyle supplements. The marketers in the company anticipated that a positive, celebratory newspaper does, in many ways, foster a sense of well-being. The reader has a sense of reassurance and control that all is well with the world. This, in turn, boosts consumption and promotes aspiration.

As Pradeep Guha shared with me, 'We "created" celebrities in the columns of our supplements. It became a sort of an artificial stimulus to churn up an upbeat, buoyant, sanguine environment. Advertisers would, of course, appreciate this as they know that gloom pulls down consumption.

'We would bring out golfers, fashion designers, socialites, starlets, talented but less known artistes in Bombay, for instance. We would build events around them. We'd give it a very happening feel, with the *TOI* at the centre of it all,' he noted. It was a clever marketing move. But a sense of joy and celebration was indeed created.

The paper had to exude optimism, even as it reported reality without distortion. Sports, leisure, lifestyle issues were important for the middle class. These had to get their due prominence in the paper. Agriculture, by the same token, was a distant theme for the urban reader. Despite its acknowledged importance for the economy and the country, it was relegated to the lowest in the priority list.

These changes obviously caused discomfort. It was not just the selection of news but also the approach and manner of reporting that had to change. More importantly, the journalist's self-image as the 'moulder of public opinion' and as one pontificating on issues of national importance, received a severe blow.

It was easy to misunderstand this move, or to miss its full significance. Many saw this shift as pandering to the interest of the advertiser. Bring in trendy themes, put aside the real issues from the newspaper, sex up the pages, and you can attract the younger and affluent classes, the kinds that advertisers love to communicate with. To an extent this was true. The paper was trying to aggregate relevant audiences for advertisers. Some themes were in, some others which were 'in national interest' but irrelevant for the urban affluent reader, were definitely out.

But this was only one part of the picture. Coinciding with this were major upheavals in India and abroad which had created a 'trust deficit' in authority and the establishment. Globally, the scene was changing rapidly. This was the time the Berlin Wall was being brought down. Authority and establishment were under serious scrutiny. Citizens were losing faith in the conventional governance structures, seeking transparency and wanting to empower themselves.

Urban India was starting to get cynical about the whole socialist and pro-poor rhetoric. The model of state-led development was being questioned and there was general dissatisfaction with governance. Caste and communal issues were dominating politics, leading to disillusionment among the middle class. Economic reforms were changing people's world view and priorities, especially in the metros.

In many ways, the new approach to content was in keeping with these social and economic changes. At the first instance, it was probably overdone. The paper, in trying to break the rigid hierarchies of the past, turned frivolous. Another oft-repeated criticism was that in creating relevance, it had ended up 'dumbing down' issues.

It had perhaps erred on the other extreme. But over the years, it sought to achieve a balance. After some initial hesitation, most newspapers followed suit. Leisure, lifestyle and celebrity became an integral part of news coverage. Interpretative reporting replaced stenographic accounts.

'*The Times* felt the pulse of the era, which was set to change. There was too much emphasis on policies. There was also an overdose of politics. Perhaps people were disgusted,' noted a senior marketing manager who didn't want to be identified as he had worked both at *HT* and *TOI*.

Even a rival publisher acknowledged that *The Times of India* had anticipated change and led the change in content. 'Both Delhi Times and Bombay Times are innovative. They saw the shift in the readers' tastes much ahead of us,' he conceded.

'The condemnation, if any, for changing the format and content of newspapers is not deserved. There was a time when even sport was considered insignificant, almost infra dig, to merit a mention on the front page of newspapers. It was tucked away inside the paper. But things changed,' he acknowledged.

*The Times of India* brought in unconventional areas into the main newspaper. Earlier, romance and film news appeared only in the vernacular press. But slowly, that became a part of mainline English newspaper. Issues such as health and fitness became mainline news.

In fact, the approach to content that Samir Jain experimented with in Delhi became more pronounced when the group went about capturing leadership in Bangalore a few years later. 'The importance of the local agenda was brought in at *TOI*, Bangalore,' says Bachi Karkaria, who was closely involved with the Bangalore edition. All the elements of proximity to the reader were introduced. 'We went completely and truly local,' recalls Karkaria.[9] 'We covered local cultural events. We visited schools and colleges and tapped all retail outlets. In eight months, circulation tripled.'

In Bangalore too the paper was sensitive to the profound change that the middle class was going through. 'We decided to fill in this void, which is created by the exit of the old culture and the onset of the new culture,' notes the editor. 'Most importantly, of course, we changed the perspective of our stories from the seller's point of view to the buyer's point of view. We looked at the user's perspective.'

In many ways, Bangalore was Delhi all over again.

Even as it used supplements, content changes and aggressive marketing to strengthen its position in Delhi, BCCL was working on extending its reach on the ground. Realizing that *HT* had a strong and committed readership in Delhi, BCCL started to explore the markets around it. These markets were traditionally dominated by local and vernacular newspapers. But over the years, many of these areas had acquired a sizeable readership for English-language dailies. National dailies from Delhi had paid little attention to these markets.

Reaching out to these areas required the national dailies to strengthen the distribution network. It also meant altering production and printing schedules in Delhi to reach these markets in time. The English-language readership in these markets had not been large to justify this effort. Advertising from these markets was also limited. The national dailies focused on Delhi.

The demand for English dailies in these markets was being met by dominant regional dailies. The other option was an early edition of a national daily from Delhi. These early editions were often poor cousins of the Delhi edition. They mostly carried news of the day before, with some updates thrown in. There was no sensitivity to the local issues in these markets.

*The Times of India*'s Delhi edition was doing well in markets around the city. That was a hint that these markets could be potential opportunities. BCCL started to pay attention to improving the quality of content and production in the early editions meant for these markets. Deadlines were advanced. Correspondents were encouraged to file reports early so that the editions reaching these markets could carry the latest news as far as possible. Distribution in these markets was strengthened.

Thus, *TOI* was able to make space for itself in these markets. The regional English dailies, which had been dominating this segment of the market, had not faced serious competition. They were forced to sit up and make improvements. Over time, the *TOI* local editions came up in many of these markets.

'We started catering to various centres like Chandigarh and Dehradun, among others. That helped. We were able to encircle *HT*. Thereafter, we made breakthroughs in Jammu and Bhopal among other regions,' A.N. Sen, who was at one time the resident editor, *TOI*, Delhi, recalled.

During this time, *HT* also entered new markets but it was perhaps not part of any cohesive approach with any clear intent or goal. 'It was expansion for the sake of expansion,' said Naresh Mohan,[10] who was executive president of *HT* from 1985 to 1998. For example, in 1985-86, it went to Patna. It chose that market partly because its Hindi edition, *Hindustan* was already doing well there. In 1995, *HT* went to Lucknow. It left out Chandigarh because of the terrorist problem in Punjab. '*HT* stuck to its natural growth areas, while *TOI* began tapping markets around and outside Delhi,' he said.

The big offensive came in March 1994, with the 'invitation price'.

Less than a decade ago, Samir Jain had argued that value was more important than just circulation numbers. Higher circulation did not necessarily imply better value for the advertiser. It was more important to have the right kind of readership, and advertisers ought to pay more for that. Dr N. Chandra Mohan, a former business editor of *TOI* had told me during a conversation on the subject that Samir Jain wanted 'the elite and the decision makers' to subscribe to his newspapers. 'He called them the "networth people".'[11]

Besides, it was also felt in the group that circulation was a losing game. The more you printed, the more you lost. It was not the route to higher profitability. Now, a decade later, circulation was what the group was targeting – and by dropping the price at that. While there seems to be an apparent contradiction, the fact is that BCCL of the mid-1990s was a completely transformed organization from the one a decade ago. What's more, the media industry, the Indian economy, the advertiser and the consumer were barely recognizable from their counterparts of the mid-1980s.

BCCL had been able to position its papers as premium brands and emerged as a profitable entity. It had organized itself into a well-oiled, innovation machine. All facets of the company were working together cohesively towards common objectives. Invitation price, to boost circulation and thereby attract more advertisement at higher rates, seemed the next logical step. In March 1994, the price of *The Times of India* in Delhi was cut to Rs 1.50 from Rs 2.90 per day.

The idea of using a lower cover price to boost circulation had worked well with *The Economic Times* a few years ago. However, for all their apparent sameness, invitation price for *TOI* was vastly different from what it had been for *ET*. For one, the price cut for *ET* was preceded by sharp and repeated increases in its price. It was recognized as a premium and aspirational product, priced at Rs 4.50 in Delhi, before the price reduction came. Besides, it faced no serious competition in its category. The idea was to convert its readers into buyers and tap into the latent potential for a business newspaper. Most of this did not apply to *TOI*.

On the face of it, reducing the cover price of the newspaper to boost its circulation did not look like a good idea. There were many questions against such a move. The first of these, of course, was whether loyal readers could be induced to switch their newspaper for Rs 45 a month. Perhaps a daily newspaper was not the kind of product where a price change would lead to a major switch in customer preference. It appeared that demand for a newspaper is, to a large extent, inelastic to its price changes.

Those opposing the move argued that a monthly bill of Rs 90 is a very small percentage of the total expenditure of a household subscribing to an English newspaper. On the other hand, the newspaper was a way of life, almost a habit, for the family. People had grown up with it. Would they give it up to save a tiny amount? Any price cut is risky, and this one more so. If people's preferences stayed where they were, the *TOI* would end up selling the same newspaper to the same people and recover from them only half of what it used to. There was no point rocking the boat. Besides, as in any price cut, there was a possibility that the perception of the brand may be adversely impacted. Customers and advertisers might see it as a cheap, discounted and down-market brand. This perception had to be prevented. The challenge was to project the invitation price as a move by a leader who cares for his people.

The counter-argument was that saving on half the monthly newspaper bill would be attractive enough for a household. They would not mind switching to another newspaper which met the same needs, if not in a better way. The idea was to get readers of *HT* to sample *TOI*, compare the two and then choose one or the other.

There was also the benefit, intangible but vital, of creating a buzz in the market. Like with its other initiatives, BCCL felt that this move would create excitement and boost the brand. Even among subscribers of *HT* who eventually decide to remain with it, *TOI* would have garnered valuable mind space. It would enter their consideration set. Thereafter, any slip-up in quality or service by *HT* could induce them to switch. (In fact, in evaluating the invitation price for *ET*, BCCL had noted that one of the benefits would be to capture mind space without having to spend on advertising the brand!)

There was, of course a third possibility. A price reduction of *TOI* could prompt other newspapers, notably *HT*, to reduce their price as well. Readers could be either indifferent to this battle, in which case both papers would lose. Or, in a more positive scenario, they could decide to subscribe to two newspapers for the same monthly bill as before.

Before effecting a price cut, the group had to tackle resistance from distributors. Their commission was linked to the cover price. Besides compensating them upfront, BCCL held out the promise of a larger circulation to mollify them. When the company went ahead and announced the invitation price, there was euphoria. Once again, the reaction was palpable among readers, advertisers and would-be subscribers of the newspaper. It turned out that a significant number of people considered it worth their while to switch papers for that extra saving.

The company did not confine itself to a lower cover price, though. It went ahead and sweetened the package further. Four pages were added to the newspaper. Satellite television had just caught on in the country. But there was no comprehensive list available of the programme schedule. The company brought out a supplement called E-Times, listing the schedule of programmes on the main satellite channels for the week, and distributed it free with *TOI*. In addition, the paper began carrying a coupon for advertisers once a week in its Delhi edition. This coupon offered 'special drawing rights' (in other words, a discount) to people wanting to advertise in the paper. It was attacking its rival from all sides.

*HT* did not react to the invitation price for the first three months. It was not sure whether its *rival* would be able to sustain this offer. But it was losing subscribers all this while. Finally, it followed suit and dropped its cover price by half. 'The real change happened with the price war. We reacted late,' commented Naresh Mohan.

He went on to point out: 'But I also realized that the gap was closing not so much in Delhi as it was elsewhere. The circulation figures show that *TOI* has added readers in Orissa, in Calcutta and in the North-east. Take the circulation figures for January–June 2000, for instance. *The Times of India* in northern India sold 549,960 copies with Delhi accounting for just 322,738. The *Hindustan Times* sold 458,000. But take the figure for Orissa. The *TOI* is at 32,000 while *HT* is only 7000 copies ahead. Do you see? Readership has grown.' After 1994, it has become a duplicate readership, he acceded.

Over the next few years, both papers gained from this move. With families going nuclear, the demand for newspapers experienced a natural growth. Besides, more families were comfortable with an English-language newspaper. And, of course, the lower price had helped expand the market as many households chose to buy two papers with the same money as before. But it is likely that *TOI* gained much more. As a challenger, and as the one who initiated the invitation price, theirs was a moral victory.

The benefits were reflected in hard numbers as well. In 1993, for example, *TOI's* circulation in Delhi was about 163,000 copies. By 1995, it had crossed 300,000 copies. By August 1996, *TOI* had touched 431,000 copies in Delhi, a stupendous growth of 164 per cent over three years. In the past, the paper had been growing at a rate of around 4 per cent annually. Following the invitation price, this rate jumped to 16 per cent and then to 40 per cent in subsequent years. This was supported by a sharp growth in newspaper readership in Delhi, especially among the youth.

The price cuts by the two leading newspapers led to sharp increase in demand and readership during the next few years. The National Readership Survey (NRS) of October 1995 showed that readership of English newspapers in Delhi grew by a whopping 49 per cent, with *TOI* growing by 81.6 per cent and *HT* by 50.6 per cent. Students as a category, especially those in the 15–24 age group, saw stellar growth.

Over the next few years, readership continued to show strong growth though at a slower rate. According to the NRS 1997, *TOI* had a combined readership of 39.1 lakhs. It had gained 6.30 lakh readers between NRS 1995 and NRS 1997. Its Delhi edition was the fastest growing edition in the city. With a readership of 5.93 lakhs, it had grown by 22 per cent over the previous NRS. The average growth rate of readership of English dailies in Delhi was 11 per cent. Though these NRS numbers were contested by HT, the fact is that the price reduction, combined with certain demographic factors, led to a sharp increase in interest in English dailies.

During the decade of 1985–95, *TOI* was able to pose a credible challenge to *HT*. In terms of circulation, *HT* continued to lead, though the gap had narrowed considerably. But in terms of perception or 'top of the mind' brand, *TOI* had edged out the leader. The latter was compelled to copy several initiatives taken by *TOI*, and formulate its independent damage control plan to counter it.

While the *HT* had formidable equity and goodwill in Delhi, *TOI* was helped by the fact that it had a free run in the lucrative Bombay market. *HT* or any other major paper did not venture into the Bombay market during the 1990s to challenge the supremacy of *TOI*. The latter could concentrate a large part of its resources and attention on attacking *HT* in Delhi, secure in the knowledge that its cash cow was undisturbed. Besides, for a long time, *HT* did not anticipate the severity of the challenge. Such intense competition had been relatively unknown in Indian industry, not to speak of the media space.

'*The Times of India* had a strategy. The *HT* did not. And that made all the difference in the Delhi market,' admitted a senior marketing manager at *HT*, who has also served with *The Times of India*.

Although both the papers had coexisted for decades, they were two very different organizations. 'The *HT* was good at cost-cutting measures. It would be able to reduce newsprint costs and keep staff salaries low. But beyond that, we could not see much happening,' he said.

Vijay Jindal is more candid. '*HT* ran like a printing press. It was a legacy asset, which was never proactive. It was one-sided and pro-government and it had been some sort of a social enterprise for a long time.' While *TOI* had made efforts to evolve into a modern, professional corporate, *HT* was still in the traditional mould. 'Just to give you a very simple illustration: people are always addressed as Mr XYZ at *TOI* and as XYZ*ji* at *HT*,' he said.

But the decade ending 1995 was only the first round of battle between the two papers. 'Frankly, *HT* realized only in 1997 that it was because of its stagnation that the *TOI* was getting ahead,' admitted a senior editor at *HT* who had also worked at *TOI*.

'It ordered a revamp. Marketing consultants were called in. The old guard was eased out. *HT* followed a multi-pronged approach, copied from *The Times of India* in places, introduced its own value additions and established its lead again,' he pointed out.

Much later, *HT* went on to start a Mumbai edition, posing a direct and formidable challenge to *TOI* there. It also revamped content, look and approach. The battle between the two giants resulted in both papers becoming more lively and youthful, making it worthwhile for the reader and advertiser. And they continue to lock horns over their domination of the newspaper market, highlighting different elements from the National Readership Survey figures.

Take the latest face-off, for example, that was out in January 2013. *The Times of India* led with the headline: 'TOI adds readers, wins lead.' And *Hindustan Times* reported: '*HT* is No. 1 choice in Delhi-NCR again.' *TOI* talks about its national domination and mentions Delhi in passing. *HT* reiterates that it continues to be number one in Delhi, for the eleventh time in a row. They continue to spar. Keep watching that space!

# EPILOGUE

AFTER MORE THAN A decade of transformation, BCCL had clearly emerged as the top media house of the country by the late 1990s. Its leadership was not just in terms of size and profitability. More than that, its profound impact on the psyche of the industry, its self-image and approach to the business accorded it a leadership position beyond numbers.

On 7 July 2002, *The Times of India* informed its readers that their newspaper had become the world's largest-selling English broadsheet[1] daily with a certified circulation of 2,144,842 copies. This put it ahead of the previous front runner *USA Today*, by 24,485 copies. While these and other numbers are regularly contested, the fact is that BCCL had established itself as a major force.

At the start of this century, India's media industry was on the threshold of major transformation. The first decade was about the explosive growth of satellite television. The twenty-four-hour news format and the proliferation of channels completely redefined the way news was gathered, sifted, prioritized, presented and distributed.

Together with this, the Internet explosion and the rapid shift towards convergence in communication have impacted the way news is accessed and consumed. These profound, almost 'revolutionary' changes were bound to have implications for the print medium. Against this background, it is interesting to see how BCCL, as the leading print house, responded to these changes in the landscape.

During the past decade or so, BCCL has expanded itself into what is now The Times Group, comprising other media interests covering radio, Internet and television. The publishing business, BCCL, has largely stuck to the trajectory, though the scale of its actions is now much bigger. It retains its basic principles of boosting profitability by trying to enhance value for the advertiser. This, in turn, has meant attracting the relevant readership audience for its publications.

In recent years, India's media has seen frantic activity including restless cacophony. Amidst all this, it appears that the core of The Times Group remained unchanged: an innovation machine, with a clear focus on the spaces where the group wishes to operate and doing all it takes to win relevant audiences for the advertiser.

There is a view among peers – and some former insiders – that after its success in the 1990s, the group just did not do enough to expand and grow its business. After 2000, this has, after all, been the most eventful decade for the media ever. Opportunities have exploded like never before, within and across mediums.

At the start of that decade, critics argue, The Times Group was the leader in the media space. It was hugely profitable, with abundant cash reserves. Some of the strongest brands in the media were in its portfolio. Above all, it had large reserves of talent. Innovation was in its DNA. It had the ability and potential to be the first mover. Given all that, did it make the most of the opportunities that came up in the past decade?

Besides the growth of the media industry, the Indian economy entered a new growth trajectory. Some of the corporate growth across sectors is on account of the buoyancy in the economy and growth of the middle class. For all its initiatives, did The Times Group achieve its potential?

One view in the corporate sector is that BCCL's success has

been much less than that of the other leaders of corporate India. The Times Group pales in comparison to Wipro, HUL, Infosys, Reliance Industries, the Aditya Birla Group and the Tatas.

'The Times Group is a success when compared with companies in the print medium. As an organization, purely in the print space, it is far ahead of anyone else in the country. But in comparison with the total media, it is still lagging. The Times Group may not be growing as fast as its competitors are.

'Strangely, the group was never professionally organized. There were no structured plans or mega objectives set for the future. That may have limited its growth,' a former company director, who did not want to be quoted on the subject said.

Although there has always been a reservoir of talent, the group has revolved around the proprietor. It is every inch a family concern, closely held. Perhaps a clearly articulated set of strategic objectives, with professionally executed initiatives, would have sent the group looking for new opportunities beyond print.

'The group does not have a long-term blueprint for its growth,' said the former company director. 'It did not exist in the 1980s and it did not exist post-2000 either. I do believe that the group's profits are relatively paltry. It can do much better, given the fact that it has such a great talent pool,' he argued.

Further, unlike leading companies in certain other sectors, it never considered entering markets overseas. In fact, all media companies in India have moved in a narrow base, a narrow tunnel. They cannot really be compared with successful Indian companies like, say, the Reliance Industries. These media companies have been conservative in their approach.

Samir Jain's focus on core competence and the late entry into television in particular, may have limited the group's growth. Although the group has since established itself in both the news and entertainment genre, it was a late entrant in the television sector. 'Television was at odds with Samir Jain's emphasis on profitability. To start with, he had a basic dislike for the medium. Given that most TV houses today are in the red, he may have been vindicated for now,' noted the former director.

The proprietor of a rival newspaper group had, strictly off the record, said, 'Sometimes, I feel that there is no vision at The Times Group.' He added, 'Vision, to me, would mean going global and planning for the future. Vision would mean having newspapers in London and New York.'

'I would have done that,' he stressed. 'I would have gone out and conquered the world with their kind of money. I wouldn't have just remained in the country. Had I been the *TOI*, I would have gone international. I would have had two editions. I would've gone straight for television (in the 1990s itself). I would've taken BCCL's surplus and invested it in the industry. One needs effort and enterprise consistently,' he asserted.

So, how would you eventually judge Samir Jain, I asked him. 'By his performance,' he retorted. 'In a nutshell, Samir Jain has weakened the editorial product as an entity. He has not protected his flanks and he has not made use of his investible surplus. And, if at all *The Times* is bigger than us, I take it as my humbling failure,' he admitted.

'In spite of all the opportunities presented to him, Samir Jain is not the king of the media. He may be a baron. But he is definitely not the king. And, now, that position too might be getting challenged. Samir Jain has not gone into the next orbit. He and I – we are citizens of the same orbit,' he claimed.

Almost everyone I met acknowledged, if somewhat grudgingly, that *The Times of India* made a sweeping success of itself between the 1980s and 1990s. But the question is: from here on, will it be able to repeat the magic, in a vastly different setting.

Sizing up *The Times of India*'s success, the editor-owner of a rival group, which has interests in television as well, told me: '*The*

*Times of India* operated in a bigger market where the advertising pie was bigger (and continues to be so). It exploited these favourable circumstances. It was entrepreneurial. And if I do brand building, I can as well get a disproportionate sum of the advertising money spent. That is what it did well.

'Fundamentally, *The Times of India*'s success came from its dominance of some of the wealthiest regions of the country. They controlled first Bombay and then Delhi. Almost 99 per cent of their success came from these places.... It does not necessarily follow that if we had control over these markets, we'd have done as well or all of us would have done far better', he said.

'Of course, it was to the *TOI*'s credit that they had a strong marketing team and that they exploited their control over the Bombay market, which has been doing very well. They have had good market share. They have also had in place great infrastructure in Bombay, for which I give them a 100 on 100. If you judge Samir Jain's personal performance, only in the context of the newspaper business, it is brilliant,' he added.

But now in 2013, the paradigm may have shifted. In the print era of the 1980s, The Times Group was the biggest player in the largest market (Bombay). In the era of television and digital, however, it appears to be just one of the participants in the fastest-growing segments of the media space.

I had two meetings with Aveek Sarkar, chief editor of the Kolkata-based Ananda Bazar Patrika group during the course of this study; the first in August 2002, in Kolkata, and the second in January 2013 in Delhi. This is the sum and substance of what he said: 'Decidedly, *The Times of India* is the dominating player in the print medium. However, print is a declining empire. By choosing to expand on a segment that is in terminal decline, one could argue that The Times Group lost its larger focus and ceded the territory to outsiders like Star, Zee or Sony.

'If you look at Rupert Murdoch, for example, his bulk business comes from entertainment, television and movies. Murdoch still remains in print perhaps only out of vanity; it does not bring him any real money. A director of News Corp did point out during their latest controversy that "print is 10 per cent of the business but 90 per cent of the headache".

'I may be totally wrong but I think that the *TOI* is fighting the wrong battle with the wrong people. We are not their opponents. And whether they beat us or not, this is not the battle they must engage in. If Dara Singh were to go to a Montessori and wrestle someone there, and win, would that amount to much? Their competition, even for the advertising rupee, is not with us. It is with the likes of Star and Zee. Subhash Chandra, Uday Shankar and Mukesh Ambani are his real competition. Not *HT*, *The Hindu* or the *ABP*,' Sarkar explained.

A media analyst who did not want to be named said The Times Group is vulnerable because while it has a vast war chest, it essentially still depends on print. And print actually gets very little advertising. This is a real transition. 'Print is a shrinking violet. It could even end up being like the "mom-and-pop stores",' he cautioned.

'With our known world crumbling and a new world emerging, it does seem likely that the focus of media houses might completely change. Several newspapers in the West such as *The Guardian* and the *Financial Times* are going through tough times. Even *The Times* and *The Sun* have been hived off into a separate division. Most media groups are putting their monies on potential thoroughbreds and exiting shaky territories', he said.

But that may not entirely be the story in India and the jury still is out on this issue. It is a fact that industrial houses, many of them with far deeper pockets than The Times Group, are carefully positioning themselves to take control of the media space. And compared to new entrants like Mukesh Ambani, and the India Today–Kumar Mangalam Birla combine, The Times Group could be much smaller. The advertising revenue is indeed going into entertainment and television channels, and advertising in print is declining compared to its inflow into the digital medium, cable, satellite and sport.

Does The Times Group have a well-diversified portfolio outside of print or, as a rival put it, will it prove to be 'the tallest tree that shall sway the most in a fierce storm'?

But there are as yet no clear winners in the digital and television space in India. The Times Group could emerge as the one. Although it entered this space late, it seems to be catching up. It could leverage its brand leadership, ample reserves and its penchant for innovation to establish dominance in the emerging spaces.

Since the mid-1980s when Samir Jain took centre stage, The Times Group has targeted the urban, English-speaking, broadsheet audience. That has been its domain throughout. It has been steadfast in this focus, resisting the temptation to go deep into the hinterland or invest in new newspaper brands. In the 1990s, this urban focus had meant devoting resources to Bombay and Delhi, the country's most lucrative markets and where the group already seemed to have a sizeable presence.

In the past decade, the domain seems to have remained the same for The Times Group. Of course, the definition of urban has expanded to include not just the metro cities, but also the top cities and in some cases, even the tier-two space. Hence, after several false starts, it made a foray into Chennai, a market dominated by *The Hindu.* It has always wanted to have a dominant voice in Kerala and West Bengal. Now, it has expanded its presence into Kolkata and Hyderabad.

But the biggest story has, undoubtedly, been the Bangalore market. The group was able to use its tried and tested formula of local coverage, attractive combo rates for advertisers and aggressive newspaper pricing to dislodge the incumbents in this market and emerge the leader. In Chennai too, it has made its presence felt, appealing essentially to the youth who chose it over the staid and conservative, though erudite, *Hindu*.

At the same time, the group has faced stiff challenge in its home turf, Mumbai, from the time *DNA* (*Daily News & Analysis*) and the *Hindustan Times* launched their editions there. *HT* made inroads with a good editorial product. *DNA* initially captured the imagination of the people with its look and feel, and aggressive brand building.

Although *The Times of India* remains the clear number one in Mumbai, this has come at a cost. By the group's own admission, profit growth has steadied. It can no longer dictate terms to advertisers in the way it did a decade ago. Besides the new entrants in the Mumbai newspaper market, other changes have also weakened *The Times of India*'s monopoly position. In the 1990s, it had established itself as the most potent if not the only route to reach out to young audiences. That is, obviously, no longer the case and it is competing in a far wider arena.

With the emergence of Internet, radio, mobile, below-the-line events and outdoors, advertisers have many more options now. Although The Times Group is the dominant player in many of these spaces, and the market for advertising has increased manifold, it is no longer in a position to command prices for its print space as it did in the earlier decade.

But even critics concede that despite the explosive growth of alternative mediums, The Times Group and other print houses have been able to hold their own in the media industry. On numerous occasions, they were written off. It was argued that as in the West, the emergence of twenty-four hour news channels would leave only two options for newspapers: either they become niche products offering insightful, interpretative coverage of events, or succumb to tabloidization.

Neither seems to have happened so far. Newspapers, no doubt, have had to reorient and align themselves to a world cluttered with twenty-four-hour news channels. They can no longer survive on objective, spot reports of events. They have had to pay more attention to packaging and presentation. In some ways, newspaper coverage has had to pick up from where television leaves off.

At the same time, they have charted their own distinct course, focusing on news breaks and offering more insightful and in-depth analysis of events that television may have failed to do. Newspapers have retained their relevance and distinctiveness among advertisers and consumers. They have also gained from the fact that Internet penetration and use in the country continues to be limited.

The Times Group has been helped along by innovations in both content and pricing. It has continued to build on the tried and tested formula of Mastermind and invitation prices. By offering its various newspapers at concessional combo rates to buyers, the group has been able to retain the attraction among the subscribers.

During the 1990s, there was growing criticism that the group was compromising on the quality of content. To attract new categories of readers, it was alleged, the group was 'dumbing down' news. At *The Times of India*, issues that were not on the narrow radar of the urban middle class were left out of the coverage. Similarly, the paper appeared to refrain from issues that were complex or required in-depth analysis.

Journalists of the old school, including some who served as editors with BCCL, felt that the idea of connecting with new readers had been taken too far. While earlier, the newspaper industry's self-styled role of a guardian of democracy was overdone, *The Times of India* had gone to the other extreme of focusing singularly on commerce. It had failed to balance the roles.

'There is a distinction between news you want to know and news you ought to know,' said a former editor of the group, who wanted to remain anonymous. 'For the former, there is always a strong pull from readers and the community. In the case of the latter, the paper has to use its judgement and ensure that those issues do not suffer and receive adequate exposure in the paper,' he added.

For some years, the group operated in the belief that if there was an issue of national importance but did not concern the daily life of its reader, it could be kept out. 'The Times Group, with its focus on "news you can use", was a breath of fresh air. But it progressively neglected the aspect of "news you ought to know" and the balance was lost.'

Senior people in the group today concede that the criticism was not entirely out of place. In their endeavour to make content lively, relevant and easy to comprehend, they may have ended up trivializing developments. Even in the choice of content and reportage, they may have gone too far in pandering to the narrow and immediate interests of the urban readership. In the process, social issues of national importance may have been ignored.

In one phase, for example, the group decided that *The Times of India* would report corporate developments in great detail. Government departments, policymaking units and public sector companies would no longer get coverage. The intention may have been to address the urban readership in their role as consumers and nascent investors. But what it meant was that, overnight, top public sector companies like NTPC and BHEL found that there was no space any longer for them in the columns of the paper. The future of key areas like railways was uncertain. Agriculture was out.

It took a while for the balance to be restored, helped no doubt by the fact that public sector companies and government departments are also big budget advertisers. The pressure on editorial space, to make way for advertisements, may have also contributed to these omissions.

In the recent past, there have been conscious efforts to restore the balance, though. For example, *The Times of India* has come up with a high-quality supplement, Crest, to demonstrate its commitment to editorial content. Started particularly for Samir Jain's artist daughter Trishla to get her interested in the newspaper business, it is not taking too many ads since that would 'spoil the beauty of the product', as a contributing writer to Crest, who works for The Times Group, put it.

The supplement was a success, touching a circulation of five lakh copies. But priced at Rs 5 – when cost worked out to rupees twenty per copy – made it a losing proposition. Circulation has been scaled down to three lakh copies, but price has been kept low and the ads have been restricted. 'Samir Jain is dead against increasing its price. He will keep saying, "Let's keep it as low as is possible,"' the writer said.

'Crest is an experiment to see if a product can sustain itself on content and quality, without advertising revenue. One must give the group points for trying this out. It isn't easy,' he argued. 'As for Trishla Jain, she was involved in it for a while. Thereafter, she chose to return to art.'

Another approach to restore the equilibrium has been to give more attention to social issues. The coverage is now more broad-based. In addition to the change in news content or approach, a flurry of trendsetting social campaigns backed by the group has been launched to bring about a balance.

That has been a conscious approach by the group. Their assessment is that modern Indian youth, while being socially conscious, want to express themselves in constructive ways. They want to take concrete action to impact their immediate surroundings, as opposed to just read, analyse and discuss the issues. As such, instead of just enhancing coverage of social issues in news content, it is better to channelize this sentiment through campaigns on issues.

In line with this thinking, the group has been able to design a format for social campaigns which it seems to be replicating across themes. This format normally includes high-voltage coverage in the form of opinions and articles on the chosen issue which normally resonates strongly with the urban middle class. There is a celebrity component to create a bigger pull. This is complemented with ground-level events, where the urban middle class can participate without upsetting their routines very much. All this is backed by focused local coverage, mostly built around the participants and beneficiaries of the campaign.

The Teach India campaign which invited people to spread literacy in the neighbourhood, the leadership campaign to choose honest and competent candidates for politics, a campaign to promote India-Pakistan relations are all efforts to provide a forum for urban middle class to do their bit for society. In the process, the group is able to balance its intense market focus with social consciousness.

The group has evolved an interesting view of empowerment, which covers both the citizen and the consumer. In line with this, its newspapers are not supposed to be in awe of any authority, whether it is governments or corporate houses. They see no merit in merely reporting the pronouncements of politicians or policymakers. Rather, they report developments from the point of view of the citizen.

The group sees itself as communicating with civil society and upholding its interests vis-à-vis all forms of authority and establishment. It is out there on behalf of civil society, bringing to it news and information that is of relevance and value. It is also willing to take up cudgels on behalf of civil society, in the latter's fair battles against the establishment. The cynic would view this as pop assertiveness. But the group is determined that in doing all this, it is not to be awed, or even swayed, by government, corporate or any other form of authority.

This means that news is chosen on the basis of its relevance for the reader. Similarly, it is reported and written in a way that makes sense to the reader. The newspaper ought to be an empowering force; an energizing, elevating one, which strives to understand and engage the reader. Most important, the reportage brings in multiple perspectives, not just those of authority or the state.

Similarly, where policy or business issues are concerned, its newspapers do not report them in a stand-alone manner. Instead, they consistently interpret developments in a way that is relevant to the reader as a consumer. So rather than hold forth on 'tightening liquidity' and 'upward bias in interest rates', its newspapers report on how much more a middle-class family will have to pay on their home loan every month.

The Times Group does deserve credit for this view of 'empowerment'. Indeed, it has marked a departure from the Indian media's obsession with politics, bureaucracy and corporate honchos. It has tried to place the reader at the centre in its coverage. This is in contrast to the traditional approach where newspapers either talked down to readers, or carried on conversations unconcerned about them.

In some ways, this has also shown the way for others in the media. These have become more open, inclusive and sensitive to the changing profile and needs of the reader. It is not easy to stick to this approach. It does lead to situations where the media may be trivializing or oversimplifying complex issues. But by and large, readers are better off.

Besides innovation in content, the group has also created new 'tools' to offer more value to the advertiser. Like in the past, these initiatives have had their share of controversy. One of them has been Medianet, which gives advertisers access to editorial space – for a fee – to 'communicate' about their products and brands. It is difficult for the reader to discern that this space is paid for and the article can easily pass off as the independent view of a journalist.

The editorial content in newspapers traditionally enjoys much higher credibility than pure advertising by a company. It is assumed that unlike an advertisement, which is paid communication by the company and hence likely to be one-sided, the editorial piece is an independent, third-party account. The journalist would have exercised balance and judgement in reporting it. This distinction between the two forms of communication has always been sacrosanct.

Through Medianet, The Times Group has blurred this distinction. It makes the advertiser's communication appear exactly like a report by a journalist. There is little to distinguish between the two. In fact, the group has a team that helps the advertiser cast his message in the same format and flow as a journalist's news report or feature article. Its subtlety and close resemblance to an 'authentic', unbiased report makes it even more difficult to distinguish. While this makes it more valuable for the advertiser, it abuses the confidence that the reader places in the news content of his newspaper.

The group may have taken it too far. The move wasn't exactly anodyne. Medianet stirred up controversy not only among rival publications but also within the group as well. There was a strong view within the group that the paper could not mix news and advertising to a degree that they would become synonymous. Even as it pursues its commercial interest, the sanctity of news had to be maintained. Further, passing off paid content as news was unethical, even a betrayal of the reader's implicit trust. In fact, it has been suggested that Pradeep Guha quit the group on this single issue.

To be sure, the group has its view, justifying Medianet. For one, it claims that this facility for advertisers is limited to only a few sections of the newspaper, mostly the lifestyle pull-outs. Ravi Dhariwal, then executive director of BCCL, in an edit piece in *The Times of India* had indicated that Medianet aimed to lift the veil of double-speak off the content that is offered in the lifestyle supplements of the main newspaper. He argued that advertorials and sponsored features and write-ups were a legitimate part of content as long as they came with a full disclosure. He noted that the vetting of such pieces was rigorous, structured and severe, and that all such articles went through a litmus test before being given space in the supplements. Stories that did not live up to scrutiny got summarily chopped, he pointed out.[2] Delhi Times now carries a disclosure below the masthead on its front page that it is an advertorial, entertainment and promotional feature.

Ravi Dhariwal also reassured that 'not only is every article that is routed through Medianet credited, it also has to pass the most stringent editorial filter, the commitment to which is unflinching in The Times Group. So if the editor of a lifestyle or city supplement of *The Times of India* feels the story is not worth the advertising it is riding on, it gets dropped'.

Besides, not all companies and brands can buy space in these columns and advertise through this route. The group is choosy about which brands would be allowed to avail of it. The brand should not be disconnected from the overall profile and values of the newspaper. It should typically be a lifestyle or 'upmarket' brand.

Medianet stirred a stormy debate, kicked off by Aroon Purie who wrote in his column, 'From the Editor-in-Chief', in *India Today*[3] that you could pay to get yourself featured in the editorial columns of *The Times of India*. The *Hindustan Times* had articles from top journalists on this issue under a series called 'the state of the media debate' in February 2003.

Writing in the *HT*, T.N. Ninan, then editor, *Business Standard* mentioned: 'Bennett, Coleman and Company as the largest publisher (of *The Times of India* and other titles) has chosen to take the aggressive line on profit maximization.'[4] He also noted: 'People get into publishing because they have some regard for the news and for the reader. If they don't, they might as well sell soap. The problem with our newspapers today is that some publishers don't see the difference.'[5]

The *Hindustan Times*' former editor, Vir Sanghvi, refrained from directly attacking *The Times of India* on this issue, preferring to talk about the 'larger media debate' of paid news.

In his column in the Sunday edition of *HT* at the height of the debate, Sanghvi wondered, 'Why are some Indian newspapers willing to sell editorial space? Why are they so ready to cheat their readers into believing that stuff that has been paid for has the credibility of news.... The people who are selling off their news pages run some of the most profitable papers in the country.'[6]

*The Times of India* defended its stand in its own columns. It spoke at length of how it had always been a leader in innovation and how its competitors were 'plagued by bankruptcy of innovative ideas' and hence started this 'acrimonious tirade'.

But more to the point, the main counter-argument forwarded by the group, though, is that many of the editorial articles are also inspired by corporate releases. Corporates, or their agencies, are able to influence the editorial teams to insert their communication in reports and articles, no longer keeping them as third-party, independent views. This, the group argues, is low-cost advertising by proxy, with the value migrating to intermediaries like public relations agencies who charge a hefty fee from corporates for making this possible. Rather than have the corporate do it through a third party, they can approach the newspaper directly and have it done more professionally for the same fee or less.

The late Sabina Sehgal Saikia in an edit piece in *The Times of India* argued that Medianet had not kicked-off the practice of planting stories in the supplement. It had instead made the process of sharing information rather transparent, she said. That, she believed, eliminated the tendency toward puffery in journalism, and removed the scope for quid pro quo. Space in the newspaper wasn't meant to be traded for personal or petty gains, she noted. And, articles went through an exacting process of selection, and were open about the fact that they had been sponsored, she said.[7]

Whatever the defence by the group, the fact is that with Medianet, a section of the news columns is available for sale. Anyone who puts together the requisite cash can, with a few qualifiers, be featured in the paper. So it is not uncommon for weddings and birthday parties, which have a small-time socialite or two pulled in, to effortlessly make their way into the editorial columns of the newspaper. Similarly, products and services might find themselves adequately advertised in the garb of news features or short stories.

In February 2011, the media world was abuzz with a story about a reporter of *The Sunday Times*, London,[8] (Nicola Smith) having called Medianet, posing as the PR agent of a company that wanted coverage for a party at a shopping mall in Delhi. The story was called 'India's media demand cash to run favourable news.' A Medianet executive reportedly told her that space could be bought in Delhi Times for £27 (Rs 2,385) a centimetre on the front page and for £16 (Rs 1413) a centimetre in the inside pages. He is reported to have added that the story could be 'dressed up as a genuine news story as long as it met a celebrity quotient'. It was mentioned to her that 'celebrities were available to attend the event at an extra cost.'

This story was then picked up by *The Guardian* (The Greenslade Blog) whose piece was entitled 'India's dodgy paid news phenomenon'.

I am reminded of a comment from the celebrated 1972 film by Francis Ford Coppola, *The Godfather*, where Don Corleone tells Virgil Sollozzo: 'It makes no difference; it don't make any difference to me what a man does for a living, you understand. But your business is a little dangerous.'

The other controversial move to boost value for the advertiser is the 'private treaties' route. Companies can enter into an arrangement whereby they get advertising in return for offering an equity stake to The Times Group.

This is a 'complete solution' offered by the group and is normally for companies that would otherwise be reluctant to advertise. These would also be companies that are not media-savvy but need media exposure to build their brands ahead of an equity issue or other funding initiatives at some point. They can receive all that from The Times Group in return for a small stake in their company. Over 200 companies have signed up for this arrangement.

The group, of course, maintains that 'private treaties' are only a way to expand the advertisers' market. Companies that do not need to advertise on a regular basis and are reluctant to set aside an advertising budget, can avail of this arrangement to get some exposure for their brands. These are companies that are not in a position to offer upfront payment for space but are quite happy to offer a stake in their companies as part of a long-term arrangement. As such, The Times Group views 'private treaties' as an innovative mechanism designed to tap this new category of potential advertisers. The group further justifies it by smugly stating that in any case criticism is fast giving way to emulation by competitors – though not as successfully.

There are still many unanswered questions. Of course, the group claims that it does not believe in 'post-mortems'. The approach is to look at the task at hand and go out and do it as best as it can. 'The innovation machine continues to generate ideas across the spectrum, tries them on the ground, fails at some and succeeds at others. We have to keep moving on,' says a young brand manager[9] of the group.

The group also claims that, contrary to corporate wisdom, it does not pay much attention to what competition does. Its focus is on what *it* wants to achieve, irrespective of what competition plans to do. 'In fact, we believe some of the competitors have not been able to do as well as expected because their focus was on us, and not on the reader or advertiser,' he noted. 'They were more concerned about destroying the enemy than creating something new and valuable.'

There may be some truth to the claim and one cannot help being struck by the uncanny success rate of the group's initiatives. And much of this success may be attributed to the guiding mantra of the group – stay relevant and profitable. What propels this media juggernaut is the eagerness to read and decode the market and its trends while keeping an eye out for competition and the willingness to experiment – taking cautious but aggressive risks. A contrarian it may seem to be in its approach, philosophy and in its many unpredictable forays into the Indian market scene but the one fact that cannot be denied is that it leaves an impact on every space it occupies, no matter what it does – good, bad or audacious.

# Notes

## Prologue

1 Following popular usage, 'media' is used as a singular noun.
2 According to the Telecom Regulatory Authority of India (TRAI)'s quarterly report, released in April 2012 there are more than 825 private satellite television channels permitted by the Ministry of Information and Broadcasting in India.
3 Rajdeep Sardesai, 'It's noise, not news', the *Hindustan Times*, 8 February 2013, p. 12.
4 The Office of the Registrar of Newspapers in India, *Press in India 2011-12*, 28 December 2012. Highlights available on the official website rni.nic.in/
5 Ibid.
6 Ibid.

## The Grand Dame of Bori Bunder

1 J. Natarajan, *History of Indian Journalism*, Delhi: Publications Division, Ministry of Information and Broadcasting, Government of India, August 1955, p.5.
2 Ibid.
3 Ibid.

4 Ramkrishna Dalmia, *A Short Sketch of My Life,* Delhi: self-published, 1973, p.173.

5 Ibid.

6 The date was mentioned by Gun Nidhi Dalmia, one of Ramkrishna Dalmia's sons, during an interaction with him, Delhi, February 2003.

7 Ramkrishna Dalmia, *A Short Sketch of My Life,* p.173.

8 Ibid., p.174.

9 Ramkrishna Dalmia, *Some Notes and Reminiscences*, Delhi: self-published, 1948; 2nd ed. 1959, p.7.

10 Ibid., p.18.

11 Interview with Alok Jain, Bharatiya Jnanpith office, Delhi, 15 January 2002.

12 Ibid.

13 Ramkrishna Dalmia, *A Short Sketch of My Life...*, p.175.

14 Interview with Ramesh Chandra Jain, Bharatiya Jnanpith office, Delhi, 11 July 2002. He passed away in September 2004.

15 Interview with R.P. Jain, Calcutta, 30 July 2002.

16 Interview with Sanjay Dalmia, Delhi, 28 August 2002. (He has tried his hand in the media with the *Sunday Mail.*)

17 Ramakrishna Dalmia, *A Short Sketch of My Life*, p.238.

Although Ramkrishna Dalmia is straightforward in mentioning the transfer of ownership of BCCL to his son-in-law, there is an undercurrent of discomfort in the family, perhaps because the company has turned out to be both a high-profile business and a money-spinner. Witness the lament by Neelima Dalmia Adhar, one of Dalmia's eighteen children from his six wives, in her book that her father's amputation from *The Times of India* was so ruthless that his name did not merit mention during the 150th-year celebrations of the newspaper. , *Father Dearest, The life and Times of R.K. Dalmia*, Namita Gokhale editions, Roli Books, Delhi, 2003, p 140. During a telephonic conversation with me (18 March 2013), Neelima Dalmia Adhar said, 'My father was very bitter, very angry about what the Jains had done. The companies had been transferred in a verbal mortgage; they had been entrusted for safe custody but they were never returned. In fact, he had said, "Let them take anything except *The Times of India* and Sawai Madhopur Cement Company." Although he kept in touch with my eldest sister (Rama Jain), he had severed all ties with the others.'

18 Ibid.

19 Ramkrishna Dalmia, *Some Notes and Reminiscences*, p.24.

20 Neelima Dalmia Adhar, *Father Dearest, The life and Times of R.K. Dalmia*, p.139. While trying to get to the source of this quote that is attributed to Jawaharlal Nehru, I asked Neelima Dalmia Adhar (on 18 March 2013 over the telephone) to give me its background. She said that the quote was a very well-known one in the family although it may not have been recorded (in writing) anywhere. Geeta Kudaisya, associate editor of the *Selected Works of Jawaharlal Nehru* believes that Pandit Nehru was not given to adopting such a tone in his speech. 'He was above all this,' she said. (Interaction at the Nehru Memorial Fund, New Delhi, 20 March 2003.)

21 In a letter dated 8 March 1953 to Mahavir Tyagi, then minister for revenue and expenditure, Nehru wrote 'the Bharat Insurance Company's monies are being used and misapplied in many ways to bolster Dalmia's other companies'. Nehru asked Tyagi to 'deal with it as rapidly as possible' so that 'legal opinion can be taken'. *Selected Works of Jawaharlal Nehru*, Second Series, Volume Twenty-One (1 Jan 1953–31 March 1953) published by Jawaharlal Nehru Memorial Fund, p.372.

22 The Government of India promulgated an order on 11 December 1956, setting up a commission of inquiry, under the Commission of Inquiries Act, 1952, to conduct investigations into the alleged malpractices of the Dalmia-Jain group of companies. Justice S.R. Tendolkar of the Bombay High Court was appointed chairman of the commission by the Union Ministry of Finance. After his death, Justice Vivian Bose, a former judge of the Supreme Court, was appointed chairman in August 1958. The commission worked for over five years before presenting its report on the investigation to the government on 18 June 1962. The Vivian Bose Commission report was presented to Parliament on 23 January 1963.

23 *The Statesman*, 24 January 1963, p.1.

24 Ibid.

25 Ibid.

26 Ibid.

27 Ibid.

28 Ibid.

29 Ibid.
30 Ibid.
31 Ibid.
32 Interview with Sanjay Dalmia, New Delhi, 28 August 2003.
33 Interview with Dr Ram Tarneja, The Ashok Hotel, New Delhi, June 2001.
34 Interview with Alok Jain, Bharatiya Jnanpith, New Delhi, 15 January 2002.
35 *India Down The Pages: The Times Group since 1838*, Mumbai: The Times Group, 2002, p.137.
36 Interview with Inder Malhotra at his Press Enclave residence, New Delhi, October 2001.
37 Interview with Baljit Kapoor, at the Observer Foundation, New Delhi, December 2001.
38 *Report of the Second Press Commission*, Vol II, Appendices I–XII, Press Council of India, Information and Broadcasting Ministry, 1982, p.369.
39 Interview with Ramesh Chandra Jain, New Delhi, 11 July 2002.
40 FICCI – The Federation of Indian Chambers of Commerce and Industry – split in 1986. ASSOCHAM – The Associated Chambers of Commerce and Industry in India – was revitalized, and the CII – Confederation of Indian Industry – emerged.
41 Interview with Dr Sanjaya Baru, New Delhi, June 2001.
42 Interview with Pritish Nandy, New Delhi, September 2001.
43 Interview with Dr Ram Tarneja, New Delhi, June 2001.
44 Interaction with the late Sham Lal in July 2001 at his Gulmohar Park residence in NewDelhi. He passed away in February 2007.
45 Based on a meeting with Sushil Pandit, New Delhi, January 2003.

## VC with a Third Eye on the Fourth Estate

1 Interview with Akhilesh Jain, New Delhi, 24 July 2002 and 10 February 2005.
2 Akhilesh did not specify whether the name is Kuku or Cuckoo. I did not ask him then as I didn't want to break that train of thought.
3 Telephonic interview with Shashank Raizada, New Delhi, February 2005.

4 Interview with Baljit Kapoor, New Delhi, December 2001.
5 Interview with Vijay Jindal, Mumbai, December 2001.
6 Interview with Priya Ranjan Dash, managing editor of the *Financial Chronicle,* New Delhi, January 2013.
7 Interaction with Gautam Adhikari, at The Oberoi's, New Delhi, 6 February 2002.
8 Two meetings with Pradeep Guha, at Le Meridien, New Delhi, August 2011.
9 Interaction with N.P. Singh, Jhandewalan, Delhi, July 2001.
10 Interaction with Ramesh Chandra Jain, New Delhi, 11 July 2002.
11 Interaction with Ramesh Chandran, Vasant Vihar, New Delhi, December 2001.
12 Three interactions with Satish Mehta; one at the Times House, New Delhi, and two at his Neeti Bagh residence in New Delhi, September 2001, August 2002, November 2002.
13 Nicholas Coleridge, *Paper Tigers: The Latest, Greatest Newspaper Tycoons and How They Won the World*, New York: Random House, 2012, p.408.
14 Interview with Jug Suraiya, the Times House, NewDelhi, July 2001.

## Building Blocks of the New Regime

1 See planningcommission.nic.in/aboutus/speech/spemsa/msa038.doc
2 Based on an interview with T.N. Ninan, New Delhi, 7 February 2003.
3 The Hindu rate of growth is a term signifying the low rate of growth – averaging about 3.5 per cent – of the Indian economy for nearly three decades from the 1950s to the 1980s, i.e., before liberalization in 1991, a lack of ambition in consumption among Indians and also a sign of the controlled economy of that era. The term is believed to have been coined by the economist Raj Krishna.
4 Interview with Sushil Pandit, Delhi, July 2002.
5 Some aggression from the BCCL stables was evident during the heydays of the *Indian Post*. Its popularity may have been discomforting. *The Times* decided to bring out a paper called *The Independent*. The idea may have been to create a flank for the *TOI*, garner some of the FMCG advertising and create a little flutter in the marketplace. This new product was aggressively pushed and prominently introduced

to the Bombay market in September 1989. (Within a month, sales reached about 10,000 copies and two months later, about 20,000. The objective was not to push sales too much but to manage to contain competition, whose sales then were about 25,000 copies. See, Satish Mehta, *Marketing to Win: Designs and Campaigns to Achieve Market Dominance,* Delhi: Pearson, 2012.

6 Based on a meeting with Gautam Adhikari, New Delhi, 6 February 2002.

7 Meeting with Dileep Padgaonkar at his Defence Colony residence, New Delhi, 2 February 2003.

8 Meeting with Bashab Sarkar, then with O & M, at his office in Okhla, Delhi, October 2001.

9 Meeting with Baljit Kapoor at the Observer Foundation, New Delhi, December 2001.

10 Meeting with N.P. Singh, New Delhi, May 2002.

## Stop Press! Reflong!

1 Sir Arthur Conan Doyle, *The Hound of the Baskervilles*, London: George Newnes Ltd, 1901, p.7.

2 Bal Gangadhar Tilak published *Kesari* and *Maratha*. Bipin Chandra Pal founded *Vande Mataram*, Jawaharlal Nehru founded the *National Herald*. Mahatma Gandhi founded *Young India* and *Harijan*.

3 Rudyard Kipling, 'The Press', in *A Diversity of Creatures*, First published in 1917. http://ebooks.adelaide.edu.au/k/kipling/rudyard/diversity/chapter12.html, accessed 15 March 2013.

4 Meeting with Sunil Jain, Delhi, March 2002.

5 Meeting with Inder Malhotra, New Delhi, 11 February 2003.

6 *Sunday* magazine, 6–12 April 1986, p.18.

7 Samir Jain had met Rupert Murdoch a few times in London in the 1990s.

8 Based on an interview with Bachi Karkaria in Mumbai, December 2001.

9 Based on an interaction with the late K.L. Nandan, Delhi, March 2005.

10 Abraham Michael Rosenthal was the executive editor of *The New York Times*' from 1977 to 1988. He had won a Pulitzer in 1960 for

international reporting and was with *The NYT* for fifty-six years, from 1943 to 1999.

11 Interview with H.K. Dua, New Delhi, June 2001. H.K. Dua had gone to the Press Council of India in July 1998 with the complaint that he had been 'wrongfully dismissed' from his job as editorial advisor of the *TOI* because he had 'refused to accede to the demand of BCCL chairman, Ashok Jain, to help him handle his alleged FERA cases by creating favourable public opinion by lobbying with the political leadership and by writing in his favour'.

'On 5 August 1998, the Press Council censured *The Times of India* "for carrying on a campaign against the Enforcement Directorate with the manifest intention of pressurizing and deflecting it from performing its lawful duties"'...according to the late Ajit Bhattacharjea, the then Director of the Press Institute of India. See *Frontline*, 29 August–11 September 1998. (Bhattacharjea had been resident editor of the *TOI*, Bombay, between 1971 and 1975. He had also been an editor with *Hindustan Times* and *The Indian Express*. He passed away in April 2011.)

12 Based on a meeting with Sunil Jain, Delhi, March 2002.

13 As told by Inder Malhotra.

14 Based on a conversation with Gautam Adhikari, New Delhi, 6 February 2002.

15 Based on a meeting with Vinita Dawra Nangia, Delhi, August 2001. (She was with the *Hindustan Times*, at that point.)

16 Based on an interview with Chandan Mitra at *The Pioneer* office, New Delhi, November 2001.

17 McManus, John H., *Market-Driven Journalism: Let the Citizen Beware*, Thousand Oaks, California: Sage Publications, 1994, p.3.

18 Based on two meetings with Pradeep Guha at Le Meridien, Delhi, August 2011.

19 Based on two meetings with Dileep Padgaonkar at his Defence Colony residence, New Delhi, July 2002 and February 2003.

20 *Sunday* magazine, 6–12 April 1986 (An Ananda Bazar group publication. Now defunct).

21 Meeting with N.P. Singh at his Jhandewalan office, Delhi, July 2001.

22 Meeting with Dileep Padgaonkar, Delhi, July 2002.

23 Dr B P Agarwal, Executive chairman of ABC Consultants, a recruitment based firm with its headquarters in Delhi, founded in 1969.
24 Based on an interaction with Satish Mehta at his Neeti Bagh home, New Delhi, August 2002.
25 Khushwant Singh wrote a review of a BCCL publication – *India Down The Pages*. See, http://www.outlookindia.com/article.aspx?220785. When I met him at his Sujan Singh Park residence in New Delhi in July 2001, he said, 'The two most unreadable newspapers in India are *The Times of India* and the *Hindustan Times*.'
26 *Sunday* magazine, cover story, 'The Paper Chase', 27 March – 2 April, 1994, p.36.
27 Ibid, p.35.
28 Based on interaction with Dileep Padgaonkar at his residence in New Delhi, July 2002.
29 During the early 1980s Welch was dubbed 'Neutron Jack' for eliminating employees while leaving buildings intact.
30 Based on a meeting with Rajnish Rikhy at the Times House, New Delhi, 23 October 2002.
31 Based on an interview with Vijay Jindal, Mumbai, December 2001.
32 Based on an interaction with V.K. Gambhir, Delhi, 2 March 2005.
33 Interaction with Pritish Nandy, New Delhi, September 2001.
34 Interview with Vimla Patil, Bombay, December 2001.

## The Price Matrix

1 William Shawcross, *Murdoch*, New York: Simon & Schuster, 1992, p.192.
2 Bagdikian, Ben Haig, *The Media Monopoly*, Boston: Beacon Press, 1983, cited in John H. McManus, *Market-Driven Journalism: Let the Citizen Beware*, Thousand Oaks, California: Sage Publication, 1994, p.20.
3 http://thinkexist.com/quotation/if-you-make-a-product-good-enough-even-though-you/397118.html accessed on 9 March 2013.
4 Based on two interviews with Pradeep Guha, a former executive director and president of BCCL, Delhi, August 2011.
5 Based on an interaction with Vijay Jindal, Mumbai, December 2001.
6 Based on an interview with Vibha Desai, Delhi, July 2001.

7 Meeting with Rajnish Rikhy, New Delhi, January 2002.
8 Interview with Bashab Sarkar, Delhi, October 2001.
9 Meeting with Nataranjan Bohidar, Delhi, August 2002.
10 Meeting with Satish Mehta, New Delhi, September 2001.
11 Interview with Rajnish Rikhy, New Delhi, January 2002.
12 Ibid.
13 Meeting with N.P. Singh, a former advertising director at BCCL, New Delhi, July 2001.
14 Meeting with Vibha Desai, Delhi, July 2001.

## Lights! Camera! Action!

1 http://www.schipul.com/quotes/881 accessed on 9 March 2013.
2 Based on two interactions with Pradeep Guha, New Delhi, August 2011.
3 Bachi Karkaria, *Behind the Times*, Delhi: BCCL, 2010, p.259.
4 http://education.howthemarketworks.com/quote-about-finance/your-premium-brand-had-better-be-delivering-something-special/ accessed on 9 March 2013.
5 *The Times of Ideas*, Delhi: published by BCCL, 2007, p.25.
6 http://thinkexist.com/quotation/an_investment_in_knowledge_always_pays_the_best/161325.html accessed on 9 March 2013.

## The Pink Panther

1 Based on two meetings with Ajit Ninan, New Delhi, April 2002 and February 2003.
2 Based on an interaction with Priya Ranjan Dash, Delhi, January2013.
3 Meeting with Paran Balakrishnan, New Delhi, 15 July 2002.
4 The newspaper was first called *Business and Political Observer*, and then, *The Observer of Business and Politics*.
5 Interview with Paran Balakrishnan, New Delhi, 15 July 2002.

## Delhi...Now!

1 'Ad Wars Contrary to Good Taste', *PCI Review*, Press Council of India, Vol 10, January 1989, No. 1, Delhi, 1989, p.77.

2 Based on a meeting with Vinita Dawra Nangia, New Delhi, August 2001.
3 An interaction with Mannika Chopra, New Delhi, January 2002.
4 Interview with Madhu Suri, New Delhi, December 2012.
5 Meeting with Umesh Anand, New Delhi, August 2001.
6 Based on an interview with A.N. Sen, New Delhi, July 2001.
7 Mathew Engel, *Tickle the Public: One Hundred Years of the Popular Press*, London: Orion, 1996. Engel was earlier with *The Guardian*.
8 Based on an interaction with Sushil Pandit, New Delhi, October 2001.
9 Based on an interview with Bachi Karkaria, Bombay, December 2001.
10 Interview with Naresh Mohan, New Delhi, July 2001. (He was the chairman of UNI then.)
11 Based on a conversation with Dr N. Chandra Mohan, Delhi, August 2001.

## Epilogue

1 A broadsheet measures about 40 × 55 cms or 16 × 22 inches and is roughly double the size of a tabloid.
2 Ravi Dhariwal, 'Much ado about Medianet,' *The Times of India*, 15 February 2003, p. 14.
3 Aroon Purie, in his column 'From the Editor-in-Chief', in *India Today*, 27 January 2003, wrote: 'Today, there are PR agencies who charge a fee to get photographs and articles on "event managed" evenings into *The Times of India*'s Page 3.'
4 T.N. Ninan, 'How advertising became news. Identity Crisis', *Hindustan Times*, 19 February 2003, p.16.
5 ______, 'All the news space that's fit to sell', *Hindustan Times*, 20 February 2003, p.18.
6 Vir Sanghvi, 'The state of the media debate', *Sunday Hindustan Times*, 16 February 2003, p.14.
7 Sabina Sehgal Saikia, 'Compete, Don't Carp ... Copycats Shouldn't Point Fingers,' *The Times of India*, 25 February 2003, p.16.
8 A story on *The Sunday Times* article was also carried by Sourav Barman in The HOOT (online) on 21 February 2011. See http://www.thehoot.org/web/home/story.php?storyid=5135&pg=1&mod=1§ionId=19. For the original article of *The Sunday Times*, see http://www.

thesundaytimes.co.uk/sto/news/world_news/Asia/article555434.ece. For comments in *The Guardian*, see http://www.guardian.co.uk/media/greenslade/2011/feb/20/press-freedom-india.

9 I sent the manuscript of the book to the Times House, addressed to Mr Samir Jain, towards the end of 2010. Rohit Khanna, senior manager, Corporate Strategy & Brand Initiative, called and asked whether I would like to come over and discuss a few things. There was one meeting with Mr Rahul Kansal, executive president, Brands, and another one with a team of three managers from the department – Khanna; chief manager, TOI Brand, Priank Mathur; and manager, TOI Brand, Rakesh Dewal. They were extremely open and courteous, and took all questions.

# Acknowledgements

*'Tasmaad asaktah satatam, Kaaryam karma samaacara,
Asakto hyaacaran karma, paramaapnoti purusah.'*

'Perform prescribed actions, without attachment, without interruption, since, by doing so, you shall achieve the highest good.'

The Bhagavadgita, Chapter 3, Verse 19.

WHAT CAN I SAY about a dream that has persisted for over twelve years; sometimes, intense and upbeat, and at other times, despondent, dormant, fearful; but always there; much like the 'Richard Parker' of my journey. It kept me struggling and learning; it kept me hungry and alert. For all that and more, I bow before this idea.

It was sometime in the autumn of 2000 that this thought entered my life, and took a grip. I decided to give into it. Writing on the media in India can be tedious. Information isn't forthcoming, although anecdotes and gossip are; and culling out details takes quite an effort. And The Times Group is very private about itself. Moreover, to work on a book on the *TOI* after having moved out of it was far more challenging. But what's the fun without a little risk!

I couldn't have pieced this story together without the generosity of the men and women who gave me their time. Most of the interviews (about a hundred in all) were conducted during the first phase, between 2001 and 2005; and the rest in 2010–13. Senior journalists and editors from within and outside the organization, marketing and advertising managers and executives, media analysts and planners, critics and some members of the extended Jain family were the narrators. Some of the people I met have passed away; yet others have moved location.

Some of you may have forgotten what you said. Yet others may have a different take now. But I thank you for sharing your experiences with me.

Three cheers for my amazing husband, Tejinder, who is my Bodhi Tree, under whose comfortable shade I was able to pursue this project for so long. He and I share similar values; it is a boon, and we sing together; that is a balm for many ailments. I would come home to my son, Avii, playing Beethoven's Fifth or Mozart's Requiem at times, and stop worrying. His music and his love are my refuge. My parents-in-law, Ramindar and H.S. Walia, have showered their abundant blessings on me, and encouraged me at all times. My wonderful siblings, Sarita and Nishant, understood my passionate involvement with this saga, and heard me out, each time. My sister-in-law, Mudita and my brother-in-law, Srinivasa, have been equally supportive. For my nephew, Vihaan, I send kisses. For Scotch, my thirteen-year-old, jet black Pomeranian, who sensed my unexpressed anxiety, I send a warm hug.

I wouldn't have half the determination that I do but for my father, Kenath Padmanabhan Menon, who taught me the value of courage, character, integrity and persistence. He encouraged me to take my own decisions and learn from my own mistakes. He passed away in December 2011 but his spirit remains with me. He would've liked to read this book, and several discussions would have followed thereafter. He was a journalist, an editor, and he wasn't enamoured of *The Times*. I must have also received my mother Ramindar Dhiman's daring, joie de vivre and sense of adventure. Or I wouldn't have given up a great job to embark upon this odyssey. My mother merits a special mention for not having imposed a stereotype on me and my sister. She always let us 'be', and she made growing up so very memorable.

*Muchas gracias* to all my friends from the National Cadet Corps especially Srikanth Mukku and Shoba Sriaiyer, who regularly enquired about this book. *Behadd shukriya* to Salim Hyder Khan who drove 25 kilometres to come to my aid. *Anek dhannobad*, Nihar Parida. Rajan Chakravarty went through a chapter and offered feedback. Sanjay Kaw wished me well. Prabhat Shunglu and I discussed poetry and short stories; that kept me sane. My guitar instructor, Herald Lawrence, prayed very hard for me. To Aniruddha Bahal, who played a crucial role, I extend my sincere *aabhaar*.

To a gang of steady friends – Supriya and Ashish Bali, Praveen and Alind Pramanick, Soniya and Sandeep Mehrotra, Anju and Jayant Verma, Suman and Chetan Kumar, Anooradha and Munish Khanna here is a couplet: '*Woh jo sulagtee hai, mere seeney mein, ek arsey sey, yeh aag; usee sey toh main roshan hoon*'. (The passion that burns within me...illuminates me.')

To my publisher, HarperCollins; chief editor and publisher V.K. Karthika and editor, Antony Thomas, I raise a glorious toast. *Prost!*

The largest share of credit, by far, goes to my dearest friend, *sakha* as well as *sarathi* – Kanwaldeep Singh – who has been unflinching in his guidance, perspective and vision for this book. He has been Krishna to my Arjuna; Socrates to my Plato, and Jedi master Yoda to my Luke Skywalker. I can't thank him enough for investing so much of himself to help me realize my dream. His dynamic mother, Kuljit Kaur, believed in this project from day one. I am fortunate to have her by my side.

Above everything else, this voyage set me on a path that the Zen Buddhists call *Satori...self-awakening*.

I give this book to you! Its time has come!

I am grateful to...Mr Sham Lal, Mr Aveek Sarkar, Mr Inder Malhotra, Mr T.N. Ninan, Mr Satish Mehta, Mr Gautam Adhikari, Mr Naresh Mohan, Dr Dileep Padgaonkar, Mr Pradeep Guha, Mr Rajnish Rikhy, Dr Sanjaya Baru, Mr M.M. Srivastava, Mr A.N. Sen, Mr Pankaj Vohra, Mr Jug Suraiya, Mr Khushwant Singh, Mr K Balakrishnan, Ms Vinita Dawra Nangia, Mr Umesh Anand, Dr N. Chandra Mohan, Mr N.P. Singh, Ms Mahashweta Ghosh Roy, Mr Pritish Nandy, Dr Ram Tarneja, Mr Sushil Pandit, Ms Vibha Desai, Mr Amitava Guha, Mr Ajit Bhattacharjea, Mr Vijay Jindal, Mr Bashab Sarkar, Dr Chandan Mitra, Mr Ramesh Chandran, Ms Bachi Karkaria, Ms Vimla Patil, Mr Baljit Kapoor, Mr Rajeev Dubey, Mr Alok Jain, Ms Mannika Chopra, Mr Sunil Jain, Mr Ram Hingorani, Mr Paran Balakrishnan, Mr Sanjoy Narayan, Mr Akhilesh Jain, Mr R.P. Jain, Mr Sanjay Dalmia, Mr Gun Nidhi Dalmia, Mr Ramesh Chandra Jain, Mr Shashank Raizada, Dr K.L. Nandan, Mr T.K. Arun, Mr Abheek Barman, Ms Madhu Suri, Mr Ajit Ninan, Mr V.K. Gambhir, Mr Bal Mukund Sinha, Mr H.K. Dua, Mr Nataranjan Bohidar, Dr John Dayal, Mr Yashwant Raj, Mr Sanjay Puri, Mr R. Chandrashekhar, Ms Mona Jain, Mr D.K. Bose, Mr Raman Parashar, Mr Praveen Puri, Mr Bobby Kunhu, Mr Rahul Kansal, Mr Priya Ranjan Dash, Mr Shubrangshu Roy, Mr Ram C. Kapoor, Mr Priank Mathur, Mr Rohit Khanna, Mr Rakesh Dewal, Ms Maya Menon, Professor M.R. Dua, Mr T.J.S. George.

(I may have forgotten some names. But I thank you.)

Throughout the ebb and flow of this ride, I had two constant companions – the art of the Impressionist painters, and poetry. Here are a few lines from a poem by John Keats, titled 'To... Hope'.

And as, in sparkling majesty, a star
Gilds the bright summit of some gloomy cloud;
Brightening the half veil'd face of heaven afar:
So, when dark thoughts my boding spirit shroud,
Sweet Hope, celestial influence round me shed,
Waving thy silver pinions o'er my head!

Sangita
New Delhi, 20 February 2013